1984

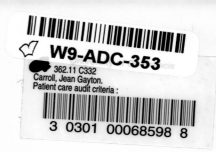
1984

PATIENT CARE AUDIT CRITERIA:

Standards for Hospital Quality Assurance

PATIENT CARE
AUDIT CRITERIA:

Standards for
Hospital Quality Assurance

FOURTH EDITION

Jean Gayton Carroll, Ph.D.

Dow Jones-Irwin
Homewood, Illinois 60430

ISBN 0-87094-392-8

Library of Congress Catalog Card No. 82-73622

Printed in the United States of America

1 2 3 4 5 6 7 8 9 0 K 0 9 8 7 6 5 4 3

FOREWORD

"... if not, why not"

The partial quotation above set the stage for many innovations related to the assessment of quality in the care of patients.

To satisfy the curiosity of the reader as to the source of this partial quotation, it came from the work of Ernest Amory Codman, a Boston surgeon, and his associates. Codman said that the skill of a hospital's staff of doctors could be judged only by the "common sense notion that every hospital should follow every patient it treats long enough to determine whether or not the treatment has been successful and then to inquire, *if not, why not.*"[1] This concept was first uttered by these physicians in 1915.

Thus has come about the quality assurance concept with the full development of the patient care audit as a key component of quality assurance programs.

The strength of a hospital's quality assurance program, especially since such a program demands the development of techniques of problem identification and problem solving, will be greatly enhanced through the utilization of this text. It has been designed to assist hospital staff in the development of the hospital-wide quality assurance program focusing on evaluation activities such as patient care audit criteria, on the identification and resolution of important problems in the provision of care, and also on incorporating quality assurance activities within the management decision-making process.

Dr. Codman played a part in the establishment of not only the American College of Surgeons, but also the Hospital Standardization Program, later to become the Joint Commission on Accreditation of Hospitals (JCAH). In 1979 the Board of the JCAH introduced a new quality assurance standard, reflecting an integrated, problem-focused approach to quality assurance which would significantly improve the quality of care provided throughout a hospital. Although this new standard eliminated the numerical requirement for patient care audits, it did not imply in any way a lessening of interest or support of auditing as a most valuable tool for evaluating patient care.

Today, the patient care review has become a sharply honed instrument which can be integrated in the hospital-wide program of quality assurance. It is a vital component of the efforts to deliver medical care of the highest quality possible.

George W. Graham, M.D.

---

[1] Loyal Davis, M.D., *A History of the A.C.S.*, Fellowship of Surgeons, 1960, p. 116.

INTRODUCTION

In his Foreword, Dr. George W. Graham has alluded to a significant issue in referring to the evolutionary development of the quality assurance standard of the Joint Commission on Accreditation of Hospitals.

Joint Commission policy requires not only that health care facilities review, or audit, the care of patients but also that they carry out whatever corrective actions may be indicated as a result of their reviews.

An audit of any sort, whether a financial audit or a review of clinical performance, is merely a systematic investigation involving the collection of data, an analysis of the findings with reference to objective criteria and the statement of conclusions based upon the results of the analysis. In general terms, the process is known as evaluation research. Evaluation research, whether in an industrial setting or a hospital, is an essential tool used in management decision making.

However, all of the well-intentioned effort put forth in conducting patient care studies will be wasted unless it takes place within an organizational framework designed and constituted in such a way as to facilitate the decision-making process and the implementation of those corrective measures that may be necessary in the interest of improving the quality of performance. Therefore, it is essential to set up a workable quality assurance plan that provides the organizational structure and the communications channels needed for the purpose of implementing the recommendations generated by the evaluation studies.

In many hospitals, quality assurance plans now exist on paper with the endorsement of boards of trustees and administration and professional staffs, but accompanied by little or no evidence of probing evaluation and behavioral change. True quality assurance demands more than this. It demands a genuine commitment to excellence coupled with a lively spirit of activism on the part of all those, including trustees, who bear responsibility for the conduct of the enterprise.

As a result of recent frequent changes in technology, pharmacology and price levels, it often is difficult for those most closely involved in patient care to stay abreast of current hospital charge structures. Therefore, as part of the research for this edition of *Patient Care Audit Criteria* we have studied the charges levied by a sample of hospitals for certain diagnostic and therapeutic procedures as well as rates for room and nursing services. The estimated charges based on the sampling are shown with the sets of review criteria.

It should be borne in mind that these estimates are merely averages based upon the 1982 charge figures obtained from a sample of hospitals in various parts of the United States. The estimated charges for rooms other than special care units reflect the 1982 charges for beds in two-bed general medical-surgical rooms. We found regional variations, as well as wide variations among hospitals in the same city, for all types of charges. In no way are these estimates to be considered as guidelines.

It is my hope that you find the material in *Patient Care Audit Criteria* helpful in your own evaluation research and that your hospital's efforts in establishing and maintaining a viable, effective quality assurance program may meet with resounding success.

Jean Gayton Carroll

ACKNOWLEDGMENTS

I am very grateful for the assitance given me by the members of various hospital committees with whom I have worked on hospital evaluation projects. In particular, I wish to acknowledge with thanks the counseling and contributions provided by each of the following individuals:

Stuart Abel, M.D.

Clinical Professor of Gynecology and Obstetrics
Northwestern University School of Medicine
Attending Staff, Prentice Women's Hospital

Proctor R. Anderson, M.D.

Associate Professor, Department of Orthopedic Surgery
Northwestern University School of Medicine
Attending Staff, Northwestern Memorial Hospital

Edward Brunner, M.D.

Professor and Chairman, Department of Anesthesiology
Northwestern University School of Medicine
Attending Staff, Northwestern Memorial Hospital

Barry Carleton, M.D.

Assistant Professor, Department of Psychiatry
Northwestern University School of Medicine
Assistant Director, Adolescent Psychiatry,
Northwestern Memorial Hospital

Donald E. Casey, M.D., D.D.S.

Professor and Chairman, Department of Oral Surgery
Northwestern University Dental School
Lecturer, Department of Surgery
Northwestern University School of Medicine
Attending Staff, Northwestern Memorial Hospital

Chicago Foundation for Medical Care[1]

Professional Standards Review Organization,
Chicago, Illinois

Francesco del Greco, M.D.

Professor of Medicine
Chief, Section of Nephrology and Hypertension
Northwestern University School of Medicine
Attending Staff, Northwestern Memorial Hospital

Sharon L. Dooley, M.D.

Assistant Professor, Department of Gynecology and Obstetrics
Section of Maternal and Fetal Medicine
Northwestern University School of Medicine
Attending Staff, Prentice Women's Hospital

Barton L. Hodes, M.D.

Professor and Chairman, Department of Ophthalmology
Milton S. Hershey Medical Center
Attending Staff, Milton S. Hershey Medical Center

Harold Laufman, M.D.

Professor Emeritus of Surgery
Albert Einstein College of Medicine of New York
Attending Staffs, Montefiore Hospital and Mount Sinai Medical Center

Peter McKinney, M.D.

Associate Professor of Clinical Surgery
Northwestern University School of Medicine
Attending Staff, Northwestern Memorial Hospital

H. Bates Noble, M.D.

Associate Professor, Department of Orthopedic Surgery
Northwestern University School of Medicine
Attending Staff, Northwestern Memorial Hospital

David Shoch, M.D.

Professor and Chairman, Department of Ophthalmology
Northwestern University School of Medicine
Attending Staff, Northwestern Memorial Hospital

Joe Leigh Simpson, M.D.

Professor of Gynecology and Obstetrics
Head, Section on Human Genetics
Northwestern University School of Medicine
Attending Staff, Prentice Women's Hospital

Cordelia Twitty, M.S.W.

Coordinator, Child Protective Services
Department of Social Services
Wyler Children's Hospital of the University of Chicago Hospitals

Florent Theriault, R.P.T.

Director of Physical Therapy Services
Henrotin Hospital

Charles Visockis, R.Ph.

Director of Pharmacy
Henrotin Hospital

[1] Grant from United States Department of Health and Human Services, Grant Number 97-P-996331-5.

June Wallace-Looby, R.R.A.

  Director of Medical Record Department
  and Director of Quality Assurance
  Northwestern Memorial Hospital

Nicholas Wetzel, M.D.

  Professor of Surgery
  Northwestern University School of Medicine
  Attending Staff, Northwestern Memorial Hospital

Dale Yoder

  Director of Environmental Services
  Henrotin Hospital

The work of Jennifer Smyth, who served as the principal research assistant on this project, was invaluable and greatly appreciated.

J. G. C.

CONTENTS

GYNECOLOGY AND OBSTETRICS

PEDIATRICS

PSYCHIATRY

INPATIENT DENTAL CARE

MODALITIES OF CARE

UTILIZATION

DEPARTMENTAL STUDIES

RECORD ANALYST'S GUIDE

APPENDIX

INDEX 325

NOTE ON THE NUMERICAL STANDARDS

You will observe that each evaluation criterion is followed by either "100%" or "0%." These are the standards that are applied by a record analyst in reviewing medical records as part of the patient care evaluation process.

The use of these two expressions is intended to imply simply that a specified element of behavior, such as a diagnostic test or a therapeutic procedure, should ordinarily be present in or absent from the record. Desirable outcomes are identified by "100%" and undesirable outcomes by "0%." These percentage notations are not intended to reflect statistical probability.

For many of the criteria, commonly applicable exceptions are listed. In record reviewing, the term "exception" is used to state a condition that excuses the record from complying with a criterion and its percentage standard.

MEDICINE

ACUTE MYOCARDIAL INFARCTION

SUGGESTED SAMPLE

Patients whose final diagnoses include, along with acute myocardial infarction, any of the following conditions.

Cardiac arrest   Persistent uncontrolled arrhythmias
Congestive heart failure   Pulmonary embolism
Pericarditis

REVIEW

Criterion	Standard	Estimated Charge
JUSTIFICATION FOR EXTENDED STAY		$ 120 supplies
1. Occurrence, following acute myocardial infarction, of (a) cardiac arrest, (b) congestive heart failure, (c) pericarditis, (d) persistent uncontrolled arrhythmias or (e) pulmonary embolism	100%	8 kit
DIAGNOSTIC AND THERAPEUTIC MEASURES TAKEN PRIOR TO EMERGENCE OF COMPLICATION		
2. Patient admitted to special care unit upon arrival at hospital or of presumptive diagnosis of AMI in hospitalized patient	100%	725 per day
3. Patient on cardiac monitor within 5 minutes of arrival at hospital or of presumptive diagnosis of AMI in hospitalized patient	100%	235
4. Laboratory and other studies ordered upon admission or presumptive diagnosis		
a. EKG	100%	48
b. Chest x-ray	100%	70
c. Cardiac enzymes	100%	75
d. Sedimentation rate	100%	12
e. CBC	100%	19
f. Urinalysis	100%	10
5. Nursing care upon admission to special care unit		
a. Immediate implementation of cardiac care plan	100%	
b. Monitoring and charting on each shift of	100%	
(1) Vital signs		
(2) Intake and output		
(3) Medications		
(4) Intravenous therapy		20
6. Follow-up studies		
a. Serial EKGs	100%	48
b. Repeat chest x-rays	100%	70
c. Serial cardiac enzymes	100%	75
7. Nuclear scan	100%	350

Exception: Patient not a candidate for full schedule of work and activity following discharge.

MANAGEMENT OF COMPLICATIONS

8. Cardiac arrest $ 125 cart

   Implementation of cardiac emergency protocol including
   - a. Cardio-pulmonary resuscitation and defibrillation   100%
   - b. Epinephrine 0.5 to 1.0 mg. every 5 minutes IV   100%
   - c. NaHCO$_3$ (44.6 mEq.) 50 ml/5 minutes IV   100%

9. Congestive heart failure
   - a. Sodium restriction and sodium depletion   100%
   - b. Diuresis   100%
   - c. Digitalis   100%

10. Pericarditis

    Supportive care with medication for relief of pain   100%

11. Persistent uncontrolled arrhythmias
    - a. Vital signs every 15 minutes   100%
    - b. EKG   100%   48
    - c. Repeat cardiac enzymes   100%   75
    - d. Anti-arrhythmic medications   100%

12. Pulmonary embolism
    - a. Confirmation by lung scan   100%   270
    - b. Determination of arterial blood gases (ABG)   100%   50
    - c. Anticoagulation   100%
    - d. Complete bed rest   100%

LENGTH OF STAY

13. Length of stay
    - a. In special care unit, 3-7 days   100%   2,370-5,390

      Exceptions: (1) In presence of persistent uncontrolled arrhythmias, until arrhythmias are controlled and condition stabilized; (2) in presence of pulmonary embolism, until resolution and stabilization of condition.
    - b. Following transfer from special care unit, 12 additional days

      Exceptions: (1) Transfer to another facility; (2) early departure against medical advice; (3) complications or other diagnoses justifying extension.   4,200

DISCHARGE STATUS

14. Patient discharged under the following conditions:
    - a. Arrhythmias under control   100%
    - b. Patient free of chest pain   100%
    - c. Temperature below 99.4 F for at least 36 hours before discharge   100%
    - d. Any complications under control   100%
    - e. Patient/family instructed re (1) activity level, (2) diet, (3) restrictions on use of tobacco and alcohol, (4) medication dosages and schedule and (5) follow-up visit to physician   100%

      Exception: Instructions on transfer form.

SUGGESTED SAMPLE

Patients whose discharge diagnoses include agranulocytosis, contractures, decubiti, gastrointestinal bleeding, tinnitus, deafness or pruritus in association with arthritis.

REVIEW

Criterion	Standard	Estimated Charge
JUSTIFICATION FOR EXTENDED STAY		$ 120 supplies
1. Occurrence, following treatment for arthritis, of (a) agranulocytosis, (b) contractures, (c) decubiti, (d) gastrointestinal bleeding, (e) tinnitus and deafness or (f) pruritus	100%	8 kit
DIAGNOSTIC STUDY		
2. History of progressive nonspecific inflammation of peripheral joints with increasing joint deformity	100%	
3. Presence of an acute episode of joint inflammation unresponsive to outpatient therapy	100%	
4. Physical examination including findings of erythematous, painful joint with some degree of joint deformity	100%	
5. Laboratory and other studies including		
a. CBC, urinalysis and admission panel	100%	125
b. Serology	100%	11
c. Rheumatoid factor titer	100%	16
d. Antinuclear antibody titer (ANA)	100%	35
e. Erythrocyte sedimentation rate	100%	12
f. Chest x-ray within past 6 months with report in record	100%	70
g. X-ray of affected joint	100%	50-75
h. Gc culture	0%	40

Exception (Indication): Contributory history.

MANAGEMENT

6. Medications as indicated   100%

  a. Salicylates

    Exception: History of gastrointestinal bleeding tendency.

  b. Phenylbutazone

    Exception: History of depression or gastrointestinal bleeding tendency.

  c. Indomethacin

    Exception: History of gastrointestinal bleeding tendency.

  d. Corticosteroids

    Exception: Presence of cardiovascular disease or hypertension.

  e. Water soluble gold compounds in presence of documented rheumatoid arthritis

Exceptions: (1) Absence of documented rheumatoid arthritis; (2) presence of pronounced joint destruction in absence of current inflammatory reaction; (3) history of renal or hepatic disease, blood dyscrasia or gastrointestinal bleeding; (4) acute systemic lupus erythematosis.

7. Physical therapy as indicated, including: 100%
   a. Hot packs $ 25
   b. Passive range of motion exercises   25
   c. Ultrasound therapy   29
   Exception to Criterion No. 7: Presence of another diagnosis contraindicating physical therapy.

8. Nursing care, including
   a. Patient assessment including vital signs, brief relevant history and present complaint   100%
   b. Formulation of care plan based on assessment and objectives   100%
   c. Patient orientation to care and procedures to be used   100%
   d. Skin care provided, including   100%
      (1) Pressure points checked for erythema daily
      (2) Patient repositioned every 3-4 hours
      (3) Patient encouraged to turn in bed
      (4) As indicated, pressure relieved with special mattress, foam rubber or sheepskin   72
      (5) Cleanliness and dryness maintained
   e. Documentation of patient's tolerance for activity   100%
   f. Patient monitored for side effects of medications, such as tinnitus and gastrointestinal discomfort   100%

9. Management of complications and side effects of medications
   a. Agranulocytosis
      Suspension of treatment with gold compounds   100%
   b. Contractures
      (1) Joint mobility maintained with passive ROM exercises   100%   25
      (2) Patient positioned appropriately   100%
      (3) Analgesics to relieve pain and facilitate mobility   100%
   c. Decubiti
      (1) Affected area left exposed   100%
      (2) Application of protective coating of silicone or compound benzoin tincture   100%
      (3) Patient positioned to relieve pressure   100%
      (4) High-protein, high-calorie, high-vitamin diet given   100%
      (5) Conservative debridement of necrotic tissue   100%
   d. Gastrointestinal bleeding
      (1) Suspension of administration of salicylates, gold compounds, phenylbutazone or indomethacin   100%
      (2) In presence of severe bleeding, patient typed and cross matched for possible transfusion   100%   50-65
      Exception: Bleeding controlled early.

e. Tinnitus and/or deafness

Suspension of administration of salicylates, gold compounds, phenylbutazone or indomethacin   100%

f. Pruritus

(1) Suspension of treatment with gold compounds   100%

(2) In presence of pruritus with development of rash and evidence of toxicity, therapy with dimercaprol, penicillamine or corticosteroids   100%

Exception: Pruritus controlled early in absence of rash.

10. Dietetic management

a. Four small balanced meals per day   100%

b. Menu including foods high in gastric buffering capacity   100%

c. Patient and family given instruction in choosing appropriate foods in relation to medication program   100%

LENGTH OF STAY

11. Length of stay

a. Osteoarthritis as primary diagnosis, 6-9 days   100% $2,100-3,150

b. Rheumatoid arthritis as primary diagnosis, 7-11 days   100%   2,450-3,850

Exceptions: (1) Early departure against medical advice or (2) complications or other diagnoses justifying extension.

DISCHARGE STATUS

12. Patient discharged under the following conditions:

a. Relief of symptoms and signs present at admission   100%

b. Patient ambulatory with temperature below 99.6 F for 24 hours before discharge   100%

c. Patient/family instructed re (1) medication schedule and dosage as applicable, (2) activity level, (3) diet and (4) follow-up visit to physician   100%

Exception: Instructions on transfer form.

SUGGESTED SAMPLE

Patients whose discharge diagnoses include acute respiratory distress, atelectasis, pneumonia or pneumothorax in association with bronchitis.

REVIEW

Criterion	Standard	Estimated Charge
JUSTIFICATION FOR EXTENDED STAY		$ 120 supplies
1. Presence of acute respiratory distress, atelectasis, pneumonia or pneumothorax in association with bronchitis	100%	8 kit
DIAGNOSTIC STUDY		
2. History including upper respiratory infection with a combination of any two of the following conditions:	100%	
a. Respiratory distress		
b. Hemoptysis		
c. Cough producing purulent sputum		
d. Chest pain		
e. Cyanosis		
f. Persistent fever unresponsive to therapy		
g. Impaired fluid balance		
h. Concomitant disease		
i. Absence of appropriate care at home		
j. Failure of patient to respond to outpatient management		
3. Physical examination report with specific reference to type of respiratory problem present	100%	
4. Laboratory and other studies including		
a. CBC, urinalysis and admission panel	100%	95
b. Electrolyte levels	100%	25
c. Nasopharyngeal culture and sensitivity test	100%	75
d. Sputum culture and sensitivity test	100%	75
e. Posterior-anterior and lateral x-rays of chest on admission	100%	70
f. EKG	100%	48
Exception: Patient under 40.		
g. Pulmonary function test	100%	11
h. Arterial blood gases	100%	70
5. Special procedures		
a. Heterophil agglutination test for infectious mononucleosis	0%	25
Exceptions (Indications): Presence of lymphadenopathy and/or tonsillar exudate.		
b. Blood culture	0%	40
Exception (Indication): Persistent fever with inability to raise sputum for culture.		

c. Cold agglutinin study Exception (Indication): Presumptive diagnosis of viral pneumonia.	0%	$ 23

MANAGEMENT

6. Anti-infective agents as indicated by culture and sensitivity *Record Analyst: Review culture and sensitivity reports and compare with drugs administered.*	100%	
7. Medications including cough mixture as indicated	100%	
8. Expectorants, steam and/or vasodilator aerosols as indicated to facilitate raising of sputum	100%	12
9. Intravenous fluids as indicated for dehydration Exception (Indication): Presence of dehydration.	0%	20
10. Oxygen as indicated Exception (Indication): Presence of respiratory distress.	0%	26
11. Bed rest with bathroom privileges	100%	
12. Nursing care		
a. Patient assessment including vital signs, brief relevant history and present complaint	100%	
b. Formulation of care plan based on assessment and objectives	100%	
c. Patient orientation to care and procedures to be used	100%	
d. Maintenance of graphic chart, medication chart and intravenous flow chart if IV therapy is employed	100%	
e. Patient monitored for evidence of complications	100%	
13. Dietetic services		
a. Report of dietician's conference with patient	100%	35
b. Provision of high calorie soft diet meeting nutritional requirements	100%	
Record Analyst: Review hospital's Dietetic Service sample menus for high calorie soft diet to obtain documentation of nutritional elements provided.		
14. Physical Therapy or Respiratory Therapy services Postural drainage 10-15 minutes, 4-5 times a day as indicated	100%	28-35
15. Respiratory Therapy services		
a. Mist therapy, either ultrasonic or heated nebulizer with bronchodilator aerosol, 3-4 times a day	100%	66-88
b. Intermittent positive pressure breathing treatment	100%	20
16. Management of complications		
a. Acute respiratory distress with arterial pCO_2 above 55 or pH of arterial plasma below 7.38		
(1) Assisted ventilation with endotracheal tube	100%	222 per 24 hours
(2) Where endotracheal tube is required for more than 48 hours, tracheostomy Exception: Tube not required more than 48 hours.	100%	
b. Atelectasis		
(1) Chest x-rays to confirm diagnosis	100%	70
(2) In presence of obstruction due to bronchial secretions, intermittent positive pressure breathing to induce coughing or use of suction to dislodge and remove plug	100%	20

(3)	Following failure of efforts to remove plug by other means, bronchoscopy with aspiration of secretions	100%	$106-125
(4)	Culture and sensitivity tests of sputum	100%	75
(5)	Antibiotic consistent with culture and sensitivity	100%	

c. Pneumonia

(1)	Chest x-ray to confirm diagnosis	100%	70
(2)	Culture and sensitivity of sputum	100%	75
(3)	Antibiotic consistent with culture and sensitivity	100%	
(4)	Intravenous fluids for dehydration	100%	20
	Exception: Absence of dehydration.		
(5)	Serial chest x-rays for evaluation	100%	70

d. Pneumothorax

(1)	Oxygen during acute phase to relieve dyspnea	100%	73 per 24 hours
(2)	Chest x-ray to confirm diagnosis	100%	70
(3)	Chest tube with suction to induce rapid re-expansion of lung	100%	53 22 per day
(4)	Medication to control residual pain	100%	
	Exception: Presence of minimal degree of collapse.		

LENGTH OF STAY

17.	Length of stay 4-6 days	100%	1,400-2,100

Exception: (a) Early departure against medical advice; (b) complications or other diagnoses justifying extension.

DISCHARGE STATUS

18. Patient discharged under the following conditions:

a.	Relief of symptoms present on admission	100%
b.	Absence of respiratory distress	100%
c.	Temperature below 99.6 F for at least 36 hours before discharge	100%
d.	Absence of complications	100%
e.	Patient/family instructed re (1) activity level, (2) diet, (3) dosage and schedule of any medications and (4) follow-up visit to physician	100%
	Exception: Instructions on transfer form.	

CARCINOMA OF THE COLON AND RECTUM
MEDICAL MANAGEMENT

SUGGESTED SAMPLE

Patients whose discharge diagnoses include bleeding, diarrhea or urinary tract infection in association with carcinoma of the colon or rectum not operated upon during this admission.

REVIEW

Criterion	Standard	Estimated Charge
JUSTIFICATION FOR EXTENDED STAY BEYOND LENGTH OF STAY ASSIGNED FOR STUDY AND ESTABLISHMENT OF DIAGNOSIS		$ 120 supplies 8 kit
1. Presence of bleeding, diarrhea or urinary tract infection in association with carcinoma of the colon	100%	
INDICATIONS FOR ADMISSION		
2. History of any of the following conditions:	100%	
a. Acute or chronic blood loss from gastrointestinal tract with hypotension and/or severe anemia with Hgb. less than 10 gms. %		
b. Obstruction associated with vomiting and resultant dehydration		
c. X-ray or other evidence of obstruction		
d. Change in bowel habits accompanied by abdominal pain, distension or cramps in lower abdomen		
e. Gastrointestinal bleeding, diarrhea or urinary tract infection in the presence of a previously established diagnosis of carcinoma of the colon or rectum		
DIAGNOSTIC AND THERAPEUTIC MEASURES		
3. History with specific reference to contributory factors	100%	
4. Physical examination including digital rectal and pelvic examinations	100%	
5. Laboratory and other studies including		
a. CBC, urinalysis and admission panel	100%	125
b. Stools tested for gross and occult blood	100%	4
c. Chest x-ray within the previous 6 months with report in record	100%	70
d. Gastrointestinal x-ray series	0%	482
Exceptions (Indications): (1) Complaint of symptoms longer than 3 weeks; (2) unexplained weight loss; (3) family history of carcinoma; (4) any anemia; (5) severe lower abdominal pain; (6) occult blood in stools.		
6. Special procedures		
a. Proctoscopy	100%	95-127
Exception: Not needed for diagnosis and location of lesion.		
b. Sigmoidoscopy	100%	157
Exception: Not needed for diagnosis and location of lesion.		

MEDICAL MANAGEMENT

7. Modified diet   100%
   Exception: General diet tolerated.
8. Antineoplastic drugs as indicated   100%
9. Medications for pain   100%
   Exception: Patient not complaining of pain.
10. Referral for surgery   100%
    Exception: Patient not a suitable candidate for surgery.
11. Nursing care
    a. Patient assessment including vital signs, brief relevant history and present complaint   100%
    b. History of allergies and drug sensitivities   100%
    c. Formulation of nursing care plan based on assessment and objectives   100%
    d. Patient orientation to care and procedures to be used   100%
    e. Observation and documentation of the patient's acceptance and tolerance of any modified diet, medications and procedures employed   100%
    f. The following monitored and maintained per care plan   100%
       (1) Intravenous therapy $ 20
       (2) Drains if present   52
       (3) Foley catheter if present   28
       (4) Medications
    g. Site of intravenous line changed every 3 days   100%
    h. Vital signs checked and recorded per care plan   100%
    i. Care plan revised to reflect any changes in needs and objectives   100%
    j. Patient monitored for evidence of complications or deterioration   100%
12. Management of complicating conditions
    a. Bleeding
       (1) Endoscopy for determination of source   100%   95-157
       (2) Patient's blood typed and cross matched   100%   50
       (3) Transfusion as indicated   100%   45-88 per unit   45 infusion fee
    b. Diarrhea
       (1) Fluids in presence of dehydration   100%
       (2) Medications to inhibit intestinal motility   100%
           Record Analyst: Such medications might include Donnitol, Librax or Lomotil, among others.
    c. Urinary tract infection
       (1) Culture and sensitivity of urine   100%   75
       (2) Antibiotic consistent with culture and sensitivity   100%

LENGTH OF STAY

13. Length of stay to study problem and establish diagnosis, 5-7 days   100%   1,750-2,450
    Exceptions: (a) Early departure against medical advice; (b) complications or other diagnoses justifying extension.

DISCHARGE STATUS

14. Patient discharged under the following conditions:
    a. Temperature below 99.6 F for at least 24 hours before
       discharge   100%
    b. Subsidence of symptoms   100%
    c. Completion of diagnostic survey   100%
    d. Plan for post-hospital care formulated and documented in
       medical record   100%
    e. Patient/family instructed on (1) any applicable dietary
       restrictions, (2) medications, (3) activity level and (4)
       follow-up visit to physician
       Exception: Instructions on transfer form.

CEREBRAL VASCULAR ACCIDENT

SUGGESTED SAMPLE

Patients whose discharge diagnoses include cardiac arrest, decubiti, dehydration or urinary tract infection in association with recent cerebral vascular accident.

REVIEW

Criterion	Standard	Estimated Charge
JUSTIFICATION FOR EXTENDED STAY		$ 120 supplies
1. Presence of any of the following in association with recent cerebral vascular accident:	100%	8 kit
a. Cardiac arrest		
b. Decubiti		
c. Dehydration		
d. Urinary tract infection		
DIAGNOSTIC AND THERAPEUTIC MEASURES		
2. History with specific reference to hypertension, seizures, stroke, vascular disease and use of oral contraceptives	100%	
3. Physical examination report with specific reference to pupillary changes, papilledema, signs of stroke damage or paralysis, reflex condition and bladder control	100%	
4. Laboratory and other studies including		
a. CBC, urinalysis and admission panel	100%	125
b. Within 12 hours of admission,		
(1) Blood sugar level	100%	14
(2) Electrolytes	100%	25
Exception: Patient not comatose		
c. EKG	100%	48
d. Chest x-ray	100%	70
e. Skull series	100%	120-140
f. EEG	100%	140
5. Attempts to control and/or lower blood pressure where diastolic pressure is higher than 110 mm Hg	100%	
6. Nursing care including		
a. Patient assessment covering vital signs, level of consciousness, control of bladder and bowels, history of allergies and drug sensitivities, estimate of weight and level of anxiety shown	100%	
b. Formulation of care plan based on assessment and objectives	100%	
c. Patient orientation to care and procedures to be used	100%	
Exception: Patient comatose.		
d. Procedures performed and documented:		
(1) Vital signs per care plan	100%	
(2) Blood pressure twice a day (BID)	100%	

(3) Presence of diastolic blood pressure higher than 120 mm Hg reported to physician in a timely manner	100%	
(4) Intake and output charted	100%	
e. Hygiene maintained, including		
(1) Catheter care, including routine culture	100%	$ 40
(2) Perineal care	100%	
(3) Oral care	100%	
f. Skin care provided		
(1) Pressure points checked for erythema (redness) daily	100%	
(2) Patient repositioned every 3-4 hours	100%	
(3) Where feasible, patient encouraged to turn in bed	100%	
(4) Pressure relieved with special mattress, foam rubber or sheepskin	100%	70
(5) Cleanliness and dryness maintained	100%	
g. When side rails on bed are up, this fact documented	100%	
7. Physical Therapy services		
a. Patient assessed and treatment plan developed, including objectives of treatment	100%	20
b. Exercise and treatment plan carried out, as indicated, including as needed (1) passive range of motion exercises, (2) gait training and (3) training in activities of daily living	100%	25 per day
8. Social Services		
a. Discharge planning initiated upon admission	100%	
b. During hospitalization, documentation of progress in discharge planning	100%	
Exception: In judgment of physician and social worker, patient is self-sufficient.		
9. Management of complications		
a. Cardiac arrest		125 cart
Implementation of cardiac emergency protocol, including		
(1) Cardio-pulmonary resuscitation and defibrillation	100%	
(2) Epinephrine 0.5 to 1.0 mg every 5 minutes by intravenous route (IV)	100%	
(3) $NaHCO_2$ (44.6 mEq) 50 ml per 5 minutes IV	100%	
b. Decubiti		
(1) Affected area left exposed	100%	
(2) Application of protective coating of silicone or compound benzoin tincture	100%	
(3) Patient properly positioned to eliminate pressure	100%	
(4) High-protein, high-calorie, high-vitamin diet with supplementary protein hydrolysates IV	100%	90 per day 30 per 2 days dressings
(5) Conservative debridement of necrotic tissue	100%	
c. Dehydration		
(1) Fluids pushed	100%	
(2) Intravenous fluids maintained	100%	20
(3) Intake and output monitored and charted	100%%	

       d. Urinary tract infection
           (1) Culture and sensitivity of urine   100% $ 75
           (2) Antibiotic consistent with culture and sensitivity   100%

LENGTH OF STAY

10. Length of stay 12-25 days   100%   4,200-8,750
     Exception: (a) Early departure against medical advice;
     (b) earlier transfer to extended care facility; (c) complications
     or other diagnoses justifying extension.

DISCHARGE STATUS

11. Patient discharged under the following conditions: 100%
     a. Neurologic function stable   100%
     b. Vital signs stable   100%
     c. Patient free of decubiti   100%
     d. Normal bowel function established   100%
     e. Maximum benefit obtained from in-hospital physical therapy   100%
     f. Patient/family instructed re (1) diet, (2) medications as
         applicable, (3) activities of daily living, (4) follow-up visit to
         physician   100%
         Exception: Instructions on transfer form.
     g. Referral made and contact established with such additional
         services as may be needed, such as Meals on Wheels, Visiting
         Nurse Association, providers of occupational or speech therapy
         and sources of equipment needed for the patient's care   100%
         Exceptions: (1) Such sources not required, or (2) patient
         transferred to extended care facility.

SUGGESTED SAMPLE

Patients who have experienced severe persistent pain with muscle spasm and limitation of motion and/or paresthesias associated with an acute episode of cervical syndrome.

REVIEW

Criterion	Standard	Estimated Charge
JUSTIFICATION FOR ADMISSION		$ 120 supplies 8 kit
1. The presence of either of the following conditions in a patient with an acute episode of cervical syndrome:	100%	
a. Severe pain with muscle spasm and limitation of motion unresponsive to conservative outpatient therapy for a period of at least 7 days		
b. Paresthesias unresponsive to outpatient therapy		
DIAGNOSTIC STUDY		
2. History of one or more of the following:	100%	
a. Recent trauma		
b. Numbness or tingling of hands and fingers		
c. Pain upon movement of neck and/or shoulders		
3. Physical examination showing limitation of neck motion	100%	
4. Studies including		
a. X-ray evidence of flattening of cervical spine	100%	120
b. Electromyography	0%	200
Exceptions (Indications): (1) Presence of indications of cord compression or of space-occupying lesion; (2) demonstrated neurological deficit.		
MANAGEMENT		
5. Management of complications		
a. Persistent severe pain with limitation of motion		
(1) Immobilization with cervical collar	100%	15
(2) Application of moist heat	100%	25
(3) Ultrasound therapy	100%	25
(4) Intermittent hand-controlled traction progressing from 15 to 30 pounds for 20 to 30 minutes per day	100%	27 per day
b. Paresthesias		
(1) Immobilization with cervical collar	100%	15
(2) Intermittent hand-controlled traction progressing from 15 to 30 pounds for 20 to 30 minutes per day	100%	27 per day
6. Nursing care including		
a. Patient assessment including vital signs, history of allergies and drug sensitivities and present complaint	100%	
b. Formulation of care plan based on assessment and objectives	100%	

c.	Character of pain observed and documented	100%	
d.	Traction monitored	100%	

LENGTH OF STAY

7.	Length of stay maximum of 5 days	100%	$1,750
	Exception: Presence of other diagnoses justifying extension.		

DISCHARGE STATUS

8. Patient discharged under the following conditions:

a.	Patient ambulatory without help or pain for 48 hours before discharge	100%	
b.	Patient aware of name, dosage, frequency and side effects of his medications	100%	
c.	Patient instructed in proper body mechanics	100%	25
d.	Follow-up visit to physician scheduled	100%	

Exception to Criteria 8b, 8c and 8d: Instructions on transfer form.

SUGGESTED SAMPLE

Patients whose discharge diagnoses include respiratory failure, ventilatory failure, sepsis or bacteremia in association with chronic obstructive pulmonary disease.

REVIEW

Criterion	Standard	Estimated Charge
JUSTIFICATION FOR EXTENDED STAY		$ 120 supplies
1. The presence of any of the following conditions in association with chronic obstructive pulmonary disease:	100%	8 kit
a. Respiratory failure		
b. Ventilatory failure		
c. Sepsis or bacteremia		
DIAGNOSTIC STUDY		
2. History with reference to		
a. Respiratory symptoms including shortness of breath, orthopnea and production of sputum	100%	
b. Tolerance for exercise	100%	
c. Exposure to any occupational or other environmental agents associated with pulmonary pathology, including smoking and exposure to dusts	100%	
3. Physical examination including report on breath sounds, lung sounds, anterior-posterior chest diameter, clubbing of finger tips, cyanosis, flaring nostrils and evaluation of respiration	100%	
4. Laboratory and other studies including		
a. CBC, urinalysis and admission panel	100%	95
b. Sputum culture and sensitivity	100%	75
Exceptions: (1) Absence of evidence of infection; (2) inability to raise sputum.		
c. Posterior-anterior and lateral x-rays of chest	100%	70
d. EKG	100%	48
e. Serial arterial blood gas analysis	100%	75
f. Pulmonary function studies	100%	10
Exception: Patient unable to cooperate.		
g. Bronchoscopy	100%	106-125
Exception: Absence of suspicion of tumor.		
h. Bronchography	0%	180
Exceptions (Indications): (1) Absence of previous bronchogram; (2) Presence of suspicion of bronchiectasis.		

MANAGEMENT OF COMPLICATIONS

5. Respiratory failure
   a. Administration of oxygen .... 100% $ 26
   b. Monitoring of acid base balance 100% 40

6. Ventilatory failure
   a. Chest x-rays for evaluation of obstruction 100% 70
   b. Serial blood gas analysis 100% 75
   c. Culture and sensitivity of sputum 100% 75
   d. EKG 100% 48
   e. Administration of oxygen 100% 26
      Exception: PaO_2 above 60.
   f. Bronchodilatation and airway clearing with powered nebulizer ... 100% 24
   g. Antibiotic consistent with sputum culture and sensitivity 100%
   h. Monitoring of acid base balance 100% 40
   i. In absence of improvement on conservative therapy, tracheal
      intubation 100% 38
      Exception: Presence of clinical improvement on conservative
      measures.

7. Sepsis or bacteremia following intubation
   a. Culture and sensitivity of blood 100% 75
   b. Broad spectrum antibiotic, followed by antibiotic consistent
      with culture and sensitivity 100%

8. Severe alkalosis
   a. Monitoring of acid base balance 100% 40
   b. After restoration of adequate ventilation, administration of
      potassium chloride 100%

9. Nursing care including
   a. Patient assessment, including vital signs, history of allergies and
      drug sensitivities and present complaint 100%
   b. Formulation of care plan based on assessment and objectives ... 100%
   c. Maintenance of patent airway 100%
   d. Tracheal suction equipment at bedside, with nasal or oral
      suction every hour and P.R.N. 100%
   e. Respirations, quality and rate, checked every hour ... 100%
   f. Auscultation for breath sounds with areas of abnormal sounds
      noted 100%
   g. Blood pressure, temperature and apical pulse checked every
      2-4 hours and P.R.N. 100%
   h. Intake and output measured and charted 100%
   i. Level of consciousness observed every 2 hours ... 100%
   j. Patient positioned in semi- to high-Fowler's position ... 100%
   k. Postural drainage and deep breathing carried out as ordered ... 100% 28-35
   l. Patient monitored for evidence of complications ... 100%
   m. Patient assisted in coughing and deep breathing every 2 hours,
      with type of cough, color and character of sputum noted ... 100%
   n. Oral hygiene administered every 2-4 hours P.R.N. ... 100%
   o. Emotional support provided 100%

LENGTH OF STAY

10. Length of stay maximum 12 days   100% $4,200
    Exception: Presence of further complications or additional diagnoses justifying extension.

DISCHARGE STATUS

11. Patient discharged under the following conditions:
    a. Patient free of respiratory distress for at least 24 hours before discharge   100%
    b. Arterial blood gas values improved   100%   75
    c. Patient relieved of edema for at least 24 hours before discharge   100%
    d. Temperature below 99.6 F for at least 24 hours before discharge   100%
    e. Patient/relative able to repeat the name, purpose, dosage, frequency and side effects of any medication to be taken   100%
    Exception: Instructions and information on transfer form.

SUGGESTED SAMPLE

Patients whose discharge diagnoses include reference to fluid retention with electrolyte abnormality, gastrointestinal bleeding, hepatic coma or pre-coma, infection, peritonitis or renal failure in association with cirrhosis.

REVIEW

Criterion	Standard	Estimated Charge
JUSTIFICATION FOR EXTENDED STAY		$ 120 supplies
1. The presence of any of the following conditions in association with cirrhosis:	100%	8 kit
a. Fluid retention with electrolyte abnormality		
b. Gastrointestinal bleeding		
c. Hepatic coma or pre-coma		
d. Infection		
e. Peritonitis		
f. Renal failure		
DIAGNOSTIC STUDY		
2. History with reference to hepatitis, nutritional habits including consumption of alcohol, any vomiting or weight loss	100%	
3. Physical examination including reference to any splenomegaly, edema or jaundice	100%	
4. Laboratory and other studies including		
a. CBC, urinalysis and admission panel	100%	125
b. Serology	100%	11
c. Direct bilirubin	100%	29
d. Creatinine clearance	100%	26
e. Prothrombin time	100%	14
f. Stool analysis for occult blood	100%	4
g. Chest x-ray	100%	70
Exception: Chest x-ray within past 3 months with report in record.		
MANAGEMENT		
5. Management of complications		
a. Fluid retention with electrolyte abnormality		
(1) Determination of electrolyte and albumin levels in blood	100%	42
(2) Fluid and sodium restriction	100%	
(3) Diuretics and aldosterone antagonists	100%	
(4) Administration of potassium supplements	100%	
(5) In presence of massive ascites, abdominal paracentesis	100%	66 tray
Exception: Presence of clinical improvement on conservative therapy.		50

b. Gastrointestinal bleeding
  (1) X-ray and esophagogastroduodenoscopy to evaluate presence, site and extent of active bleeding — 100% — $ 525
  (2) Repeat coagulation profile — 100% — 64
  (3) Correction of any coagulation defect observed — 100%
  (4) Tamponade of esophageal varices — 100%
  (5) Replacement of blood loss and steps to prevent or reverse shock — 100% — 50
    per type
    45-88
    per unit
    45
    infusion fee
  (6) Surgical procedures as indicated to reduce portal blood pressure — 100%
c. Hepatic coma or pre-coma
  (1) Determination of blood ammonia level — 100% — 47
  (2) Determination of neurological status — 100% — 80
  (3) Measures to reduce blood ammonia level, including cathartics and/or enemas to remove blood from gastrointestinal tract — 100% — 8
  (4) Control of gastrointestinal hemorrhage — 100%
  (5) Esophageal tamponade to stop any variceal bleeding — 100%
  (6) Discontinuance of diuretics — 100%
  (7) Treatment of renal failure if present — 100%
  (8) Paracentesis — 100% — 66
    tray
    50
d. Peritonitis
  (1) Paracentesis with culture and sensitivity of material obtained — 100% — 110
  (2) Antibiotic consistent with culture and sensitivity — 100%
  (3) Drainage of peritoneal cavity — 100% — 52
e. Renal failure
  (1) Repeat blood chemistries — 100% — 50
  (2) Fluid intake restricted to volume consistent with urine output, measured extrarenal loss and allowance for insensible loss — 100%
  (3) Electrolyte composition of fluids controlled in accordance with patient's requirements as indicated by blood chemistries — 100% — 23
  (4) Protein intake eliminated — 100%
  (5) Mannitol infusion administered — 100% — 22

6. Nursing care, including
a. Patient assessment including vital signs, history of allergies and drug sensitivities, brief relevant history and present complaint — 100%
b. Formulation of care plan based on assessment and objectives — 100%
c. Patient orientation to care and procedures to be used — 100%
d. Social Service personnel informed of any special needs of patient — 100%
e. Patient monitored for evidence of complications — 100%

LENGTH OF STAY

7. Length of stay 8-14 days   100% $2,800-
                                                                                        4,900

    Exceptions: (a) Early departure against medical advice; (b) trans-
    fer to extended care facility; (c) complications or other diagnoses
    justifying extension.

DISCHARGE STATUS

8. Patient discharged under the following conditions:
    a. Clearing of sensorium   100%
    b. Absence of bleeding   100%
    c. Control of or absence of fluid retention   100%
    d. Patient ambulatory with temperature below 99.6 F on day of
        discharge   100%
    e. Patient/relative instructed re (1) avoidance of alcohol, (2)
        dietary needs, (3) special counseling recommended and sources
        listed for patient and (4) follow-up visit to physician   100%
        Exception: Instructions on transfer form.
    f. Social Service referral made to appropriate community agencies
        as indicated   100%
        Exception: Patient transferred to extended care facility.

CONGESTIVE HEART FAILURE

SUGGESTED SAMPLE

Patients who experienced cardiac arrest, digitalis toxicity, persistent arrhythmias, pulmonary embolism, hypokalemia or venous thrombosis associated with congestive heart failure.

REVIEW

Criterion	Standard	Estimated Charge
JUSTIFICATION FOR EXTENDED STAY		$ 120 supplies 8 kit
1. The presence of any of the following conditions in association with congestive heart failure:	100%	
a. Cardiac arrest		
b. Digitalis toxicity		
c. Persistent arrhythmias		
d. Pulmonary embolism		
e. Hypokalemia		
f. Venous thrombosis		
DIAGNOSTIC STUDY		
2. History	100%	
3. Physical examination findings including reference to any evidence of respiratory distress or cardiac arrhythmias	100%	
4. Laboratory and other studies including		
a. CBC, urinalysis and admission panel	100%	125
b. EKG	100%	48
c. Chest x-ray	100%	70
d. Blood cholesterol level	100%	16
e. Serum electrolytes	100%	25
f. Daily recording of blood pressure	100%	
MANAGEMENT		
5. Bed rest	100%	
6. Sedation as needed	100%	
7. Oxygen as needed	100%	26
Exception: Absence of respiratory distress.		
8. Diuretics as needed	100%	
Exception: Absence of fluid retention.		
9. Low sodium diet	100%	
10. Digitalis derivatives as needed	100%	
Exception: Presence of thyrotoxicosis.		
11. Nursing care including		
a. Patient assessment including vital signs, history of allergies and drug sensitivities and present complaint	100%	

24

b. Formulation of care plan based on assessment and objectives	100%	
c. Patient orientation to care and procedures to be used	100%	
d. Patient positioned to minimize breathing difficulty	100%	
e. Calf massage or gentle leg exercises	100%	
f. Monitoring and maintenance of intravenous and drug therapies	100%	
g. Patient monitored for evidence of complications	100%	
h. Evaluation of patient's tolerance for activity	100%	

12. Management of complications

    a. Cardiac arrest

       Implementation of hospital's cardiac arrest plan including $ 125

(1) Administration of oxygen	100%	
(2) Administration of vasopressors	100%	
(3) Isoproterenol, sodium bicarbonate and lidocaine in conjunction with resuscitative measures	100%	

    b. Digitalis toxicity

(1) Digitalis medication discontinued	100%	
(2) Serum digoxin level determined	100%	30
(3) Serum potassium level determined	100%	20
(4) Administration of potassium chloride as indicated	100%	

       Exception: Compromised renal function.

    c. Persistent arrhythmias

(1) Anti-arrhythmic medication	100%	
(2) Cardioversion as indicated	100%	400
(3) Where arrhythmias persist, pacemaker implantation	100%	700

       Exception: Satisfactory response to conservative measures.

    d. Pulmonary embolism

(1) Blood gas analysis	100%	70
(2) Lung scan for evaluation	100%	270
(3) Chest x-ray	100%	70
(4) Anti-coagulation	100%	

    e. Hypokalemia

(1) Monitoring of electrolyte levels	100%	25
(2) Administration of potassium as indicated	100%	

    f. Deep venous thrombosis

(1) Administration of anticoagulants	100%	
(2) Complete bed rest with affected extremity elevated above heart level	100%	
(3) Application of warm moist packs to affected area	100%	
(4) Culture and sensitivity, followed by appropriate anti-biotic	100%	75

       Exception: Absence of evidence of infection.

LENGTH OF STAY

13. Length of stay 7-11 days   100%   2,450-3,850

    Exceptions: (a) Early departure against medical advice; (b) complications or other diagnoses justifying extension.

25

DISCHARGE STATUS

14. Patient discharged under the following conditions:

    a. Patient ambulatory with temperature below 99.4 F for 36 hours before discharge   **100%**

    b. Patient free of (1) respiratory distress, (2) cyanosis and (3) edema   **100%**

    c. EKG stabilized   **100%**

    d. Presence of x-ray evidence of improvement in pulmonary congestion and pleural effusion   **100%**

    e. Patient/family instructed re (1) activity level, (2) diet, (3) any applicable restrictions on use of tobacco or alcohol, (4) medication dosages, schedule and side effects as applicable and (5) follow-up visit to physician   **100%**

        Exception: Instructions on transfer form.

SUGGESTED SAMPLE

Patients who were admitted primarily for the treatment of previously known or recently diagnosed diabetes and for stabilization of their condition.

REVIEW

Criterion	Standard	Estimated Charge
JUSTIFICATION FOR ADMISSION		$ 120 supplies
1. Presence of one of the following conditions:	100%	8 kit
a. Blood glucose 325 mg/100 ml or greater		
b. Ketoacidosis with		
(1) Acetonuria 1+ or greater		
(2) CO_2 below 20 mEq		
(3) Arterial blood pH below 7.35		
c. Insulin reaction		
d. Insulin allergy		
e. Insulin resistance		
STATUS UPON DISCHARGE		
2. Stabilization of blood glucose (plasma glucose) for at least 48 hours before discharge, with either of the following:	100%	
a. Fasting plasma glucose between 90 and 180 mg/ml or		9
b. 2 hour postprandial plasma glucose below 200 mg/100 m		9
3. Urine acetone no higher than 1+	100%	3
4. Absence of reports of urine acetone equal to or higher than 1+ for at least 48 hours before discharge	100%	3
5. The patient or significant other:	100%	
a. Demonstrating ability to test urine for sugar and acetone		
b. Showing ability to administer insulin		
Exception: Patient not insulin dependent.		
c. Showing ability to provide skin and foot care		
d. Showing ability to administer medications and to identify early signs of adverse reactions		
e. Instructed in diet restrictions and given copy of diet		35
f. Instructed in weight controls or goals		
Exception: Weight change not necessary.		
g. Instructed in restrictions on exercise		
Exception: No restrictions indicated.		
h. Instructed with respect to follow-up appointment with physician		
Exception: Instructions on transfer form.		
LENGTH OF STAY		
6. Length of stay 3 to 7 days	100%	1,050-2,450
Exceptions: (a) Early departure against medical advice; (b) presence of complications or other diagnoses justifying extension.		

27

SUGGESTED SAMPLE

Patients whose discharge diagnoses include hemorrhage, obstruction, pancreatitis or perforation associated with duodenal or gastric ulcer.

REVIEW

Criterion	Standard	Estimated Charge
JUSTIFICATION FOR EXTENDED STAY		
1. The presence of any of the following in conjunction with duodenal or gastric ulcer:	100%	$ 120 supplies 8 kit
a. Hemorrhage		
b. Obstruction		
c. Pancreatitis		
d. Perforation		
DIAGNOSTIC STUDY		
2. History with specific reference to (a) pertinent drug-related history (aspirin, aspirin-related compounds, Butazolidin, Indocin, Motrin, steroids), (b) use of tobacco, alcohol and caffeine	100%	
3. Physical examination	100%	
4. Laboratory and other studies including		
a. CBC, urinalysis and admission panel	100%	125
b. Serology	100%	11
c. Chest x-ray within past 3 months with report in record	100%	70
d. Upper gastrointestinal tract x-ray studies	100%	200
Exceptions: (1) UGI performed within past 3 months and documented in record; or (2) endoscopy revealing duodenal or gastric ulcer done prior to UGI; or (3) patient taken to surgery before UGI could be performed.		
e. Endoscopy with or without biopsy	0%	325
Exceptions (Indications): (1) UGI negative or equivocal; (2) radiologist reports malignant appearance on x-ray; (3) endoscopy needed to determine source of bleeding; (4) other lesions suspected in esophagus or stomach; (5) endoscopy needed prior to surgery.		
f. Serum gastrin study	0%	60
Exception (Indication): Suspicion of presence of Zollinger-Ellison peptic ulcer syndrome.		
g. Gastric analysis	0%	18
Exceptions (Indications): (1) Endoscopy not available; (2) peptic ulcer syndrome suspected; (3) data needed before surgery.		
h. Serum calcium study	0%	20
Exception (Indication): Admission blood panel shows elevated serum calcium.		

MANAGEMENT

5. Administration of antacids — 100%

6. Ulcer diet — 100%

7. Bed rest with bathroom privileges — 100%

8. Follow-up upper gastrointestinal series — 100% — $ 200

   Exceptions: (a) Patient treated surgically; (b) hospital stay less than 14 days; (c) presence of clinically good response to therapy.

9. Follow-up with endoscopy — 0% — 190

   Exceptions (Indications): (a) Persistent symptoms despite optimal therapy; (b) occurrence of hemorrhage.

10. Management of complications

    a. Hemorrhage

       (1) Administration of skimmed milk with an antacid hourly — 100%

           Exception: Presence of vomiting.

       (2) Patient's blood typed and cross matched for transfusion — 100% — 50

       (3) Transfusion of whole blood or of individual units of plasma — 100% — 45-88 per unit / 45 infusion fee

       (4) Surgical repair following failure of conservative measures to control hemorrhage within 24 hours — 100%

    b. Obstruction

       (1) Continuous nasogastric aspiration — 100% — 27

       (2) Intravenous fluids to correct dehydration, acid base imbalance and hypoproteinemia — 100% — 20

       (3) Surgical correction of obstruction in absence of response to conservative measures — 100%

    c. Pancreatitis

       (1) Continuous nasogastric suction — 100% — 27

       (2) Administration of non-aspirin analgesics — 100%

    d. Perforation

       (1) Continuous nasogastric aspiration — 100% — 27

       (2) Immediate measures to prevent shock, including intravenous dextrose and saline — 100% — 20

       (3) Prompt surgical repair — 100% — 1,300 OR / 260 anesthesia / 190 RR

    e. Failure of signs of healing after 2 weeks of intensive medical therapy in hospital

       Referral of patient for surgery — 100%

11. Nursing care, including

    a. Patient assessment, including vital signs, history of allergies and sensitivities, brief relevant history and present complaint — 100%

    b. Formulation of care plan based on assessment and objectives — 100%

    c. Patient orientation to care and procedures to be used — 100%

    d. Patient monitored for evidence of complications — 100%

    e. Intravenous therapy monitored and maintained — 100%

29

LENGTH OF STAY

12. Length of stay
    a. Duodenal or gastric ulcer without complications, 4-8 days   100% $1,400-2,800
    b. Complicated by hemorrhage, 14 days   100%   4,900
    c. Complicated by obstruction, unoperated, 10 days   100%   3,500
    d. Complicated by pancreatitis with resolution, 10 days   100%   3,500
    e. Complicated by perforation, 14 days postoperative   100%   4,900

    Exceptions: (1) Early departure against medical advice, or (2) other complications or additional diagnoses justifying extension.

DISCHARGE STATUS

13. Patient discharged under the following conditions:
    a. Complications absent   100%
    b. Patient recovered from any surgery performed   100%
    c. Patient tolerating solid diet   100%
    d. Hgb greater than 9 gms % and Hct stable   100%
    e. Patient ambulatory, with temperature below 99.6 F on day of discharge   100%
    f. Pain relieved or any residual pain accounted for   100%
    g. Patient/family instructed re (1) diet, (2) dosage and schedule of any applicable medications and (3) follow-up visit to physician   100%

    Exception: Instructions on transfer form.

SUGGESTED SAMPLE

Patients whose discharge diagnoses include congestive heart failure or hemolytic transfusion reaction in association with iron deficiency anemia.

REVIEW

Criterion	Standard	Estimated Charge
JUSTIFICATION FOR EXTENDED STAY		$ 120 supplies
1. Presence of either of the following conditions in association with iron deficiency anemia:	100%	8 kit
a. Congestive heart failure		
b. Hemolytic transfusion reaction		
DIAGNOSTIC STUDY		
2. Documented investigation of etiology of blood loss including:		
a. Menstrual history and pelvic examination	100%	
Exception: Male patient.		
b. Stool guaiac study	100%	4
c. Sigmoidoscopy	100%	157
d. Upper gastrointestinal series	100%	210
e. Barium enema	100%	185
f. Esophagogastroduodenoscopy	100%	190
General Exception to Criteria Nos. 2b, 2c, 2d, 2e and 2f: Female patient with other etiology identified and documented.		
MANAGEMENT		
3. Oral iron administered	100%	
Exceptions: Presence of (a) colostomy, (b) acute inflammatory bowel disease, (c) intolerance to oral iron, (d) active peptic ulcer, (e) erosive gastritis or (f) malabsorption syndrome.		
4. Management of complications		
a. Congestive heart failure		
(1) Transfusion with packed red cells	100%	50 type, 45-88 per unit, 45 infusion fee
(2) Bed rest with patient positioned to minimize breathing difficulty	100%	
(3) Oxygen as needed	100%	26
Exception: Absence of respiratory distress.		
b. Hemolytic transfusion reaction		
(1) Transfusion stopped	100%	
(2) Patient's body kept warm	100%	

(3) Infusion of 10% mannitol solution at rate of 10-15 ml/min. until 1,000 ml have been administered	100%	$20
(4) Re-typing and cross-matching of pre-transfusion specimens of patient's and donor's blood	100%	55
(5) Re-typing and cross-matching of post-transfusion specimens of patient's and donor's blood	100%	

Record Analyst: Hemolytic transfusion reaction will be manifested by temperature higher than 101F, chills and renal shutdown with urinary output below 20 ml/hour, and/or presence of hemoglobin in serum or urine. Find data in nursing notes, progress notes and laboratory reports.

5. Nursing care, including

a. Patient assessment including vital signs, history of allergies and drug sensitivities and present complaint	100%	
b. Formulation of care plan based on assessment and objectives	100%	
c. Patient orientation to care and procedures to be used	100%	
d. Patient monitored for evidence of complications	100%	

LENGTH OF STAY

6. Length of stay

a. In absence of complications, 5-7 days	100%	1,750-2,450
b. In presence of congestive heart failure, 7-11 days	100%	2,450-3,850
c. In presence of hemolytic transfusion reaction, 8-10 days	100%	2,800-3,500

DISCHARGE STATUS

7. Patient discharged under the following conditions:

a. Temperature below 99.4F for 24 hours before discharge	100%	
b. Complications absent	100%	
c. Response to therapy satisfactory as manifested by	100%	

    (1) Hgb level above 8 gms % or Hgb increase of 1.5 gms % over an admission level higher than 8 gms %, and

    (2) Reticulocyte count increase of 2 percentage points

d. Presence of normal renal function	100%	
e. Patient/family instructed re (1) diet, (2) dosages and schedules of medications and (3) follow-up visits to physician	100%	

Exception: Instructions on transfer form.

LUMBOSACRAL SPRAIN, ACUTE

SUGGESTED SAMPLE

Patients who have experienced severe persistent lower back pain with muscle spasm and limitation of motion, intervertebral disc abnormality, or neurological deficit associated with an acute lumbosacral sprain.

REVIEW

Criterion	Standard	Estimated Charge
JUSTIFICATION FOR ADMISSION		
1. The presence of any of the following conditions in a patient with an acute lumbosacral sprain:	100%	$ 120 supplies 8 kit
a. Severe pain with muscle spasm and limited motion unresponsive to conservative outpatient therapy for a period of at least 7 days		
b. Established intervertebral disc abnormality		
c. Segmental neurological deficit		
DIAGNOSTIC STUDY		
2. History of one or more of the following:	100%	
a. Recent trauma		
b. Recent lifting of heavy object		
c. Recent unexpected twisting or sudden bending		
d. Low back pain radiating to posterior thigh, calf and foot, aggravated by coughing, sneezing or defecation		
3. Physical examination showing at least one of the following:	100%	
a. Positive straight leg raising test in conjunction with low back pain radiating to posterior thigh, calf and foot, aggravated by coughing or sneezing		
b. Depression of deep tendon reflexes, hypesthesia and loss of muscle tone in conjunction with straight leg raising test and low back pain		
c. Tenderness over lumbosacral area		
4. Studies including		
a. X-ray evidence of flattening of lumbar lordosis	100%	220
b. Electromyography	0%	200
Exceptions (Indications): (1) Presence of indications of cord compression or of space-occupying lesion; (2) demonstrated neurological deficit; (3) demonstrable muscle atrophy.		
c. Myelography	0%	510
Exceptions (Indications): (1) Presence of indications of cord compression or of space-occupying lesion; (2) demonstrated neurological deficit; (3) demonstrable muscle atrophy.		
d. Scan	0%	390
Exception (Indication): Required to locate site of suspected or confirmed lesion.		
MANAGEMENT		
5. Management of complications		
a. Persistent severe pain with limitation of motion		

(1) Bed rest in position of greatest comfort	100%		
(2) Administration of analgesics and muscle relaxants	100%		
(3) Application of moist heat	100%	$	25
(4) Ultrasound therapy	100%		27

b. Disc abnormality

(1) Bed rest in position of greatest comfort	100%	
(2) Administration of analgesics and muscle relaxants	100%	
(3) Local heat	100%	25
(4) Pelvic or lower extremity traction	100%	30
(5) Surgical treatment in presence of any of the following conditions:	100%	

      (a) Progressive damage to nerve tissue

      (b) Failure of chronic symptoms to respond to conservative treatment

      (c) Absence of improvement in acute episode after 4 to 6 weeks of bed rest

c. Neurological deficit as reflected in numbness or loss of bladder or bowel function

(1) Electromyography for evaluation and localization	100%	200
(2) In presence of progressive damage to nerve tissue, surgical treatment of extruded or protruding disc	100%	

6. Nursing care, including

a. Patient assessment including vital signs, history of allergies and drug sensitivities and present complaint	100%
b. Formulation of care plan based on assessment and objectives	100%
c. Character of pain observed and documented	100%
d. Patient monitored for evidence of complications including neurological abnormalities	100%
e. Traction monitored where applicable	100%

LENGTH OF STAY

7. Length of stay

a. Lumbosacral sprain on conservative management, maximum of 6 days	100%	2,100
b. Lumbar laminectomy, postoperative stay 7-11 days	100%	2,450-3,850

Exceptions: (1) Early departure against medical advice; (2) presence of complications or other diagnoses justifying extended stay.

DISCHARGE STATUS

8. Patient discharged under the following conditions:

a. Patient ambulatory without help or pain for 48 hours before discharge	100%
b. Patient aware of name, dosage, frequency and side effects of his medications	100%
c. Patient instructed in proper body mechanics, documented in record	100%
d. Follow-up visit to physician scheduled	100%

Exception to Criteria 8b, 8c and 8d: Instructions on transfer form.

SUGGESTED SAMPLE

Patients whose discharge diagnoses include atelectasis, bronchiectasis, lung abscess, metastatic infection or pleural effusion in association with bacterial or viral pneumonia.

REVIEW

Criterion	Standard	Estimated Charge
JUSTIFICATION FOR EXTENDED STAY		$ 120 supplies
1. The presence of any of the following conditions in association with bacterial or viral pneumonia:	100%	8 kit
a. Atelectasis		
b. Bronchiectasis		
c. Lung abscess		
d. Metastatic infection		
e. Pleural effusion		
DIAGNOSTIC STUDY		
2. History including report of any two of the following:	100%	
a. Cough		
b. Persistent fever		
c. Purulent sputum		
d. Hemoptysis		
e. Chest pain		
f. Cyanosis		
3. Physical examination report	100%	
4. Laboratory and other studies including		
a. CBC, urinalysis and admission panel	100%	125
b. Electrolytes	100%	25
c. Blood culture and sensitivity	100%	75
d. Sputum culture and sensitivity	100%	75
e. Chest x-ray on admission showing some pneumonic infiltrate excluding aspiration and interstitial pneumonia	100%	70
f. Cold agglutinin	0%	
Exception (Indication): Presumptive diagnosis of viral pneumonia.		
5. Special procedures		
a. Bronchoscopy	0%	106-125
Exceptions (Indications): (1) Presence of lobar pneumonia unresolved after 1 week of treatment; (2) to rule out carcinoma.		
b. Thoracentesis	0%	
Exception (Indication): Pleural fluid shown on x-ray.		

MANAGEMENT

6. Antibiotics appropriate for specific organism — 100%
7. Intravenous fluids for dehydration — 100% — $ 20
   Exception: Absence of dehydration.
8. Follow-up chest x-rays — 100% — 70
9. Bed rest — 100%
10. Management of complications
    a. Atelectasis
       (1) Bronchoscopy with aspiration of secretion — 100% — 106-125
       (2) Intermittent positive pressure breathing exercise — 100% — 22
       (3) Administration of broad spectrum antibiotic from outset — 100%
    b. Bronchiectasis
       (1) Postural drainage at least twice a day — 100% — 16
       (2) Antibiotic — 100%
    c. Lung abscess
       (1) Culture and sensitivity — 100% — 75
       (2) Antibiotic consistent with sensitivity — 100%
       (3) Postural drainage — 100% — 32
       per 24 hours
    d. Metastatic infection
       (1) Drainage — 100% — 57
       (2) Culture and sensitivity — 100% — 75
       (3) Antibiotic consistent with sensitivity — 100%
    e. Pleural effusion
       Thoracentesis — 100% — 135
       40
       tray
11. Nursing care including
    a. Patient assessment including vital signs, history of allergies and drug sensitivities and present complaint — 100%
    b. Formulation of care plan based on assessment and objectives — 100%
    c. Patient orientation to care and procedures to be used — 100%
    d. Patient positioned to facilitate drainage as indicated in presence of atelectasis, bronchiectasis, lung abscess or metastatic infection — 100%
    e. Patient monitored for evidence of complications — 100%
    f. Intravenous therapy and medications monitored and maintained — 100%

LENGTH OF STAY

12. Length of stay in presence of
    a. Pneumonia, uncomplicated: 5-8 days — 100% — 1,750-2,800
    b. Atelectasis: 8-10 days — 100% — 2,800-3,500
    c. Bronchiectasis: 8-10 days — 100% — 2,800-3,500
    d. Lung abscess: 10-15 days — 100% — 3,500-5,250
    e. Metastatic infection: 8-10 days — 100% — 2,800-3,500
    f. Pleural effusion: 10-15 days — 100%
    Exceptions: (1) Early departure against medical advice; (2) complications or other diagnoses justifying extended stay.

DISCHARGE STATUS

13. Patient discharged under the following conditions:
    a. Temperature below 99.4 F for at least 36 hours before discharge   100%
    b. Relief of symptoms present at admission   100%
    c. Clearing of, or marked improvement in, radiologic evidence of infiltrate   100%
    d. Absence of complications   100%
    e. Patient/family instructed in (1) activity level, (2) diet, (3) dosage and schedules of any applicable medications and (4) follow-up visit to physican   100%
       Exception: Instructions on transfer form.

SUGGESTED SAMPLE

Patients whose discharge diagnoses include congestive heart failure, hemorrhage resulting from the use of anticoagulants, or shock in association with pulmonary embolism.

REVIEW

Criterion	Standard	Estimated Charge
JUSTIFICATION FOR EXTENDED STAY		$ 120 supplies
1. The presence of any of the following conditions in association with pulmonary embolism:	100%	8 kit
a. Congestive heart failure		
b. Hemorrhage due to anticoagulants		
c. Shock		
DIAGNOSTIC STUDY		
2. History including reference to (a) dyspnea, (b) cough and pleural pain, (c) cough with bloody streaking, (d) hemoptysis, (e) findings suggestive of pneumonia, (f) pleural effusion or (g) thrombophlebitis	100%	
3. Physical examination report including reference to (a) accentuation of pulmonary second sound, (b) tachypnea, (c) rales and decreased breath sounds, (d) cyanosis and/or (e) gallop rhythm or tachycardia	100%	
4. Laboratory and other studies including		
a. Elevated SGOT and LDH	100%	46
b. Serum bilirubin greater than 1.5 gms.	100%	25
c. Blood gas analysis	100%	70
d. CBC, urinalysis and admission panel	100%	125
e. Chest x-ray showing evidence of pulmonary embolism	100%	70
f. Radioisotope lung scan, pulmonary angiography or venogram showing findings consistent with pulmonary embolism	100%	270 scan 340 other
g. EKG	100%	48
MANAGEMENT		
5. Bed rest	100%	
6. Anticoagulants	100%	
7. Oxygen	100%	26
Exception: Absence of respiratory distress		
8. Daily repeat prothrombin time studies during anticoagulant therapy	100%	15
9. Follow-up lung scan	100%	270
10. Ambulation when fully anticoagulated and asymptomatic	100%	
11. Surgical embolectomy	0%	
Exception (Indication): Presence of continuing shock.		
12. Management of complications		
a. Congestive heart failure		
(1) Bed rest with bathroom privileges	100%	

(2) Administration of diuretics	100%	
(3) Cautious digitalization	100%	

b. Hemorrhage resulting from use of anticoagulants

(1) Anticoagulant therapy terminated	100%	
(2) Protamine sulfate therapy started	100%	
(3) Vitamin K administered	100%	

c. Shock

(1) Administration of either	100%	
(a) Meteraminol 100 mg/L DW or		$ 20 IV
(b) Isoproterenol 2-4 mg/L DW		
(2) Cautious digitalization	100%	
(3) Surgical embolectomy	0%	850 OR
		230 anesthesia

Exception (Indication): Failure of response to conservative therapy.

13. Nursing care including

263 RR

a. Patient assessment including vital signs, history of allergies and drug sensitivities and present complaint — 100%

b. Patient orientation to care and procedures to be used — 100%

c. Formulation of care plan based on assessment and objectives — 100%

d. Maintenance of bed rest and activity level ordered — 100%

e. Intake and output measured and charted — 100%

    Exception: Not ordered.

LENGTH OF STAY

14. Length of stay in presence of

a. Pulmonary embolism without additional complications: 10-14 days — 100% — 3,500-4,900

b. Pulmonary embolism with complications such as congestive heart failure, hemorrhage or shock: 17-23 days — 100% — 7,450-9,550

    Exceptions: (1) Early departure against medical advice; (2) complications or other diagnoses justifying extended stay.

DISCHARGE STATUS

15. Patient discharged under the following conditions:

a. Patient free of indications for admission, with pain decreased or absent — 100%

b. Patient stable on anticoagulant therapy — 100%

    Exception: Anticoagulants not indicated.

c. Temperature below 99.6 F for 36 hours before discharge — 100%

d. Patient tolerating general diet — 100%

    Exception: Presence of other condition requiring modified diet.

e. Patient free of complications of pulmonary embolism — 100%

f. Patient/family instructed re (1) avoidance of any alcohol or aspirin products during anticoagulant program; (2) avoidance of any drug interacting with anticoagulant; (3) dosage, schedule and effects of anticoagulant; (4) follow-up visit to physician — 100%

    Exception: Instructions on transfer form.

URINARY TRACT INFECTION

SUGGESTED SAMPLE

Patients whose discharge diagnoses include septicemia, allergic reactions to anti-infective agents or allergic reactions to intravenous pyelogram contrast medium in association with urinary tract infection.

REVIEW

Criterion	Standard	Estimated Charge
CRITERION FOR INCLUSION IN THIS STUDY		$ 120 supplies
1. Urine culture showing 100,000 colonies or more of any organism, on clean catch or catheterization specimen of urine	100%	8 kit
DIAGNOSTIC STUDY		
2. Review of history with special reference to any history of (a) urinary tract infection due to bacteria, (b) recent urinary tract infection, or (c) urinary tract manipulation such as catheterization	100%	
3. Physical examination with special reference to urinary symptoms and any other abnormalities	100%	
4. Laboratory and other studies including		
a. Urine culture and sensitivity	100%	75
b. Fasting blood sugar or 2-hour postprandial blood sugar	100%	14
c. Intravenous pyelogram	100%	128
Exception: First episode of urinary tract infection in a female.		
d. In females, pelvic examination with search for cystocele	100%	
Exception: Documentation of recent pelvic examination in record.		
e. In males, digital examination to evaluate prostate	100%	
Exception: Documentation of recent digital examination in record.		
MANAGEMENT		
5. Anti-infective agents consistent with culture and sensitivity findings	100%	
6. Follow-up urine culture in hospital in absence of improvement	100%	75
7. At least one repeat blood pressure determination	100%	
Exception: BP within normal limits on first determination.		
8. Re-assessment of need for indwelling catheter after 3 days' use	100%	
Exception: (a) Absence of indwelling catheter; (b) presence of long-term problem such as neurogenic bladder.		
9. Gynecological consultation	0%	
Exception (Indication): Presence of previously unevaluated or large cystocele.		
10. Urological consultation	0%	
Exception (Indication): Presence of a genitourinary abnormality not previously evaluated.		
11. Management of complications		
a. Allergic reaction to anti-infective agent		

(1) Medication stopped	100%	
(2) Another appropriate anti-infective agent substituted	100%	
b. Allergic reaction to intravenous pyelogram contrast medium		
(1) Chart labeled	100%	
(2) Patient informed of his sensitivity	100%	

12. Nursing care

 a. Patient assessment including vital signs, history of allergies and drug sensitivities and present complaint   100%

 b. Patient orientation including explanation of any special devices and procedures to be applied   100%

 c. Formulation of care plan based on assessment and objectives   100%

 d. Patient encouraged to take ample amounts of fluids   100%

 e. Catheter care as applicable

  (1) Closed system Foley catheter used, size 16 where feasible   100% $ 40

  (2) Aseptic technique employed at insertion

   (a) Sterile gloves worn   100%

   (b) Parts swabbed with iodine   100%

   (c) Catheter lubricated with sterile lubricant from catheter kit   100%

    Contraindicated: Use of unsterile lubricant from previously opened pack.

  (3) Constant downward flow maintained, with collection bag hanging below bladder level at all times   100%

    Contraindicated: Collection bag resting on floor below bed.

  (4) In presence of indwelling catheter, meatal hygiene twice a day   100%

  (5) Monitoring for formation of plug   100%

  (6) Where specimen needed, collection port swabbed and sterile needle and syringe used each time   100%

  (7) Manual irrigation   0%

    Exception (Indication): Written order by physician.

  General Exception to Criterion 12e: Absence of catheter.

LENGTH OF STAY

13. Length of stay 4-6 days   100% 1,400-2,100

 Exceptions: (a) Early departure against medical advice; (b) complications or other diagnoses justifying extension; (c) need for endoscopy or corrective surgery.

DISCHARGE STATUS

14. Patient discharged under the following conditions:

 a. Urine culture sterile   100% 75

  Exception: Presence of documented plan for continued antibiotic therapy and follow-up urine culture.

 b. Absence of symptoms and signs of urinary tract infection such as chills, fever, dysuria and frequency   100%

 c. Patient/family instructed re (1) need for increased fluid intake, (2) dosage and schedule of medications as applicable and (3) follow-up visit to physician   100%

  Exception: Instructions on transfer form.

SUGGESTED SAMPLE

Patients whose discharge diagnoses include gastrointestinal bleeding or hepatic decompensation in association with viral hepatitis A or B.

REVIEW

Criterion	Standard	Estimated Charge
JUSTIFICATION FOR EXTENDED STAY		$ 120 supplies
1. The presence of either of the following conditions in association with viral hepatitis A or B:	100%	8 kit
a. Gastrointestinal bleeding		
b. Hepatic decompensation		
DIAGNOSTIC STUDY		
2. History with special reference to possible recent exposure to infectious hepatitis, to blood transfusions or to injections	100%	
3. Physical examination report with special reference to evidence of jaundice, gastrointestinal bleeding, coma or pre-coma	100%	
4. Laboratory and other studies including		
a. CBC, urinalysis and admission panel	100%	125
b. Electrolyte level determinations	100%	25
c. Serial blood urea nitrogen levels	100%	19
d. Creatinine level	100%	25
e. Australian antigen test	100%	46
f. Protein electrophoresis	100%	40
g. Elevated direct and indirect bilirubin	100%	54
h. Stool studies for occult blood	100%	4
i. Elevated SGOT	100%	23
j. Chest x-ray	100%	70
k. Upper gastrointestinal series	0%	210
Exception (Indication): Presence of jaundice.		
l. Cholecystogram	0%	130
Exception (Indication): Presence of jaundice.		
m. Hepatic scan	0%	314
Exception (Indication): Presence of jaundice.		
MANAGEMENT		
5. Intravenous fluids	100%	20
Exception: Patient receiving general diet.		
6. Multiple vitamins	100%	
7. Activity as tolerated	100%	

8. Management of complications
    a. Gastrointestinal bleeding
        (1) Patient's blood typed and cross-matched for transfusion — 100% — $ 50
        (2) Patient transfused with whole blood — 100% — 45-88 per unit / 45 infusion fee

    b. Hepatic decompensation
        (1) Prednisolone 50-100 mg/day administered orally — 100%
        (2) Low-fat, high-carbohydrate diet given — 100%
        (3) In presence of extreme nausea and vomiting, 10% glucose administered by intravenous route — 100% — 20
        Exception: Absence of extreme nausea and vomiting.

9. Nursing care including
    a. Patient assessment including vital signs, history of allergies and drug sensitivities and present complaint — 100%
    b. Formulation of care plan based on assessment and objectives — 100%
    c. Patient orientation to care and procedures to be used — 100%

LENGTH OF STAY

10. Length of stay 8-12 days — 100% — 2,800-4,200
    Exceptions: (a) Early departure against medical advice;
    (b) complications or other diagnoses justifying extension.

DISCHARGE STATUS

11. Patient discharged under the following conditions:
    a. Presenting symptoms including jaundice absent or ameliorated — 100%
    b. Complications absent — 100%
    c. Temperature below 99.6 F for at least 24 hours before discharge — 100%
    d. Patient/family instructed re (1) diet, (2) activity level including return to work or school, (3) dosage and schedule of any medications, (4) restrictions on use of alcohol and (5) follow-up visit to physician — 100%
    Exception: Instructions on transfer form.

SURGERY

AMPUTATION—LOWER EXTREMITY

SAMPLE

Patients discharged following amputation of a lower extremity.

REVIEW

Criterion	Standard	Estimated Charge
INDICATIONS FOR ADMISSION AND PROCEDURE		$ 140 supplies 8 kit
1. Presence of one or more of the following conditions: (a) Vascular occlusion or diabetic gangrene; (b) chronic infection such as osteomyelitis unresponsive to conservative therapy; (c) severe trauma eliminating the possibility of reconstruction; (d) bone or soft tissue malignancy; (e) certain congenital anomalies incompatible with function, or severe anomalies secondary to organic disease	100%	
PREOPERATIVE STUDIES		
2. In the chart prior to surgery,		
a. History of complaints consistent with indications listed above	100%	
b. Physical examination report with documentation of the presence of any of the conditions listed above	100%	
3. Laboratory and other studies		
a. Hospital's usual admission studies including CBC, urinalysis and admission panel	100%	125
b. Coagulation profile	100%	85
c. 2-hour postprandial blood sugar	100%	14
Exception: Presence of vascular occlusion or chronic infection.		
d. Chest x-ray within past 4 weeks with report in record	100%	70
e. EKG	100%	48
Exception: Patient under 40 years of age.		
f. Arteriogram	100%	100
Exceptions: (1) Absence of vascular occlusion, diabetic gangrene or chronic infection; (2) presence of allergy to dye.		
PREOPERATIVE CARE		
4. Preoperative nursing care		
a. Admission assessment of patient	100%	
b. Notification of Rehabilitation and Social Service of impending amputation	100%	
c. Patient instructed concerning		
(1) Routine postoperative care	100%	
(b) Positioning in bed	100%	
(3) Use of trapeze	100%	
(4) Body image and phantom pain	100%	
(5) Post-anesthesia deep breathing and coughing	100%	

d. Trapeze installed on bed	100%	$ 12
e. Physician's orders and special procedures explained and implemented	100%	

5. Physical Therapy Services

Implementation of pre-amputation routine including

a. Assessment of patient with respect to strength, range of motion of all extremities, abilities in activities of daily living and balance	100%	40
b. Establishment of patient's potential for use of prosthesis	100%	
c. Instruction in gait training with crutches or walker	100%	25
d. Explanation of postoperative program to patient	100%	

6. Social Service program

Assessment covering at least:

a. Psychological evaluation	100%	
b. Environmental evaluation and inquiry about home setting	100%	
c. Evaluation of patient's economic capacity to cope with any special home care expenses that will be incurred	100%	

Exception to Criteria Nos. 5 and 6:   Emergency surgery for trauma.

7. Anesthesiologist's preoperative evaluation of patient including specification of ASA class and risk level	100%	

MANAGEMENT

1,450
OR

8. Below-knee amputation	100%	345 RR

Exception: Absence of adequate viable below-knee tissue to allow for flap healing.

307
anesthesia

9. Posterior flap on lower extremity.	100%	30 instruments

Exception: Prohibited by presence of infection, location of trauma, or tumor.

10. Guillotine or delayed closure	0%	

Exception (Indication):   As indicated in presence of infection.

11. Report by operating surgeon of (a) preoperative diagnosis, (b) procedures performed, (c) description of tissues and findings, dictated or written immediately after surgery	100%	
12. Pathologist's report consistent with preoperative diagnosis	100%	195

13. Management of complications

a. Wound infection

(1) Culture and sensitivity	100%	75
(2) Incision and drainage	100%	20
(3) Appropriate antibiotic	100%	
(4) Intensified wound care	100%	

b. Stump necrosis (dead flap)

1,450
OR

(1) Revision of amputation, followed by	100%	345 RR
(2) Postoperative management as outlined under Postoperative Care and Management	100%	307 anesthesia

30
instruments

c. Urinary tract infection

(1) Culture and sensitivity of urine	100%	75
(2) Appropriate antibiotic	100%	

d. Decubiti
   (1) Intensification of skin care — 100%
   (2) Frequent re-positioning of patient — 100%
   (3) Culture and sensitivity of lesions, followed by appropriate antibiotic — 100% $ 75

POSTOPERATIVE CARE AND MANAGEMENT

14. Anesthetist's postoperative evaluation following discharge from Recovery Room — 100%

15. Stump care: In presence of an infected stump with guillotine amputation, frequent dressing changes and debridement as indicated — 100%

16. Postoperative nursing care
  a. Pulse and respiration every 15 minutes until stable, then hourly for 4 hours, or per nursing care plan — 100%
  b. Patient monitored for evidence of complications such as sudden changes in vital signs, sudden apprehension, or redness, swelling, hematoma of or drainage from stump — 100%
  c. Physician notified promptly of any complications — 100%
  d. Prevention of contractures by means of positioning — 100%
  e. Special care in Jobst air boot — 100%
   (1) Proper pressure maintained in boot — 34 boot
   (2) Prevention of moisture collection and maceration of skin
   Exception: Jobst air boot not used. — 95 cast
  f. Elastic bandage removed and stump rewrapped every 6 hours — 100%   25 per day
  g. Patient demonstrating ability to engage in graduated activity such as bed exercises, chair exercises, exercise program designed by Physical Therapy Service and, when indicated, crutch walking — 100%
  h. Nurse's evaluation of condition of wound documented at time of dressing change — 100%

17. Postoperative Physical Therapy services provided
  a. 48 hours postoperative, wrapping begun to shrink and shape stump in anticipation of prosthesis and to prevent edema — 100%   25
  b. Patient trained in exercises to strengthen stump quads, adductors and normal leg, and in range of motion exercises to stump as indicated — 100%   25 per day
  c. Pain management initiated as indicated for phantom limb pain upon consultation with attending physician — 100%   40
  d. Prosthetic evaluation obtained no later than 2 weeks post-operative — 100%   40
  e. Family member or other responsible party contacted concerning home program before discharge — 100%
  Exception: Instructions on transfer form.

18. Postoperative Social Service program
The following services provided and documented in the record
  a. Continuous psychological evaluation and support — 100%
  b. Discharge planning — 100%
  c. Referrals to appropriate community resources such as Visiting Nurse Association, Meals on Wheels, etc. — 100%

LENGTH OF STAY

19. Length of stay
    a. Preoperative stay 5 days maximum   100% $1,750

       Exception: Presence of other diagnoses justifying extension.

    b. Postoperative range of 14-25 days   100% 4,900-8,750

       Exceptions: (1) Earlier transfer of patient to rehabilitation facility, (2) early departure against medical advice, (3) complications or other diagnoses justifying extension.

DISCHARGE STATUS

20. Patient discharged under the following conditions:
    a. Presence of viable flap and healing wound   100%
    b. Stitches removed   100%
    c. Patient showing some degree of independence with use of walker 100%

       Exceptions: (1) Double amputation, (2) disability following cerebral vascular accident, or (3) upper extremity disability.

    d. Patient trained to wrap stump to prevent edema   100%

       Exception: Patient untrainable.

    e. Absence of infections and other complications   100%
    f. Patient/family instructed re (1) wound care, (2) any applicable medications and (3) follow-up visit to physician.

       Exception: Instructions on transfer form.

APPENDECTOMY

SUGGESTED SAMPLE

Patients whose discharge diagnoses include paralytic ileus, peritonitis, postoperative hemorrhage, urinary tract infection or wound dehiscence or infection following appendectomy.

REVIEW

Criterion	Standard	Estimated Charge
JUSTIFICATION FOR EXTENDED STAY		$ 90 supplies 8 kit
1. Presence of (a) paralytic ileus, (b) peritonitis, (c) postoperative hemorrhage, (d) urinary tract infection or (e) wound dehiscence or infection following appendectomy	100%	
PREOPERATIVE STUDY AND CARE		
2. In the chart prior to appendectomy,		
a. At least a brief history including reference to (1) abdominal pain and (2) nausea, vomiting or anorexia	100%	
b. Report on complete physical examination including (1) digital rectal examination, (2) pelvic examination for all females beyond menarche, (3) any rectal or pelvic tenderness, and (4) any abdominal tenderness or rebound in right lower quadrant	100%	
3. Menstrual history as applicable	100%	
Exception: Not applicable due to sex or age.		
4. Hospital's routine preoperative studies including CBC, urinalysis and admission panel	100%	95
5. Documentation of chest x-ray within past 3 months	100%	70
6. Documentation of time of last preoperative meal	100%	
7. Preoperative nursing preparation including instructions in deep breathing, coughing and turning in bed following surgery	100%	
8. Anesthesiologist's preoperative evaluation of patient with specification of ASA class and risk level	100%	
MANAGEMENT		610 OR
9. Appendectomy	100%	160 RR
10. Report by operating surgeon including (a) preoperative diagnosis, (b) procedures performed and (c) description of tissues and findings, dictated or written immediately after surgery	100%	170 anesthesia 20 instruments
11. Pathologist's report positive for appendicitis	100%	60
Exception: Incidental appendectomy.		
12. Management of complications		
a. Paralytic ileus		
(1) Nothing by mouth	100%	
(2) Nasogastric tube	100%	27
(3) As indicated, Miller-Abbott tube for decompression of small intestine	100%	85 drain set 60

(4) If ileus is minimal, peristaltic stimulants and lubricated rectal tube	100%	$ 14
b. Peritonitis		
(1) Culture and sensitivity	100%	75
(2) Appropriate antibiotic	100%	
(3) Intravenous fluids	100%	
c. Postoperative hemorrhage		50 type
Blood replacement	100%	45-88 per unit
		45 infusion fee
d. Urinary tract infection		
(1) Culture and sensitivity of urine	100%	75
(2) Appropriate antibiotic	100%	
e. Wound dehiscence or infection		
(1) Surgical repair with correction of primary cause	100%	
(2) In presence of infection, culture and sensitivity of drainage	100%	75
(3) In presence of infection, antibiotic consistent with culture and sensitivity	100%	

POSTOPERATIVE CARE

13. Anesthetist's postoperative evaluation of patient following transfer from Recovery Room — 100%

14. Postoperative nursing care
   a. Pulse and respiration every 15 minutes until stable, then hourly for 4 hours or per postoperative nursing care plan — 100%
   b. Intake and output charted — 100%
      Exception: Not ordered.
   c. Intravenous therapy and medications maintained as applicable — 100%
   d. Patient encouraged to breathe deeply, cough and turn in bed — 100%
   e. Patient monitored for evidence of complications — 100%
   f. Condition of wound monitored — 100%

LENGTH OF STAY

15. Length of stay 4-6 days — 100% 1,400-2,100
   Exceptions: (a) Early departure against medical advice; (b) complications or other diagnoses justifying extension.

DISCHARGE STATUS

16. Patient discharged under the following conditions:
   a. Wound dry and healing — 100%
   b. Normal diet tolerated — 100%
   c. Patient's temperature below 99.8 F for 36 hours before discharge — 100%
   d. Follow-up care plan documented in record, with patient/family aware of (1) need to avoid strenuous activity for 2 weeks, (2) need to avoid lifting heavy objects for at least 6 weeks, (3) wound care if wound still draining, (4) bathing instructions if stitches still present, and (5) follow-up visit to physician — 100%
      Exception: Instructions on transfer form.

SAMPLE

Patients discharged following blepharoplasty.

REVIEW

Criterion	Standard	Estimated Charge
PREOPERATIVE STUDY AND CARE		$ 90 supplies
1. In the chart prior to surgery,		8 kit
a. Documentation of the presence of (1) entropion, (2) ectropion, (3) blepharoclasis or (4) uni- or bilateral ptosis	100%	
b. History including reference to etiology of condition and patient's need for plastic surgery to maintain satisfactory self image	100%	
c. Physical examination report with documentation of indications for procedure	100%	
d. Photographs relevant to planned procedure	100%	
2. Laboratory tests including the following performed before admission		
a. CBC	100%	19
b. Urinalysis	100%	10
3. Preoperative nursing care including		
a. Patient assessment including vital signs, brief relevant history and patient's reason for surgery	100%	
b. History of allergies and drug sensitivities	100%	
c. Formulation of care plan based on assessment and objectives	100%	
d. Patient orientation and preparation	100%	
SURGICAL MANAGEMENT		725 OR 50 local anesthetic 10 instruments
4. Plastic repair of (a) entropion, (b) ectropion, (c) blepharoclasis or uni- or bilateral ptosis as indicated	100%	
5. Report by operating surgeon of (a) preoperative diagnosis, (b) procedures performed and (c) description of tissues and findings, written or dictated immediately after surgery	100%	
6. Pathologist's report on any specimens submitted	100%	
Exception: Absence of tissue specimens.		
7. Management of complications		
a. Hemorrhage		
Bleeders clamped	100%	
b. Delayed ectropion		
Surgical correction after healing of initial incisions	100%	
POSTOPERATIVE CARE		
8. Postoperative nursing care		
a. Patient's condition observed until stable	100%	
b. Positioning requirements maintained	100%	

LENGTH OF STAY

9. Length of stay maximum 2 days   100% $ 700
   Exception: Complications or other diagnoses justifying extension.

DISCHARGE STATUS

10. Wounds dry with no signs of complications   100%
11. Patient's temperature below 99.4F   100%
12. Patient instructed re (a) facial care, (b) activity level and return to work, (c) medication as applicable and (d) follow-up visit to physician   100%

    Record Analyst: The presence in the record of a copy of the surgeon's standard instruction sheet covering at least these elements, with an indication that a copy was given to the patient, satisfies this requirement.

BREAST RECONSTRUCTION

SAMPLE

Patients discharged following breast reconstruction.

REVIEW

Criterion	Standard	Estimated Charge
JUSTIFICATION FOR EXTENDED STAY		$ 90 supplies
1. Occurrence of a shift in the position of the breast implant, the loss of the flap, or infection following breast reconstruction	100%	8 kit
POSTOPERATIVE STUDY AND CARE		
2. In the chart prior to surgery,		
a. History including report of breast amputation	100%	
b. Physical examination report showing	100%	
(1) Surgical absence of breast and		
(2) Absence of contraindications to elective surgery	100%	
3. Documentation of the following:		
a. Patient's desire for reconstruction and of her level of understanding concerning the compromises involved	100%	
b. Evaluation of probability of recurrence of malignancy	100%	
c. Copy of pathologist's report following mastectomy	100%	
4. Photographs in record	100%	
5. Laboratory and other studies performed prior to admission		
a. CBC, urinalysis and admission panel	100%	125
b. Chest x-ray	100%	70
6. Preoperative nursing care including		
a. Patient assessment including vital signs, brief relevant history and present complaint	100%	
b. History of allergies and drug sensitivities	100%	
c. Patient orientation to care and procedures to be used	100%	
d. Formulation of nursing care plan	100%	
e. Preoperative instruction, preparation and medication	100%	
7. Anesthesiologist's preoperative evaluation of patient with specification of ASA class and risk level	100%	
SURGICAL MANAGEMENT		50
8. The following procedures as indicated:	100%	1,500 OR
a. In the presence of adequate tissue, an implant beneath the skin		275 anesthesia
b. As indicated for addition of skin and muscle padding, use of latissimus dorsi myocutaneous flap		190 RR
		10 instruments
		9 medications

54

9. Report by operating surgeon covering (a) preoperative diagnosis, (b) procedures performed and (c) description of tissues and findings, dictated or written immediately after surgery 100%

10. Management of complications $ 580
    OR
    a. Shift in position of implant 180
       Repositioning of implant 100% anesthesia
    10
    instruments

    b. Loss of flap 580
       OR
       Debridement and closure 100% 180
       anesthesia
    10
    instruments

    c. Infection
       (1) Culture and sensitivity of incision 100% 75
       (2) Antibiotic consistent with culture and sensitivity 100%

POSTOPERATIVE CARE

11. Anesthetist's postoperative evaluation of patient following transfer from Recovery Room 100%

12. Postoperative nursing care including
    a. Vital signs every 15 minutes until stable, then hourly for 4 hours or per postoperative nursing care plan 100%
    b. Patient encouraged to breathe deeply, cough and turn in bed 100%
    c. Wound condition noted at time of dressing change 100%
    d. Patient monitored for evidence of complications 100%

LENGTH OF STAY

13. Length of stay 3 or 4 days 100% 1,050-1,400
    Exceptions: (a) Early departure against medical advice; (b) complications or other diagnoses justifying extension.

DISCHARGE STATUS

14. Patient discharged under the following conditions:
    a. Patient's temperature below 99.5 F for 36 hours before discharge 100%
    b. Wound dry and healing 100%
    c. Complications absent 100%
    d. Patient instructed re (1) limited motion on affected side for several weeks; (2) bathing and wound care; (3) dosage and schedule of any medications ordered and (4) follow-up visit to physician 100%

CARCINOMA OF THE COLON
SURGICAL MANAGEMENT

SAMPLE

Patients discharged following resection of the colon or colectomy for carcinoma of the colon.

REVIEW

Criterion	Standard	Estimated Charge
JUSTIFICATION FOR EXTENDED STAY		$ 120 supplies
1. Presence of hemorrhage, wound dehiscence or wound infection in association with colon resection or colectomy for carcinoma of the colon	100%	8 kit
PREOPERATIVE STUDY AND CARE		
2. In the chart prior to surgery,		
a. Documentation of either	100%	
(1) Established diagnosis of carcinoma of the colon based on tissue report following previous surgery, or		
(2) Presence of 2 or more of the following elements:		
(a) Pain in left side, left iliac fossa or upper abdomen		
(b) Change in bowel habits such as mucous or mucous diarrhea or change in stool calibre		
(c) Rectal bleeding		
(d) Palpable mass in right iliac fossa		
(e) Signs of obstruction including fever, anorexia or vomiting, abdominal distension, constipation or intermittent cramps		
(f) Diagnosis of severe ulcerative colitis (pseudopolyposis of colon)		
(g) Feeling of incomplete evacuation		
(h) Weakness or weight loss		
b. History with specific reference to contributory factors	100%	
c. Physical examination report including digital rectal and pelvic examinations	100%	
3. Laboratory and other studies performed before admission or within 1 day before surgery,		
a. Routine preoperative tests including CBC, urinalysis and admission panel	100%	125
b. Serology	100%	11
c. Coagulation profile	100%	85
d. Stools tested for gross and occult blood	100%	4
e. Chest x-ray either on the present admission or within 2 weeks before the present admission	100%	70
f. EKG either on present admission or within 2 weeks before the present admission	100%	48

4. Preoperative nursing care
   a. Patient assessment including vital signs, weight estimate, brief relevant history and present complaint — 100%
   b. Patient orientation to care and procedures to be used — 100%
   c. History of allergies and drug sensitivities — 100%
   d. Formulation of care plan based on assessment and objectives — 100%
   e. Instruction in deep breathing, coughing and turning in bed following surgery — 100%
   f. Preoperative preparation and medication — 100%
5. Anesthesiologist's preoperative evaluation of patient with specification of ASA class and risk level — 100%

SPECIAL PROCEDURES

6. Proctosigmoidoscopic examination with biopsy — 100% — $ 350

SURGICAL MANAGEMENT

7. Primary resection of colon with anastomosis — 100%
   Exceptions: (a) In presence of perforation or abscess formation, abscess drained and colostomy performed; growth resected and colostomy closed at a later date; or (b) presence of extensive tissue invasion making it impossible to remove the lesion in toto.

   2,200 OR
   317 anesthesia
   345 RR
   30 instruments

8. Transverse colectomy with end-to-end anastomosis — 0%

   Exception (Indication): Absence of tissue invasion, permitting removal of lesion in toto.

   2,200 OR
   317 anesthesia
   345 RR
   30 instruments

9. Report by operating surgeon of (a) preoperative diagnosis, (b) procedures performed and (c) description of tissues and findings dictated or written immediately after surgery — 100%

   165

10. Pathologist's report reflecting presence of carcinoma — 100%

    150

11. Management of complications
    a. Hemorrhage
       (1) Bleeding arrested or controlled — 100%
       (2) Patient's blood typed and cross-matched for transfusion — 100% — 50
       (3) Closure re-evaluated and source of bleeding identified — 100%
       (4) Definitive surgical measures taken to arrest bleeding — 100%
    b. Wound dehiscence
       (1) Surgical closure — 100%

       850 OR
       170 anesthesia
       160 RR
       30 instruments

       (2) Elimination of causative factor — 100%
    c. Wound infection
       (1) Drainage of wound — 100% — 52
       (2) Culture and sensitivity of drainage — 100% — 75
       (3) Appropriate antibiotic — 100%

POSTOPERATIVE CARE

12. Anesthetist's postoperative evaluation of patient following transfer
    from Recovery Room   100%

13. Postoperative nursing care
    a. Vital signs every 15 minutes until stable, then hourly for 4
       hours, then per postoperative care plan   100%
    b. Intravenous therapy, Foley catheter and medications
       monitored and maintained   100%
    c. Character and amount of any discharge from wound or
       drainage tube observed and documented   100%
    d. Care plan revised to reflect postoperative needs and objectives   100%
    e. Patient monitored for evidence of complications   100%
    f. Patient encouraged to breathe deeply, cough and turn in bed   100%

LENGTH OF STAY

14. Length of stay
    a. In presence of established diagnosis, preoperative stay
       maximum 2 days   100% $ 700
    b. To establish diagnosis, 5 days   100%   1,750
    c. Postoperative stay 12-16 days   100%   4,200-5,600

    Exceptions: (1) Early departure against medical advice; (2)
    complications or other diagnoses justifying extension.

DISCHARGE STATUS

15. Patient discharged under the following conditions:
    a. Good bowel function established   100%
    b. Patient tolerating solid diet   100%
    c. Complications absent   100%
    d. Patient's temperature below 99.6F for 36 hours before
       discharge   100%
    e. Patient/family instructed re (1) diet, (2) medications if
       applicable, (3) care of wound or colostomy and (4) plan for
       follow-up care including visit to physician   100%   35
       Exception: Instructions on transfer form.

CARCINOMA OF THE LUNG
SURGICAL MANAGEMENT

SUGGESTED SAMPLE

Patients whose discharge diagnoses include atelectasis, intractable pain, pneumonia, pneumothorax or wound infection in association with surgery for carcinoma of the lung.

REVIEW

Criterion	Standard	Estimated Charge
JUSTIFICATION FOR EXTENDED STAY		$ 120 supplies
1. Presence of atelectasis, intractable pain, pneumonia, pneumothorax or wound infection following surgery for carcinoma of the lung	100%	8 kit
PREOPERATIVE STUDY AND CARE		
2. In the chart prior to surgery,		
a. Documentation of either of the following elements:	100%	
(1) X-ray or bronchoscopic evidence of lung tumor		70-190
(2) Positive sputum cytology report		110
b. History including any history of smoking and of any exposure to industrial or other environmental carcinogens		
c. Physical examination report		
3. Laboratory and other studies including		
a. Routine preoperative tests including CBC, urinalysis and admission panel	100%	125
b. Serology	100%	11
c. Coagulation profile	100%	85
d. Chest x-ray	100%	70
e. EKG	100%	48
f. Sputum cytology	100%	110
g. Sputum culture for fungi and tuberculosis	100%	75
h. Bronchogram	100%	145
i. Bronchoscopy	100%	190
General Exception to Criteria Nos. 3f, 3g, 3h and 3i: Documentation in record of studies performed shortly before admission.		
j. Type and cross match for transfusion	100%	50
4. Preoperative nursing care including		
a. Patient assessment including vital signs, weight estimate, brief relevant history and present complaint	100%	
b. History of allergies and drug sensitivities	100%	
c. Formulation of care plan based on assessment and objectives	100%	
d. Patient orientation to care and procedures to be used	100%	
e. Patient given preoperative instructions based on anesthesia plan and anticipated surgical procedures	100%	

5.	Anesthesiologist's preoperative evaluation of patient with specification of ASA class and risk level	100%	

SURGICAL MANAGEMENT

6.	Excisional biopsy	100%	$ 880 OR 220 anesthesia
	Exception: Extensive local spread of neoplasm making excision of neoplasm impossible.		
7.	Resection	100%	2,060 OR 350 anesthesia 395 RR 30 instruments
	Exceptions: (a) Extension of neoplasm beyond the lung; (b) presence of distant metastases; (c) presence of severe pulmonary or cardiac disability.		
8.	Report by operating surgeon of (a) preoperative diagnosis, (b) procedures performed and (c) description of tissues and findings, dictated or written immediately after surgery	100%	
9.	Pathologist's report reflecting carcinoma of the lung	100%	110-200
10.	Palliative roentgenotherapy	0%	
	Exception (Indication): Presence of non-resectable lesion.		
11.	Chemotherapy	0%	
	Exception (Indication): Presence of extensive inoperable primary carcinoma of the lung.		
12.	Management of complications		
	a. Atelectasis		
	(1) Mechanical aspiration	100%	45
	(2) Culture and sensitivity	100%	75
	(3) Antibiotic consistent with culture and sensitivity	100%	
	b. Intractable pain		
	Chlorpromazine in conjunction with other sedatives as needed	100%	
	c. Pneumonia		
	(1) Culture and sensitivity	100%	75
	(2) Antibiotic consistent with culture and sensitivity	100%	
	d. Pneumothorax		
	Supportive care with medication for pain	100%	
	e. Wound infection		
	(1) Culture and sensitivity of drainage	100%	75
	(2) Antibiotic consistent with culture and sensitivity	100%	

POSTOPERATIVE CARE

13.	Anesthetist's postoperative evaluation of patient following transfer from Recovery Room	100%	
14.	Postoperative nursing care including		
	a. Vital signs every 15 minutes until stable, then hourly for 4 hours or per postoperative nursing care plan	100%	
	b. Intravenous therapy and medications monitored and maintained	100%	
	c. Intake and output measured and charted daily	100%	
	d. Weight recorded at least once after admission documentation	100%	

	e.	Drainage system, underwater or other, monitored	100%	
	f.	Patient monitored for evidence of complications	100%	

LENGTH OF STAY

15. Length of stay

	a.	For diagnostic study only, 3-7 days	100%	$1,050-2,450
	b.	Excisional biopsy only, maximum of 7-9 days postoperative	100%	2,450-3,150
	c.	Resection, maximum of 14 days postoperative	100%	6,580

Exceptions: (1) Early departure against medical advice; (2) complications or other diagnoses justifying extension.

DISCHARGE STATUS

16. Patient discharged under the following conditions:

	a.	Patient's temperature below 99.6 F for 24 hours before discharge	100%
	b.	Wound dry and healing	100%
	c.	Complications absent	100%
	d.	Patient/family instructed re (1) activity level, (2) wound care, bathing and personal hygiene, (3) diet as applicable, (4) medications as applicable, (5) community resources for assistance as needed and (6) follow-up visit to physician	100%

Exception: Instructions on transfer form.

CARCINOMA OF THE PROSTATE
SURGICAL MANAGEMENT

SUGGESTED SAMPLE

Patients whose discharge diagnoses include any of the following in association with surgery for carcinoma of the prostate.

Fistula	Sepsis
Hemorrhage	Urinary retention
Renal failure	Wound infection

REVIEW

Criterion	Standard	Estimated Charge
JUSTIFICATION FOR EXTENDED STAY		$ 100 supplies
1. Presence of any of the following conditions after surgery for carcinoma of the prostate:	100%	8 kit
a. Fistula		
b. Hemorrhage		
c. Renal failure		
d. Sepsis		
e. Urinary retention		
f. Wound infection		
PREOPERATIVE STUDY AND CARE		
2. In the chart prior to surgery,		
a. Documentation of at least 1 of the following conditions:	100%	
(1) Finding on digital rectal examination of stony hard prostatic nodule, or		
(2) Presence of progressive symptoms or signs of obstruction such as frequency, hesitancy, nocturia, slow urinary stream, dribbling or acute or chronic urinary retention with overflow		
b. Urinary history supporting diagnosis	100%	
c. Physical examination report including precise description of size, consistency and configuration of prostate	100%	
3. Laboratory and other studies including		
a. Hospital's routine preoperative tests including CBC, urinalysis and admission panel	100%	125
b. Coagulation profile	100%	85
c. Electrolytes	100%	25
d. Urine culture and sensitivity	100%	75
e. Documentation of presence of elevated blood acid phosphatase from specimen drawn more than 48 hours after any prostatic massage	100%	23
f. EKG	100%	48
g. Chest x-ray	100%	70

h. Intravenous pyelogram with post-voiding film	100%	$ 360
i. Cystogram and ureterogram	100%	236
j. Cystoscopy	100%	90

4. Preoperative nursing care including

a. Patient assessment including vital signs, brief relevant history and present complaint	100%	
b. History of allergies and drug sensitivities	100%	
c. Formulation of care plan based on assessment and objectives	100%	
d. Patient orientation to care and procedures to be used	100%	
e. Patient instructed to breathe deeply, cough and turn in bed following surgery	100%	
f. Preoperative preparation and medication	100%	

5. Anesthesiologist's preoperative evaluation of the patient with specification of ASA class and risk level — 100%

SURGICAL MANAGEMENT

6. Biopsy and frozen section study — 100% — 580
OR
170
anesthesia

7. Total prostatovesiculectomy — 100% — 1,500
OR
295
anesthesia
345
RR

   Exception: Presence of advanced carcinoma that has been demonstrated to be hormone-resistant.

8. Conservative prostatectomy — 0% — 1,300
OR
265
anesthesia
345
RR
30
instruments

   Exception: Presence of advanced hormone-resistant carcinoma.

9. Report by operating surgeon of (a) preoperative diagnosis, (b) procedures performed and (c) description of tissues and findings dictated or written immediately after surgery — 100%

10. Pathologist's report confirming carcinoma of the prostate — 100% — 110

11. Management of complications

   a. Fistula — 30

   (1) Catheter repositioned — 100% — 567
   OR
   (2) Fistula excised and repaired — 100% — 170
   anesthesia
   190
   RR

   b. Hemorrhage

   (1) Blood replacement — 100% — 95
   45-88
   per unit
   (2) In presence of persistent bleeding, surgical exploration and repair — 100% — 1,140
   OR
   210
   anesthesia
   300
   RR

c. Renal failure
   (1) Diuretics   100%
   (2) Peritoneal dialysis   100% $ 540

d. Sepsis
   (1) Culture and sensitivity   100%   75
   (2) Antibiotic consistent with culture and sensitivity   100%

e. Urinary retention
   (1) Catheterization   100%   40
   (2) Conservative management   100%

f. Wound infection
   (1) Culture and sensitivity   100%   75
   (2) Antibiotic consistent with culture and sensitivity   100%

POSTOPERATIVE CARE

12. Anesthetist's postoperative evaluation of patient following transfer from Recovery Room   100%

13. Antibiotics to combat any pre-existing urinary tract infection   100%
Exception: Absence of urinary tract infection.

14. Blood transfusion   0%   95
Exceptions (Indications): (a) Surgical blood loss exceeding 500 cc's or (b) Hgb less than 10 gms %.   45-88 per unit

15. Postoperative nursing care including
a. Vital signs every 15 minutes until stable, then hourly for 4 hours or per postoperative care plan   100%
b. Monitoring and charting of fluid intake and output   100%
c. Monitoring of intravenous therapy and medications   100%
d. Documentation of Foley catheter care   100%
e. Patient encouraged to breathe deeply, cough and turn in bed   100%
f. Patient monitored for evidence of complications   100%

LENGTH OF STAY

16. Length of stay
a. Total prostatovesiculectomy, 12-16 days   100%   4,200-5,600
b. Conservative (transurethral) prostatectomy, 8-10 days   100%   2,800-3,500
Exceptions: (1) Early departure against medical advice; (2) complications or other diagnoses justifying extension.

DISCHARGE STATUS

17. Patient discharged under the following conditions:
a. Patient's temperature below 99.6 F for 24 hours before discharge   100%
b. Voiding adequate   100%
c. Renal function stable   100%
d. Wound healing   100%
e. Patient's physical condition permits care at home or in extended care facility   100%
f. Complications absent   100%
g. Patient/family instructed re (1) diet, (2) activity level and return to work, (3) applicable medication dosages and schedule, (4) wound care and (5) follow-up visit to physician   100%
Exception: Instructions on transfer form.

CARCINOMA OF THE RECTUM
SURGICAL MANAGEMENT

SUGGESTED SAMPLE

Patients whose discharge diagnoses include wound dehiscence or wound infection following surgery for carcinoma of the rectum.

REVIEW

Criterion	Standard	Estimated Charge
JUSTIFICATION FOR EXTENDED STAY		$ 120 supplies
1. The presence of wound dehiscence or wound infection following surgery for carcinoma of the rectum	100%	8 kit
PREOPERATIVE STUDY AND CARE		
2. In the chart prior to surgery,		
a. Documentation of	100%	
(1) Established diagnosis of carcinoma of the rectum, or		
(2) Presence of 2 or more of the following conditions: (a) Pain in left side, left iliac fossa or upper abdomen; (b) change in bowel habits such as presence of mucous or mucous diarrhea or change in stool calibre; (c) rectal bleeding; (d) palpable mass in right iliac fossa; (e) signs of obstruction including fever, anorexia, vomiting, abdominal distention, constipation or intermittent cramps; (f) diagnosis of severe ulcerative colitis (pseudopolyposis of colon); (g) feeling of incomplete evacuation or (h) weakness or weight loss		
b. History with specific reference to contributory factors	100%	
c. Physical examination report including digital rectal and pelvic examinations	100%	
3. Laboratory and other studies including		
a. Hospital's routine preoperative tests including CBC, urinalysis and admission panel	100%	125
b. Coagulation profile	100%	85
c. Serology	100%	11
d. Stools tested for gross and occult blood	100%	4
e. Barium and air contrast x-rays of colon	100%	185
f. Chest x-ray	100%	70
g. EKG	100%	48
4. Preoperative nursing care		
a. Patient assessment including vital signs, weight, brief relevant history and present complaint	100%	
b. History of allergies and drug sensitivities	100%	
c. Formulation of initial care plan based on assessment and objectives	100%	

d. Patient orientation to care and procedures to be used	100%	
e. Preoperative instruction in deep breathing, coughing and turning in bed following surgery	100%	
f. Preoperative preparation and medication	100%	
5. Anesthesiologist's preoperative evaluation of patient with specification of ASA class and risk level	100%	

SURGICAL MANAGEMENT

6. Anterior resection of rectum with preservation of anal sphincter in the presence of either of the following indications:	100%	$2,240 OR 415 anesthesia
a. Presence of tumor of low grade malignancy in upper rectum, or		345 RR
b. Resection intended as a palliative measure in the presence of distant metastases and a patient totally averse to colostomy		30 instruments
7. Excision of rectum with terminal colostomy	0%	2,240 OR 415 anesthesia
Exceptions (Indications):		
a. Presence of tumor in lower half of rectum, less than 10 inches (25.4 cm) from the anal verge, or		345 RR
b. In the presence of high grade malignancy where no distant metastases are noted		30 instruments
8. Report by operating surgeon of (a) preoperative diagnosis, (b) procedures performed and (c) description of tissues and findings dictated or written immediately after surgery	100%	
9. Pathologist's report confirming presence of carcinoma	100%	160-200
10. Management of complications		
a. Wound dehiscence		
(1) Bleeding controlled or arrested	100%	
(2) Patient's blood typed and cross matched for transfusion	100%	50
(3) Closure re-evaluated and source of bleeding identified	100%	610
(4) Closure repaired	100%	
b. Wound infection		
(1) Wound drained	100%	52
(2) Culture and sensitivity of drainage	100%	75
(3) Antibiotic consistent with culture and sensitivity	100%	

POSTOPERATIVE CARE

11. Anesthetist's postoperative evaluation of patient following transfer from Recovery Room	100%	
12. Postoperative nursing care including		
a. Vital signs every 15 minutes until stable, then hourly for 4 hours or per postoperative nursing care plan	100%	
b. Maintenance of intravenous therapy and medications	100%	
c. Daily charting of intake and output	100%	
d. Documentation of quantity and character of wound drainage	100%	
e. Patient monitored for evidence of complications	100%	

LENGTH OF STAY

13. Length of stay
    a. In presence of established diagnosis, preoperative stay maximum
       of 3 days   100% $1,050
    b. To establish diagnosis, 5 days   100%   1,750
    c. Postoperative stay, maximum of 15 days   100%   5,250
    Exceptions: (1) Early departure against medical advice;
    (2) complications or other diagnoses justifying extension.

DISCHARGE STATUS

14. Patient discharged under the following conditions:
    a. Presence of good bowel function   100%
    b. Presence of ability to tolerate solid diet   100%
    c. Good wound healing   100%
    d. Adequately functioning colostomy   100%
       Exception: Absence of colostomy.
    e. Absence of complications   100%
    f. Patient's temperature below 99.6 F for 36 hours before discharge 100%
    g. Patient/family instructed re (1) diet, (2) medications as
       applicable, (3) care of wound or colostomy, (4) bathing and
       personal hygiene and (5) follow-up visit to physician   100%   35
       Exception: Instructions on transfer form.

SUGGESTED SAMPLE

Patients discharged with the diagnosis of dislocation of implant, flat anterior chamber, intraocular infection or wound separation following cataract extraction, with or without lens implantation.

REVIEW

Criterion	Standard	Estimated Charge
JUSTIFICATION FOR EXTENDED STAY		$ 45 supplies
1. Presence of dislocation of implant, flat anterior chamber, intraocular infection or wound separation following cataract extraction	100%	8 kit
PREOPERATIVE STUDY AND CARE		
2. In the chart prior to surgery,		
a. History showing (1) the course of the visual loss, (2) any drug intake and (3) family history, if any, of cataracts	100%	
b. Physical examination report including reports on (1) slit lamp examination, (2) ophthalmoscopic examination, (3) visual acuity in person over 5 years of age, (4) tonometry and (5) visual field examination, all performed prior to admission	100%	

Record Analyst: Note that even though the above studies were performed before admission, reports of the findings must be included in the medical record.

Criterion	Standard	Estimated Charge
3. Laboratory and other studies performed prior to admission		
a. Routine preoperative tests including CBC, urinalysis and admission panel	100%	95
b. Chest x-ray within past 30 days with report in record	100%	70
c. EKG	0%	48

Exceptions (Indications): (1) Patient over 60, (2) history of cardiovascular disease, (3) presence of chronic disease such as diabetes or hypertension.

Criterion	Standard	Estimated Charge
4. Preoperative nursing care including		
a. Patient assessment including vital signs, brief relevant history and present complaint	100%	
b. History of allergies and drug sensitivities	100%	
c. Formulation of care plan based on assessment and objectives	100%	
d. Patient orientation to care and procedures to be used	100%	
e. Preoperative preparation, medications and instructions consistent with anesthesia plan	100%	
5. Anesthesiologist's preoperative evaluation of patient	100%	

Exception: Local anesthesia planned.

SURGICAL MANAGEMENT

6. Cataract extraction, intracapsular or extracapsular, with or without lens implantation — 100% — $ 135 OR 10 instruments

7. Report by operating surgeon of (a) preoperative diagnosis, (b) procedures performed and (c) description of tissues and findings, dictated or written immediately after surgery — 100% — 19 medications 55 anesthesia

8. Management of postoperative complications

   a. Dislocation of lens implant

      Patient returned to operating room for repositioning of implant — 100% — 135 OR 10 instruments

      55 anesthesia

   b. Flat anterior chamber

      (1) Conservative, supportive care for 4-7 days — 100%

      (2) In absence of spontaneous resolution after 4-7 days, wound resutured — 100% — 135 OR 10 instruments 55 anesthesia

   c. Intraocular infection

      (1) Return to operating room for aspiration of aqueous and vitreous for culture and sensitivity — 100% — 135 OR 10 instruments

      (2) Administration of antibiotic consistent with culture and sensitivity — 100%

   d. Wound separation

      Patient returned to operating room for resuturing of wound — 100% — 135 OR 10 instruments 55 anesthesia

POSTOPERATIVE CARE

9. Postoperative evaluation of patient by anesthetist — 100%
   Exception: Local anesthesia used.

10. Daily inspection of the eye and change of dressing — 100%

11. Postoperative nursing care

    a. Nursing Service to instruct Hospital's telephone operators not to route any calls to patient's phone until further notice — 100%
       Exception: Private duty nurse on duty.
       This recommendation is intended to apply to the immediate postoperative period, until the patient is fully alert.

    b. Daily charting of vital signs and medications per care plan — 100%

    c. Patient monitored for evidence of complications — 100%

LENGTH OF STAY

12. Length of stay
    a. Intracapsular extraction, 4-5 days   100% $1,400-
                                                                                            1,750

    b. Other extraction, 3-4 days   100%   1,050-
                                                                                            1,400

    c. Extraction with lens implantation, 4-5 days   100%   1,400-
                                                                                            1,750

    Exceptions: (1) Early departure against medical advice;
    (2) complications or other diagnoses justifying extension.

MANAGEMENT OF DELAYED COMPLICATIONS

13. Presence of corneal endothelial touch   135
                                                                                              OR
    a. Patient re-admitted to hospital   100%   10
    b. Corneal touch evaluated and removed   100%   instruments
    c. Lens implant repositioned as indicated   100%   55
                                                                                          anesthesia
    d. Length of stay 4-5 days   100%   1,400-1,750

    Exceptions: (1) Early departure against medical advice;
    (2) complications or other diagnoses justifying extension.

DISCHARGE STATUS

14. Patient discharged under the following conditions:
    a. Eye(s) healing   100%
    b. Patient's temperature below 99.6 F   100%
    c. Patient comfortable with any pain controlled with oral
       medication   100%
    d. Complications absent   100%
    e. Patient/family instructed re (1) prohibition against lifting heavy
       objects, (2) daily eye care, (3) follow-up visit to physician   100%
    Exception: Instructions on transfer form.
    *Record Analyst: The presence in the record of the surgeon's
    standard instruction sheet with an indication that the patient
    has received a copy satisfies this requirement.*

SUGGESTED SAMPLE

Patients whose discharge diagnoses include paralytic ileus, pneumonitis or wound infection following cholecystectomy.

REVIEW

Criterion	Standard	Estimated Charge
JUSTIFICATION FOR EXTENDED STAY		$ 75 supplies
1. Presence of paralytic ileus, pneumonitis or wound infection following cholecystectomy	100%	8 kit
PREOPERATIVE CARE		
2. In the chart prior to surgery,		
a. Documentation of	100%	
(1) Previously established diagnosis of gallstones or non-functioning gallbladder, with patient admitted at this time for surgery, or		
(2) Presence of an acute abdominal problem requiring hospitalization in conjunction with one or more of the following:		
(a) Nausea, vomiting, dehydration and pain of gallbladder colic		
(b) History of recurrent pain or gallbladder attacks		
(c) Fever associated with any of the above symptoms		
(d) Jaundice		
(e) Pain or tenderness in the right upper quadrant		
(f) Leucocytosis		
b. History supporting preoperative diagnosis	100%	
c. Physical examination report	100%	
3. Laboratory and other studies performed prior to admission		
a. Routine preoperative tests including CBC, urinalysis and admission panel	100%	125
b. Coagulation profile	100%	85
c. Serology	100%	11
d. Chest x-ray	100%	70
e. EKG	100%	48
Exception: Patient under 40 years of age.		
f. Liver function studies	100%	80
g. Gastrointestinal x-ray series	100%	210
h. Cholecystogram	100%	130
i. Pancreatic function tests	0%	22
Exception (Indication): History of jaundice or diabetes.		

4. Preoperative nursing care including
   a. Patient assessment including vital signs, brief relevant history and present complaint 100%
   b. History of allergies and drug sensitivities 100%
   c. Formulation of care plan based on assessment and objectives 100%
   d. Patient orientation to care and procedures to be used 100%
   e. Documentation of degree of patient's acceptance of modified diet 100%
      Exception: Patient on general diet.
   f. Preoperative instruction in breathing deeply, coughing and turning in bed following surgery 100%
   g. Preoperative preparation and medication 100%
5. Anesthesiologist's preoperative evaluation of patient with specification of ASA class and risk level 100%

SURGICAL MANAGEMENT

6. Surgical procedure either .... 100% $ 930 OR
   a. Cholecystectomy or   215 anesthesia
   b. Cholecystectomy with exploration of common duct   225 RR
7. Report by operating surgeon of (a) preoperative diagnosis, (b) procedures performed and (c) description of tissues and findings dictated or written immediately after surgery .... 100%   20 instruments
8. Pathologist's report confirming preoperative diagnosis 100%   110-200
9. Management of complications
   a. Paralytic ileus
      (1) Nothing by mouth 100%
      (2) Nasogastric tube employed 100%   10
      (3) In presence of minimal ileus, peristaltic stimulants and lubricated rectal tube 100%
   b. Pneumonitis
      (1) Culture and sensitivity of sputum 100%   75
      (2) Antibiotic consistent with culture and sensitivity 100%
   c. Wound infection
      (1) Culture and sensitivity of drainage from wound 100%   75
      (2) Antibiotic consistent with culture and sensitivity 100%

POSTOPERATIVE CARE

10. Anesthetist's postoperative evaluation of patient following transfer from Recovery Room 100%
11. Postoperative nursing care including
    a. Vital signs every 15 minutes until stable, then hourly for 4 hours or per postoperative nursing care plan 100%
    b. Intravenous therapy and medications maintained and monitored 100%
    c. Vital signs, intake and output documented daily per plan 100%
    d. Character and amount of any wound discharge documented 100%
    e. Patient monitored for evidence of complications 100%

LENGTH OF STAY

12. Length of stay 8-11 days   100% $2,800-
     Exceptions: (a) Early departure against medical advice;   3,850
     (b) complications or other diagnoses justifying extension.

DISCHARGE STATUS

13. Patient discharged under the following conditions:
     a. Patient tolerating general diet   100%
     b. Patient's temperature below 99.0 F on day of discharge   100%
     c. Incision dry and healing   100%
     d. Patient/family instructed re (1) any applicable dietary
         restrictions, (2) activity level, (3) bathing or showering and
         (4) follow-up visit to physician   100%
         Exception: Instructions on transfer form.

SUGGESTED SAMPLE

Patients whose treatment for facial cellulitis was complicated by the presence of an allergic reaction to an anti-infective agent, the development of a resistant strain of bacteria or of a supra infection, or by respiratory complications.

REVIEW

Criterion	Standard	Estimated Charge
JUSTIFICATION FOR EXTENDED STAY		$ 95 supplies 8 kit
1. The presence of an allergic reaction to an anti-infective agent, the development of a resistant strain of bacteria or of a supra infection, or of a respiratory complication in association with facial cellulitis	100%	
PREOPERATIVE STUDY AND CARE		
2. In the chart prior to surgery,		
a. Documentation of the presence of 2 or more of the following:	100%	
(1) Facial cellulitis or abscess		
(2) Pre-existing condition predisposing patient to infection		
(3) Combination of neck or pharyngeal swelling with difficulty in swallowing and impending airway obstruction		
(4) Extension of cellulitis to mediastinum		
(5) Failure to respond to outpatient management		
b. History with specific reference to trauma, lesions, fever, nausea, chills, vomiting or other systemic symptoms	100%	
c. Physical examination report including determination of extent of cellulitis or abscess	100%	
3. Laboratory and other studies including		
a. CBC, urinalysis and admission panel	100%	95
b. The following specified cultures of the abscess	100%	
(1) Anaerobic		150
(2) Aerobic		75
(3) Fungus		73
Exception: Recent or concurrent course of an antibiotic.		
c. Gram stain study	100%	9
Exception: Absence of abscess subject to aspiration.		
d. Serology	100%	11
e. Chest x-ray within past 6 months with report in record	100%	70
f. X-ray of facial sinuses	100%	125
g. Dental x-rays	100%	112
h. EKG	100%	48
Exception: Patient under 40.		
i. Blood gas analysis	0%	70
Exception (Indication): Presence of impending airway obstruction.		

4. Preoperative nursing care including
   a. Patient assessment including vital signs, brief relevant history and present complaint ... 100%
   b. History of allergies and drug sensitivities ... 100%
   c. Formulation of care plan based on assessment and objectives ... 100%
   d. Patient orientation to care and procedures used ... 100%
   e. Preoperative instruction consistent with anesthetic plan ... 100%
   f. Preoperative preparation and medication ... 100%
5. Anesthesiologist's preoperative evaluation of patient ... 100%
   Exception: General anesthesia not planned.

SURGICAL MANAGEMENT

6. Either or both of the following procedures: ... 100%
   a. Incision and drainage with culture and sensitivity study ... $ 20 supplies
      Exception: Infection not resolved with formation of discrete abscess. ... 130 OR 10 instruments

   b. Biopsy and removal of etiologic agent. ... 100% ... 20 supplies
7. Report by operating surgeon of (a) preoperative diagnosis, (b) procedures performed and (c) description of tissues and findings, dictated or written immediately after surgery ... 100% ... 130 OR 10 instruments
8. Pathologist's report on all tissue specimens submitted ... 100% ... 60

POSTOPERATIVE CARE

9. Anesthetist's postoperative evaluation of patient following transfer from Recovery Room ... 100%
   Exception: General anesthesia not used.
10. Antibiotics as indicated by culture and sensitivity tests ... 100%
11. Postoperative nursing care including
    a. Daily graphic charting of vital signs per nursing care plan ... 100%
    b. Maintenance of intravenous therapy and medications ... 100% ... 20
    c. Patient encouraged to breathe deeply, cough and turn in bed ... 100%
    Exception: General anesthesia not used.
    d. Revision of care plan to reflect patient's condition ... 100%
12. Management of complications
    a. Allergic reaction to antibiotic
       (1) Antibiotic discontinued ... 100%
       (2) Antihistamine administered ... 100%
       (3) Appropriate antibiotic substituted ... 100%
    b. Development of resistant strain of bacteria or of supra infection
       (1) Antibiotic discontinued ... 100%
       (2) Culture and sensitivity repeated ... 100% ... 75
       (3) Appropriate antibiotic substituted ... 100%
    c. Respiratory complication ... 130 OR

       Tracheotomy and endotracheal tube ... 100% ... 74

75

LENGTH OF STAY

13. Length of stay 5-8 days   100% $1,750-
    Exceptions: (a) Early departure against medical advice;   2,800
    (b) complications or other diagnoses justifying extension.

DISCHARGE STATUS

14. Patient discharged under the following conditions:
    a. Patient's temperature below 100 F on day of discharge   100%
    b. Resolution of cellulitis or abscess   100%
    c. Food intake adequate for nutritional objectives   100%
    d. Return of laboratory test values to essentially normal levels   100%
    e. Patient/family instructed re (1) diet, (2) medications as
       applicable and (3) follow-up visit to physician   100%
       Exception: Instructions on transfer form.

CORRECTION OF GLAUCOMA

SAMPLE

Patients discharged following surgery for the correction of glaucoma.

REVIEW

Criterion	Standard	Estimated Charge
JUSTIFICATION FOR EXTENDED STAY		$ 45 _{supplies} 8 _{kit}
1. Presence of (a) infection, (b) prolonged absence of anterior chamber, or (c) wound leak following surgery for the correction of glaucoma	100%	
PREOPERATIVE STUDY AND CARE		
2. In the chart prior to surgery,		
a. Note reporting the presence of one of the following indications for admission:	100%	
(1) In open angle glaucoma, lack of patient compliance with medical recommendations to check a diurnal curve, i.e., to check cyclic variation in intraocular pressure		
(2) In closed angle glaucoma, admission to control an attack of angle closure		
b. Note reporting the presence of one of the following indications for surgery:	100%	
(1) In open angle glaucoma, failure to control pressure with resultant progressive deterioration of visual function or impending visual loss despite optimal medical management		
(2) In closed angle glaucoma, need for iridectomy		
c. History including reference to at least one of the following:	100%	
(1) Pressure elevation with inadequate control		
(2) Progression of visual loss or deterioration of optic nerve as evidenced by enlarged cup		
(3) Sudden onset of blurred vision, haloes, pain, nausea or red eye	100%	
d. Physical examination report showing intraocular pressure high enough to cause deterioration of visual function or threat of impending visual loss from pressure elevation	100%	
3. Preoperative studies including CBC, urinalysis and admission panel performed prior to admission	100%	
4. Special procedures performed before admission and documented in the record		
a. Tonometry	100%	50-125 _{total}
b. Gonioscopy	100%	
c. Ophthalmoscopy	100%	
d. Pupillary dilatation	100%	
e. Visual field examination	100%	

77

f. Visual field acuity with and without correcting lens	100%	
Exception: Patient under 5 years of age.		
5. Preoperative nursing care		
a. Patient assessment including vital signs, brief relevant history and present complaint	100%	
b. History of allergies and drug sensitivities	100%	
c. Formulation of care plan based on assessment and objectives	100%	
d. Patient orientation to care and procedures to be used	100%	
e. Preoperative instruction and preparation	100%	
6. Anesthesiologist's preoperative evaluation of patient	100%	
Exception: Local anesthesia planned.		

SURGICAL MANAGEMENT
$ 19
supplies and medications

7. One of the following procedures as indicated		
a. In open angle glaucoma, filtration procedure	100%	135 OR
b. In closed angle glaucoma, peripheral iridectomy	100%	135 OR
Exception: Presence of chronic condition associated with permanent adhesive closure of the filtration angle.		10 instruments
		55 anesthesia
c. In closed angle glaucoma, filtration procedure	0%	135 OR
Exception: Presence of chronic condition associated with permanent adhesive closure of the filtration angle.		10 instruments
8. Report by operating surgeon covering (a) preoperative diagnosis (b) procedures performed and (c) description of tissues and findings, dictated or written immediately after surgery	100%	
9. Management of complications		
a. Infection		19 supplies
(1) Aspiration of vitreous for culture and sensitivity		135 OR
(2) Intensive therapy with antibiotic consistent with drug consistent with culture and sensitivity	100%	
b. Prolonged absence of anterior chamber		
(1) Conservative management for 5 days	100%	
(2) After 5 days without resolution, repair of surgical wound	100%	19 supplies
		135 OR
c. Wound leak		
Surgical repair of wound	100%	19 supplies
		135 OR

POSTOPERATIVE CARE

10. Anesthetist's postoperative evaluation of patient after transfer from Recovery Room	100%	
Exception: Local anesthesia used.		
11. Bed rest for 1 day postoperative	100%	350

12. Eye drops and ointments as indicated	100%	$ 18
13. Postoperative nursing care including		

a. Nursing Service to instruct Hospital's telephone operators not to route calls to patient's phone until further notice ... 100%

Exception: Private duty nurse on duty.

This recommendation is intended to apply to the immediate postoperative period, until the patient is fully alert.

b. Daily charting of vital signs and medications per care plan ... 100%

c. Patient monitored for evidence of complications ... 100%

LENGTH OF STAY

14. Length of stay

a. Filtration procedure: 3-7 days depending upon rapidity of reformation of anterior chamber ... 100% ... 1,050-2,450

b. Iridectomy: 1-2 days ... 100% ... 350-700

Exceptions: (1) Early departure against medical advice; (2) complications or other diagnoses justifying extension.

DISCHARGE STATUS

15. Patient discharged under the following conditions:

a. Eye showing no evidence of infection ... 100%

b. Anterior chamber formed ... 100%

c. Wound intact ... 100%

d. Temperature below 99.6 F on day of discharge ... 100%

e. Patient/family instructed re (1) avoidance of crowds, (2) prohibition against strenuous activity for 3 weeks, (3) prohibition against lifting heavy objects and (4) follow-up visit to physician ... 100%

Exception: Instructions on transfer form.

HEMORRHOIDECTOMY

SUGGESTED SAMPLE

Patients whose discharge diagnoses include any of the following in association with hemorrhoidectomy.

Early postoperative bleeding
Post-anesthesia headache
Postoperative urinary retention

Urinary tract infection
Wound infection

REVIEW

Criterion	Standard	Estimated Charge
JUSTIFICATION FOR EXTENDED STAY		$ 120 supplies
1. Presence of (a) early postoperative bleeding, (b) post-anesthesia headache, (c) postoperative urinary retention, (d) urinary tract infection or (e) wound infection following hemorrhoidectomy	100%	8 kit
PREOPERATIVE STUDY AND CARE		
2. In the chart prior to surgery,		
a. History	100%	
b. Physical examination report including report of digital rectal examination and of hemorrhoids with protrusion, bleeding or thrombosis	100%	
3. Laboratory and other studies performed prior to admission		
a. CBC, urinalysis and admission panel	100%	95
b. Coagulation profile	100%	85
c. Serology	100%	11
d. Chest x-ray within past 3 months with report in record	100%	70
e. EKG	100%	48
Exception: Patient under 40.		
f. Proctoscopic examination	100%	106-125
g. Barium enema x-ray	100%	185
4. Preoperative nursing care including		
a. Patient assessment including vital signs, brief relevant history and present complaint	100%	
b. History of allergies and drug sensitivities	100%	
c. Formulation of nursing care plan based on assessment and objectives	100%	
d. Patient orientation to care and procedures to be used	100%	
e. Preoperative instruction in deep breathing, coughing and turning in bed following surgery	100%	
f. Preoperative preparation and medication	100%	
5. Anesthesiologist's preoperative evaluation of patient with specification of ASA class and risk level	100%	

SURGICAL MANAGEMENT

			$ 135 OR
6.	Hemorrhoidectomy	100%	160 RR
7.	Report by operating surgeon of (a) preoperative diagnosis, (b) procedures performed and (c) description of tissues and findings, dictated or written immediately after surgery	100%	20 instruments 190 anesthesia
8.	Pathologist's report on hemorrhoidal veins in record	100%	60
9.	Management of complications		
	a. Early postoperative bleeding		
	(1) Re-examination in operating room or proctoscopy unit	100%	130 OR
	(2) Re-exploration and suture of bleeding point if bleeding is massive or persistent	100%	10 instruments
	b. Post-anesthesia headache		
	(1) Bed rest	100%	
	(2) Forced fluids orally or by intravenous route	100%	
	(3) Analgesic for pain	100%	
	(4) Re-evaluation by anesthesiologist within 12 hours	100%	
	c. Postoperative urinary retention Catheterization	100%	30
	d. Urinary tract infection		
	(1) Culture and sensitivity of urine	100%	75
	(2) Antibiotic consistent with culture and sensitivity	100%	
	e. Wound infection		
	(1) Frequent sitz baths	100%	
	(2) Culture and sensitivity of purulent discharge	100%	75
	(3) Appropriate antibiotic in presence of suppuration	100%	

POSTOPERATIVE CARE

10.	Anesthetist's postoperative evaluation of patient following transfer from Recovery Room	100%	
11.	Postoperative nursing care		
	a. Vital signs every 15 minutes until stable, then per postoperative nursing care plan	100%	
	b. Documentation of quantity and character of any drainage from wound site	100%	
	c. Patient encouraged to breathe deeply, cough and turn in bed	100%	
	d. Patient monitored for evidence of complications	100%	

LENGTH OF STAY

12.	Length of stay 5-7 days	100%	1,750-2,450

Exceptions: (a) Early departure against medical advice; (b) complications or additional diagnoses justifying extension.

DISCHARGE STATUS

13.	Patient discharged under the following conditions:		
	a. Temperature below 99.6 F on day of discharge	100%	
	b. Normal bowel function established	100%	
	c. Pain minimal or absent	100%	
	d. Complications absent	100%	
	e. Patient instructed re (1) bathing and personal hygiene and (2) follow-up visit to physician	100%	

Exception: Instructions on transfer form.

SUGGESTED SAMPLE

Patients whose discharge diagnoses include any of the following conditions in association with herniorrhaphy.

Orchitis, trauma to testis, to blood supply or to vas deferens
Postoperative wound infection
Prostatism
Pulmonary embolism
Strangulation of the bowel

REVIEW

Criterion	Standard	Estimated Charge
JUSTIFICATION FOR EXTENDED STAY		
1. Presence of any of the following conditions in association with herniorrhaphy:	100%	
a. Orchitis		
b. Postoperative wound infection		
c. Prostatism		
d. Pulmonary embolism		
e. Strangulation of bowel		$ 75 supplies
PREOPERATIVE STUDY AND CARE		
2. In the chart prior to surgery,		
a. Documentation of the presence of inguinal or femoral hernia	100%	
b. History with specific reference to contributory factors	100%	
c. Physical examination report including digital rectal examination	100%	
3. Laboratory and other studies performed prior to admission		
a. CBC, urinalysis and admission panel	100%	125
b. Coagulation profile	100%	85
c. Serology	100%	11
d. Barium enema x-ray study	100%	185
e. Chest x-ray within past 3 months with report in record	100%	70
f. EKG	100%	48
Exception: Patient under 40.		
g. Hematocele or hydrocele ruled out by means of (1) trans-illumination or (2) palpation of hernia and external inguinal ring for normal cord structure above mass	100%	
h. Sigmoidoscopy	100%	157
Exceptions: (1) Patient under 50 years of age, (2) presence of clearly visible, palpable hernia such that sigmoidoscopy is not needed for diagnosis or identification of site.		
4. Preoperative nursing care		
a. Patient assessment including vital signs, brief relevant history and present complaint	100%	

b. History of allergies and drug sensitivities	100%	
c. Formulation of care plan based on assessment and objectives	100%	
d. Patient orientation to care and procedures to be used	100%	
e. Preoperative instruction in deep breathing, coughing and turning in bed following surgery	100%	
f. Preoperative preparation and medication	100%	
5. Anesthesiologist's preoperative evaluation of patient with specification of ASA class and risk level	100%	

SURGICAL MANAGEMENT

6. Surgical repair by means of one of the following procedures:	100%	$1,112 OR
a. Indirect inguinal herniorrhaphy, bilateral or unilateral		260 anesthesia
b. Direct inguinal herniorrhaphy, bilateral or unilateral		190 RR
c. Femoral herniorrhaphy, bilateral or unilateral		
7. Report by operating surgeon of (a) preoperative diagnosis, (b) procedures performed and (c) description of tissues and findings, dictated or written immediately after surgery	100%	20 instruments
8. Management of complications		
a. Orchitis or trauma to testis, to blood supply or to vas deferens		
(1) Culture and sensitivity	100%	75
(2) Antibiotic consistent with culture and sensitivity	100%	
(3) Bed rest	100%	
(4) Scrotal support	100%	17
(5) Ice bags	100%	25[1]
(6) Anti-inflammatory enzymes	100%	
b. Postoperative wound infection		
(1) Drainage of wound	100%	52
(2) Culture and sensitivity of wound drainage	100%	75
(3) Antibiotic consistent with culture and sensitivity	100%	
c. Prostatism		
(1) Catheterization for relief of urinary retention	100%	30
(2) Culture and sensitivity	100%	75
(3) Antibiotic consistent with culture and sensitivity	100%	
(4) Cystoscopy for evaluation	100%	160
(5) Digital rectal examination for evaluation	100%	
(6) Therapy as indicated by evaluation findings	100%	
d. Pulmonary embolism		
(1) Confirmation by lung scan	100%	270
(2) Chest x-ray	100%	70
(3) Bed rest	100%	
(4) Anticoagulant therapy	100%	
(5) Monitoring of cardiac and pulmonary status	100%	
e. Strangulation of bowel		1,112 OR
(1) Fluid electrolyte balance maintained	100%	190 anesthesia
(2) Hernia repaired surgically	100%	160 RR
		20 instruments

---

[1] 8 @ $3.20 each, over 2 days.

POSTOPERATIVE CARE

9. Anesthetist's postoperative evaluation of patient following transfer from Recovery Room — 100%

10. Postoperative nursing care
    a. Vital signs every 15 minutes until stable, then hourly for 4 hours or per postoperative nursing care plan — 100%
    b. Patient encouraged to breathe deeply, cough and turn in bed — 100%
    c. Wound and dressing monitored for evidence of excessive discharge — 100%
    d. Intravenous therapy and medications maintained — 100%
    e. Intake and output charted daily — 100%
       Exception: Not ordered.
    f. Patient monitored for evidence of complications — 100%

LENGTH OF STAY

11. Length of stay
    a. Preoperative for elective surgery, 1 day maximum — 100% — $ 350
    b. Postoperative as shown below — 100%

	Unilateral	Bilateral Same Day		
Infants up to 1 year	1-2 days	1-2 days	100%	370-740
1-19 years of age	2-3	2-3	100%	700-1,050
20-64 years of age	4-6	5-7	100%	1,400-2,450
65 years and over	6-8	7-8	100%	2,100-2,800

   • Sequential repair 5-7 days apart, with total postoperative stay of 14 days, with maximum postoperative stay of 5 days following second procedure — 100% — 4,200-5,600

   Exceptions: (1) Early departure against medical advice; (2) complications or other diagnoses justifying extension.

DISCHARGE STATUS

12. Patient discharged under the following conditions:
    a. Temperature below 99.6 F for 24 hours before discharge — 100%
    b. Wound healing — 100%
    c. Normal eating, bowel function and urination patterns established — 100%
    d. Patient/family instructed re (1) diet, (2) activity level, (3) return to work or school, (4) wound care, bathing and personal hygiene and (5) follow-up visit to physician — 100%
       Exception: Instructions on transfer form.

SUGGESTED SAMPLE

Patients whose discharge diagnoses include any of the following conditions in association with fracture of the hip.

Cardiovascular complications including congestive heart failure
Hemorrhage from wound
Pulmonary complications other than embolism
Pulmonary embolism
Shock
Urinary tract infection
Wound infection

REVIEW

Criterion	Standard	Estimated Charge
JUSTIFICATION FOR EXTENDED STAY		$ 150 supplies
1. Presence of any of the following conditions following treatment for fracture of the hip:	100%	8 kit
a. Cardiovascular complications including congestive heart failure		
b. Hemorrhage from wound		
c. Pulmonary complications other than embolism		
d. Pulmonary embolism		
e. Shock		
f. Urinary tract infection		
g. Wound infection		
PREOPERATIVE STUDY AND CARE		
2. In the chart prior to surgery,		
a. Documentation of diagnosis of fracture of the hip	100%	
b. History including reference to level of ambulation and activity prior to fracture	100%	
c. Physical examination report with specific reference to pain, rotation and range of motion	100%	
3. Laboratory and other studies including		
a. Hospital's usual preoperative tests including CBC, urinalysis and admission panel	100%	125
b. X-ray of the hip	100%	100
c. Chest x-ray	100%	70
Exception: Patient under 10 years of age.		
d. Coagulation profile	100%	85
Exception: Surgery not planned.		
e. Blood typed and cross matched for transfusion	100%	50
Exception: Surgery not planned.		

4. Preoperative nursing care
   a. Patient assessment including vital signs, brief relevant history and present complaint ... 100%
   b. History of allergies and drug sensitivities ... 100%
   c. Formulation of care plan based on assessment and objectives ... 100%
   d. Patient orientation to care and planned procedures ... 100%
   e. Preoperative instruction in deep breathing, coughing and turning in bed following surgery ... 100%
      Exception: Surgery not planned.
   f. Preoperative preparation and medication ... 100%
      Exception: Surgery not planned.
5. Anesthesiologist's preoperative evaluation of patient with specification of ASA class and risk level ... 100%

SURGICAL AND OTHER MANAGEMENT

$ 60
supplies

6. Hip pinning ... 100%

   Exception: Presence of a previously non-ambulatory patient for whom pinning is not needed in the interest of improved nursing care or for relief of pain.

   1,650
   OR
   295
   anesthesia
   345
   RR
   35
   instruments
   64
   traction

7. Buck's traction as an alternative to pinning ... 0%
   Exception: Presence of a patient who is not a suitable candidate for pinning, due to general condition or other factors.

8. Report by operating surgeon of (a) preoperative diagnosis, (b) procedures performed and (c) findings, dictated or written immediately after surgery ... 100%
   Exception: Absence of surgery.

9. Management of complications
   a. Cardiovascular complications including congestive heart failure
      (1) Complete bed rest ... 100%
      (2) Oxygen, sedation and medication as indicated ... 100%
      (3) Patient monitored for evidence of complications ... 100%
      (4) Investigation of possible embolism or thrombophlebitis ... 100%

      75
      per 24 hours

   b. Decubitus
      (1) Culture and sensitivity of lesion ... 100%
      (2) Antibiotic consistent with culture and sensitivity ... 100%
      (3) Intensified care of skin ... 100%

      75

   c. Hemorrhage from surgical wound
      Transfusion ... 100%
      Exception: Blood loss less than 500 cc, with Hct 30% or above.

      50
      type
      45
      infusion
      45-88
      per unit

   d. Pulmonary complications other than embolism
      (1) Respiratory therapy services including oxygen as needed, breathing exercises and intermittent positive pressure breathing therapy as indicated ... 100%

      75
      per 24 hours
      20
      per day
      22
      per day

      (2) Culture and sensitivity of sputum ... 100%

      75

      (3) Antibiotic consistent with culture and sensitivity ... 100%

e. Pulmonary embolism

(1) Confirmation by lung scan	100%	$ 270
(2) Anticoagulant therapy	100%	
(3) Sedation	100%	
(4) Bed rest	100%	
(5) Transfer to Intensive Care Unit	100%	770 per day
(6) Patient monitored	100%	

f. Shock

(1) Patient transferred to Intensive Care Unit for monitoring	100%	770 per day
(2) Oxygen administered	100%	75 per 24 hours
(3) Plasma infused	100%	45 per infusion 45-88 per unit

g. Urinary tract infection

(1) Culture and sensitivity of urine	100%	75
(2) Antibiotic consistent with culture and sensitivity	100%	

h. Wound infection

(1) Culture and sensitivity of drainage	100%	75
(2) Antibiotic consistent with culture and sensitivity	100%	

POSTOPERATIVE CARE

Not applicable in the absence of surgery.

10. Anesthetist's postoperative evaluation of patient following transfer from Recovery Room	100%	
11. Postoperative nursing care		
a. Vital signs every 15 minutes until stable, then hourly for 4 hours or per postoperative nursing care plan	100%	
b. Intravenous therapy and medications maintained and charted	100%	
c. Intake and output charted	100%	
d. Patient encouraged to breathe deeply and cough	100%	
e. Patient monitored for evidence of complications	100%	
12. Radiological examination of hip prior to discharge	100%	210

Exception: Patient transferred to another facility for definitive care.

13. Physical Therapy services including		
a. Evaluation report prior to treatment	100%	20
b. Formulation of care plan specifying applicable weight bearing limitation and objectives	100%	
c. Treatment reports with reference to services provided, including as indicated	100%	20-40 per day
(1) Tilt table exercises		
(2) Leg raising exercises		
(3) Quadriceps setting exercises		
(4) Active dorsiflexion		
(5) Triceps exercises		

(6) Gait training
   Exception: Patient not ambulatory before fracture.
(7) Training in use of walker
   Exceptions: (a) Patient not ambulatory before fracture;
   (b) Other disability preventing use of walker.

OTHER SERVICES

14. Social Service assistance including
    a. Initial evaluation of patient's or family's ability to care for patient following discharge — 100%
    b. Identification of appropriate extended care facility — 100%
       Exceptions: (1) Patient to be discharged home; (2) patient to be transferred for definitive care; (3) patient to be returned to nursing home from which he came.
    c. Arrangements made with community agencies for provision of post-hospital services and supplies as needed (i.e., Meals on Wheels, Visiting Nurse Association, etc.) — 100%
       Exceptions: (1) Patient and family self-sufficient; (2) to be transferred to another facility.
15. Dietetic consultation including
    a. Evaluation of patient's dietary status and knowledge — 100% — $ 35
    b. Patient education, documented by notes in medical record — 100%

LENGTH OF STAY

16. Length of stay
    a. For medical management only, without surgery, 12-21 days — 100% — 4,200-7,350
    b. For surgical management, 17-22 days — 100% — 5,950-7,700
    Exceptions: (1) Early departure against medical advice; (2) transfer for definitive care; (3) complications or other diagnoses justifying extension.

DISCHARGE STATUS

17. Patient discharged under the following conditions:
    a. Nursing Service's evaluation of patient's ability in activities of daily living documented — 100%
    b. Vital signs stable with temperature below 99.6 F for at least 24 hours before discharge — 100%
    c. Condition stabilized, including resolution of any complications — 100%
    d. Pain reduced and controlled with oral medication — 100%
    e. Patient and family instructed re (1) restrictions on weight-bearing, (2) wound care as applicable, (3) bathing and hygiene, (4) any applicable medication schedule and dosages and (5) follow-up visit to physician — 100%
    Exception: Instructions on transfer form.

LUMBAR LAMINECTOMY FOR DISC DISEASE

SUGGESTED SAMPLE

Patients whose discharge diagnoses include any of the following conditions in association with lumbar laminectomy for disc disease.

Cerebral spinal fluid fistula
Neurological deficit precipitated by or aggravated by surgery
Urinary tract infection
Wound dehiscence or hematoma

REVIEW

Criterion	Standard	Estimated Charge
JUSTIFICATION FOR EXTENDED STAY		$ 148 supplies
1. Presence of any of the following conditions following lumbar laminectomy for disc disease:	100%	8 kit
a. Cerebral spinal fluid fistula		
b. Neurological deficit precipitated by or aggravated by surgery		
c. Urinary tract infection		
d. Wound dehiscence or hematoma		
PREOPERATIVE STUDY AND CARE		
2. In the chart prior to surgery,		
a. Documentation of either	100%	
(1) Spinal fluid protein greater than 50%, or		15
(2) Diagnostic myelographic, electrolyelographic or computerized tomographic abnormality corresponding to the level of clinical suspicion		530
b. In conjunction with positive diagnostic findings, history of severe sciatic leg pain with or without back pain unresponsive to a 30-day trial of conservative therapy including	100%	
(1) Traction		
(2) Bed rest at home or in hospital		
(3) Physical therapy		
(4) Medication		
Exception: History of repeated regressions and exacerbations or evidence of progressive loss of motor function.		
c. Positive physical findings including at least 2 of the following:	100%	
(1) Focal motor weakness		
(2) Focal reflex changes		
(3) Positive straight leg raising test		
3. Laboratory and other studies including		
a. CBC, urinalysis and admission panel	100%	125
b. Coagulation profile	100%	85
c. Serology	100%	11
d. Patient's blood typed and cross matched	100%	50

e. Chest x-ray within past 3 months with report in record	100%	$ 70
f. EKG	100%	48

Exception: Patient under 40.

4. Preoperative nursing care

a. Patient assessment including vital signs, brief relevant history, present complaint, degree of pain and tolerance of activity	100%
b. History of allergies and drug sensitivities	100%
c. Formulation of care plan based on assessment and objectives	100%
d. Patient orientation to care and nursing procedures	100%
e. Preoperative instruction in deep breathing, coughing and turning in bed following surgery	100%
f. Preoperative preparation and medication	100%

5. Anesthesiologist's preoperative evaluation of patient with specification of ASA class and risk level — 100%

SURGICAL MANAGEMENT

6. Lumbar laminectomy	100%	819 OR
7. Spinal fusion with bone graft	0%	200 anesthesia

Exception: Multiple level laminectomy.

25 instruments

8. Blood transfusion	0%	45 infusion

Exception: Documented surgical blood loss exceeding 500 cc's.

45-88 per unit

9. Report by operating surgeon of (a) preoperative diagnosis, (b) procedures performed and (c) description of tissues and findings dictated or written immediately after surgery

10. Pathologist's report on specimens submitted	100%

11. Management of complications

a. Cerebral spinal fluid fistula

(1) Culture and sensitivity of leakage	100%	75
(2) Antibiotic consistent with culture and sensitivity	100%	
(3) Osmotic dehydration agents	100%	
(4) Bed rest	100%	
(5) Surgical repair of fistula	100%	819 OR

189 anesthesia
25 instruments

b. Neurological deficit precipitated by or aggravated by surgery

(1) Evaluation and documentation	100%
(2) Electromyography	100%
(3) Appropriate splinting	100%
(4) Application of physical medicine and physical therapy modalities	100%

c. Urinary tract infection

(1) Culture and sensitivity of urine	100%	75
(2) Antibiotic consistent with culture and sensitivity	100%	

d. Wound dehiscence or hematoma
   (1) Drainage of wound   100% $ 52
   (2) Surgical closure of wound   100%   189
                                                anesthesia
                                                819
                                                OR
                                                25
                                                instruments

POSTOPERATIVE CARE

12. Anesthetist's postoperative evaluation of patient following transfer from Recovery Room   100%

13. Postoperative nursing care including
    a. Pulse and respiration every 15 minutes until stable, then hourly for 4 hours or per postoperative nursing care plan   100%
    b. Patient encouraged to cough and breathe deeply   100%
    c. Intravenous therapy and medications maintained and monitored   100%
    d. Patient monitored for evidence of complications   100%

LENGTH OF STAY

14. Length of stay
    a. For trial of conservative therapy, 7-11 days   100%   2,450-3,850
    b. In presence of established diagnosis with surgery planned, preoperative stay of 1-2 days   100%   350-700
    c. Postoperative stay, 7-11 days   100%   2,450-3,850

    Exceptions: (1) Early departure against medical advice; (2) complications or other diagnoses justifying extension.

DISCHARGE STATUS

15. Patient discharged under the following conditions:
    a. Patient ambulatory   100%
    b. Temperature below 99.6 F for 2 days before discharge   100%
    c. Complications absent   100%
    d. Pain controlled with minimal oral medication   100%
    e. Patient and family instructed re (1) any applicable limitations on activity, (2) progressive activity schedule, (3) dosages and schedules of any medications and (4) follow-up visit to physician   100%

    Exception to Criterion No. 15: Early transfer to another medical facility for convalescence, with discharge instructions noted on transfer form.

SUGGESTED SAMPLE

Patients whose treatment for fracture of the mandible or maxilla has been complicated by atelectasis, local infection or the vomiting and aspiration of gastric contents.

REVIEW

Criterion	Standard	Estimated Charge
JUSTIFICATION FOR EXTENDED STAY		$ 100 supplies
1. Presence of atelectasis, local infection resulting from inclusion of tooth in fracture line, or history of vomiting and aspiration of gastric contents	100%	8 kit
PREOPERATIVE STUDY AND CARE		
2. In the chart prior to surgery,		
a. History including description of recent trauma	100%	
b. Physical examination report supporting diagnosis	100%	
c. X-ray or clinical evidence of fractures of the mandible or maxilla with associated malocclusion or misalignment of facial contours	100%	
d. Laboratory and other studies including		
(1) CBC and urinalysis	100%	29
(2) X-ray studies including		
(a) Facial bone films for maxilla surgery	100%	131
(b) Four views of mandible for lower jaw surgery	100%	120
(c) Chest film	100%	70
3. Preoperative nursing care including		
a. Patient assessment including vital signs and brief relevant history	100%	
b. History of allergies and drug sensitivities	100%	
c. Formulation of care plan based on assessment and objectives	100%	
d. Patient orientation to care and planned procedures	100%	
e. Preoperative teaching based on anesthetic plan	100%	
f. Preoperative preparation and medication	100%	
4. Anesthesiologist's preoperative evaluation of patient with specific reference to ASA class and level of risk	100%	
SURGICAL MANAGEMENT		850 OR
5. Open reduction, fixation and immobilization	100%	305 anesthesia
Exception: Reduction, fixation and immobilization secured by non-operative methods	100%	300 RR
6. Report by operating surgeon of (a) preoperative diagnosis, (b) procedures performed, (c) condition of tissues and findings and (d) count of any teeth removed, dictated or written immediately after surgery	100%	12 instruments

7. Confirmatory post-reduction films	100%	$120-131
8. Medications as indicated for pain	100%	

POSTOPERATIVE CARE

9. Anesthetist's postoperative evaluation of patient following transfer from Recovery Room — 100%

10. Postoperative nursing care including
   a. Nursing Service to instruct Hospital's telephone operators not to route any calls to patient's phone until further notice — 100%
      Exception: Private duty nurses on duty.
   b. Pulse and respiration every 15 minutes until stable, then per postoperative nursing care plan — 100%
   c. Tracheotomy set in room — 100% — 65
   d. Airway precautions taken and documented — 100%
   e. Patient kept under close observation until fully alert — 100%
   f. Patient re-instructed in use of nurse call system — 100%
   g. Documentation in record showing that nursing station personnel have been informed of patient's inability to talk — 100%
   h. Intravenous therapy and medications maintained and monitored — 100%
   i. Daily local hygiene — 100%
   j. Dressings monitored for evidence of drainage or bleeding — 100%
   k. Patient monitored for evidence of complications — 100%

11. Dietetic services including
   a. Documentation of dietician's conference with patient and family member — 100% — 35
   b. Provision of liquid diet meeting nutritional requirements — 100%

12. Management of complications
   a. Atelectasis
      (1) Mechanical aspiration — 100% — 46
      (2) Culture and sensitivity — 100% — 75
      (3) Antibiotic consistent with culture and sensitivity — 100%
   b. Local infection resulting from tooth in fracture line
      (1) Removal of tooth in or near fracture line — 100% — 90 supplies 135 OR
      (2) Culture and sensitivity — 100% — 75
      (3) Anti-infective agent consistent with culture and sensitivity — 100%
   c. Vomiting and aspiration of gastric contents
      (1) Emergency tracheotomy — 100%
      (2) Aspiration of gastric contents through tube — 100% — 50
      (3) Administration of appropriate antibiotics — 100%

LENGTH OF STAY

13. Length of stay
   a. Repair of mandible, 1-4 days — 100% — 350-1,400
   b. Repair of middle third of face, 3-7 days — 100% — 1,050-2,450
   Exceptions: (1) Early departure against medical advice; (2) complications or other diagnoses justifying extension.

DISCHARGE STATUS

14. Patient discharged under the following conditions:
    a. Temperature below 99.6 F for 24 hours before discharge   100%
    b. Presence of radiologic evidence of satisfactory alignment of fractured bones   100%
    c. Complications absent   100%
    d. Patient and family instructed re (1) liquid diet, (2) oral hygiene, (3) activity level, including return to work or school, and (4) follow-up visit to physician   100%
       Exception: Instructions on transfer form.

SUGGESTED SAMPLE

Patients whose discharge diagnoses include postoperative hemorrhage, wound infection or depression, or who experienced marked and persistent restriction of arm motion on the affected side following mastectomy.

REVIEW

Criterion	Standard	Estimated Charge
JUSTIFICATION FOR EXTENDED STAY		$ 120 supplies
1. The presence of postoperative hemorrhage, wound infection, depression, or marked and persistent restriction of arm motion on the affected side following mastectomy	100%	8 kit
PREOPERATIVE STUDY AND CARE		
2. In the chart prior to surgery,		
a. Documentation of either of the following as an indication for admission and surgery:	100%	
(1) Need for biopsy to evaluate tumor mass in breast		
(2) Pathologist's report on previous biopsy positive for carcinoma		
b. History	100%	
c. Physical examination report with specific reference to (1) mass in breast, (2) nipple discharge or (3) breast skin changes	100%	
d. Laboratory and other studies performed prior to admission		
(1) CBC, urinalysis and admission panel	100%	125
(2) Coagulation profile	100%	85
(3) Serology	100%	11
(4) Differential blood count	100%	35
(5) Chest x-ray	100%	70
(6) EKG	100%	48
Exception: Patient under 40.		
(7) Mammography or xeroradiography report	100%	151
3. Preoperative nursing care including		
a. Patient assessment including vital signs, brief relevant history and present complaint	100%	
b. History of allergies and drug sensitivities	100%	
c. Formulation of nursing care plan based on assessment and objectives	100%	
d. Patient orientation to care and planned procedures	100%	
e. Instruction in breathing deeply, coughing and turning in bed following surgery	100%	
f. Preoperative preparation and medication	100%	

4. Anesthesiologist's preoperative evaluation of patient with specification of ASA class and risk level ... 100%

SURGICAL MANAGEMENT

5. Excisional biopsy ... 100% ... $ 140
   OR
   Exception: Malignancy previously confirmed by biopsy. ... 150
   In presence of ... anesthesia
   120
   RR

6. Benign tumor
   a. Excision of mass ... 100% ... 580
      OR
      Exceptions: (1) Presence of malignancy, (2) presence of ... 200
      extensive benign disease. ... anesthesia
   b. Simple mastectomy ... 0% ... 170
      RR
      Exception (Indication): In absence of malignancy, performed
      in presence of extensive benign disease.

7. Malignant disease
   a. Modified radical mastectomy ... 100% ... 800
      OR
      Exceptions: (1) Absence of malignant disease, (2) presence ... 240
      of malignancy or metastases such that simple mastectomy or ... anesthesia
      radical mastectomy with internal mammary node dissection ... 190
      is indicated. ... RR
   b. Radical mastectomy with internal mammary node dissection ... 0%
      Exception (Indication): Required to control lymph node
      metastases from inner quadrant or subareolar tumors.
   c. Simple mastectomy ... 0%
      Exception: Performed as a palliative measure in presence of
      gross malignancy or metastases.

8. Report by operating surgeon of (a) preoperative diagnosis,
   (b) procedures performed and (c) description of tissues and
   findings, dictated or written immediately after surgery ... 100%

9. Pathologist's report on tissue specimen in record ... 100%

10. Management of complications
    a. Hemorrhage
       (1) Re-evaluation and repair of closure as indicated ... 100%
       (2) Blood transfusion ... 100% ... $ 50
           type
           Exception: Estimated blood loss less than 500 cc's. ... 45
           infusion
           45-88
           per unit
    b. Wound infection
       (1) Drainage of wound ... 100% ... 52
       (2) Culture and sensitivity of drainage ... 100% ... 75
       (3) Antibiotic consistent with culture and sensitivity ... 100%
    c. Psychological depression
       (1) Enhanced efforts to provide emotional support
           documented in nursing notes and progress notes ... 100%
       (2) Psychiatric evaluation and consultation ... 100% ... 50

    d. Restriction of arm motion on affected side

(1) Institution of physical therapy exercise program	100%	$ 20 per day
(2) Introduction to community programs designed to assist mastectomy patients	100%	

POSTOPERATIVE CARE

11. Postoperative evaluation by anesthetist following transfer from Recovery Room	100%	
12. Estrogen receptor assay	100%	290

Exceptions: (a) Absence of malignancy; (b) male patient.

13. Postoperative nursing care

a. Vital signs every 15 minutes until stable, then hourly for 4 hours or per postoperative nursing care plan	100%	
b. Patient encouraged to breathe deeply, cough and turn in bed	100%	
c. Wound care given, including monitoring of (1) drains, (2) character and amount of drainage and (3) condition of dressing	100%	
d. Intravenous and drug therapy maintained	100%	
e. Nursing care plan revised to meet postoperative needs	100%	

14. Physical Therapy services

Following radical or modified radical mastectomy.

a. Evaluation of range of motion of arm on operated side, expressed in degrees	100%	20
b. Implementation of exercise program to secure optimal range of motion and strength in affected arm	100%	20 per day
c. Documentation of outcomes of physical therapy	100%	

General Exception: Absence of radical or modified radical mastectomy.

LENGTH OF STAY

15. Length of stay

a. Preoperative, 1 day maximum	100%	350
b. Postoperative		
(1) Excisional biopsy only, 2 days maximum	100%	700
(2) Excision of mass only, 2 days maximum	100%	700
(3) Simple mastectomy, 6 days maximum	100%	2,100
(4) Modified radical mastectomy, 8 days maximum	100%	2,800
(5) Radical mastectomy with internal mammary node dissection, 10 days maximum	100%	3,500

Exceptions: (a) Early departure against medical advice; (b) complications or other diagnoses justifying extension.

DISCHARGE STATUS

16. Patient discharged under the following conditions:

a. Temperature below 99.6 F for at least 24 hours before discharge	100%	
b. Wound dry and healing	100%	

c. Complications absent   100%
d. Plan for further therapy documented   100%
    Exception: Additional therapy not indicated.
e. Patient has been put in touch with community programs
    designed for rehabilitation of post-mastectomy patients   100%
    Exception: Such rehabilitation not required in absence of
    radical or modified radical mastectomy.
f. Patient has verbalized instructions on (1) bathing and personal
    hygiene, (2) applicable limitations on exercise and heavy
    physical work, (3) exercise plan as applicable and (4) follow-up
    visit to physician   100%
    Exception: Instructions on transfer form.

MAXILLARY OSTEOTOMY, ANTERIOR

SUGGESTED SAMPLE

Patients whose maxillary surgery has been complicated by the presence of atelectasis, hematoma or local infection or by the vomiting and aspiration of gastric contents.

REVIEW

Criterion	Standard	Estimated Charge
JUSTIFICATION FOR EXTENDED STAY		$ 100 supplies
1. Presence of atelectasis, hematoma, local infection or a history of vomiting with aspiration of gastric contents	100%	8 kit
PREOPERATIVE STUDY AND CARE		
2. In the chart prior to surgery,		
a. Documentation of the presence of malrelation of jaws, with repositioning required as an accessory to orthodontia	100%	
b. History including orthodontic history	100%	
c. Physical examination report showing findings consistent with indications for repositioning and absence of contraindications to elective surgery	100%	
d. Laboratory and other studies performed prior to admission, including		
(1) CBC, urinalysis and admission panel	100%	95
(2) Chest x-ray	100%	70
(3) Cephalometric x-ray studies documented with reports in record	100%	122
(4) Coagulation profile	0%	85
Exception (Indication): History of bleeding tendency or patient receiving anticoagulant.		
3. On hand for study, plaster or gypsum models of patient's jaws	100%	
4. Preoperative nursing care		
a. Patient assessment including vital signs, brief relevant history and patient's reason for surgery	100%	
b. History of allergies and drug sensitivities	100%	
c. Formulation of care plan based on assessment and objectives	100%	
d. Patient orientation to care and planned procedures	100%	
e. Preoperative teaching consistent with anesthesia plan	100%	
f. Preoperative preparation and medication	100%	
5. Anesthesiologist's preoperative evaluation of patient with specification of ASA class and level of risk	100%	

SURGICAL MANAGEMENT

6. Preoperative review of models of patient's jaws in operating room	100%	$1,250 OR
7. Repositioning and fixation of osteotomized segment	100%	35 instruments
8. Report by operating surgeon of (a) preoperative diagnosis, (b) procedures performed, (c) condition of tissues and findings and (d) count of any teeth removed, dictated or written immediately after surgery	100%	290 anesthesia 400 RR
9. Confirmatory postoperative x-ray film	100%	122
10. Medications as indicated for pain	100%	
11. Management of complications		
a. Atelectasis		
(1) Mechanical aspiration	100%	46
(2) Culture and sensitivity	100%	75
(3) Antibiotic consistent with culture and sensitivity	100%	
b. Hematoma		
Evacuation of hematoma	100%	50
c. Local infection		
(1) Culture and sensitivity	100%	75
(2) Antibiotic consistent with culture and sensitivity	100%	
d. Vomiting and aspiration of gastric contents		
(1) Emergency tracheotomy	100%	
(2) Aspiration of gastric contents through tube	100%	50
(3) Administration of appropriate antibiotics	100%	

POSTOPERATIVE CARE

12. Anesthetist's postoperative evaluation of patient following transfer from Recovery Room	100%	
13. Postoperative nursing care		
a. Nursing Service to instruct Hospital's telephone operators not to route any calls to patient's phone until further notice	100%	
Exception: Private duty nurses on duty.		
b. Pulse and respiration every 15 minutes until stable, then every 4 hours or per postoperative nursing care plan	100%	
c. Tracheotomy set in room	100%	65
d. Airway precautions taken and documented	100%	
e. Patient kept under close observation until fully alert	100%	
f. Patient re-instructed in use of nurse call system	100%	
g. Documentation in record showing that nursing station personnel have been informed of patient's inability to talk	100%	
h. Intravenous therapy and medications maintained and monitored	100%	20
i. Daily local and oral hygiene	100%	
j. Patient monitored for evidence of complications	100%	
14. Dietetic services		
a. Documentation of dietician's conference with patient and family member	100%	35
b. Provision of liquid diet meeting nutritional requirements	100%	

LENGTH OF STAY

15. Length of stay
    a. Preoperative, 1 day maximum   100% $ 350
    b. Postoperative, 4-6 days   100%   1,400-2,100
       Exceptions: (1) Early departure against medical advice;
       (2) complications or other diagnoses justifying extension.

DISCHARGE STATUS

16. Patient discharged under the following conditions:
    a. Temperature below 99.6 F for 24 hours before discharge   100%
    b. Presence of radiologic evidence of satisfactory alignment of jaws   100%
    c. Complications absent   100%
    d. Patient and family instructed re (1) liquid diet, (2) oral
       hygiene, (3) activity level including return to work or school
       and (4) follow-up visit to physician   100%
       Exception: Instructions on transfer form.

PACEMAKER IMPLANTATION

SUGGESTED SAMPLE

Patients whose discharge diagnoses include skin necrosis, hematoma, wound infection, pacemaker malfunction or pacemaker failure, in association with pacemaker implantation.

REVIEW

Criterion	Standard	Estimated Charge
JUSTIFICATION FOR EXTENDED STAY		$ 187 supplies
1. Presence of skin necrosis, hematoma, wound infection, pacemaker malfunction or failure following pacemaker implantation	100%	8 kit
PREOPERATIVE STUDY AND CARE		
2. In the chart prior to the implantation,		
a. Documentation of the presence of any one of the following:	100%	
(1) Acquired complete auriculo-ventricular block		
(2) Sinus node dysfunction		
(3) Intermittent complete heart block (right bundle branch block, left bundle branch block or bifascicular)		
(4) Acute myocardial infarction with anterior wall heart block		
(5) Congenital complete auriculoventricular block or surgical auriculoventricular block with symptoms		
(6) Recurrent ventricular tachycardia		
(7) Atrial fibrillation with slow ventricular rate (paroxysmal atrial tachycardia, Wolff-Parkinson-White Syndrome)		
(8) Bradycardia resulting from electrolyte imbalance (hyperkalemia)		
(9) Pacemaker failure		
b. History with specific reference to any of the following:	100%	
(1) Stokes-Adams attacks		
(2) Syncope and/or dizziness		
(3) Tachycardia		
(4) Bradycardia		
(5) Intractable congestive heart failure		
(6) Hypertensive vascular disease		
c. Physical examination report with findings of either	100%	
(1) Bradycardia less than 40 per minute, irregular, with EKG evidence of heart block, or		
(2) Tachycardia greater than 120 per minute not controlled by medication		
3. Laboratory and other studies including		
a. CBC, urinalysis and admission panel	100%	125
b. Coagulation profile	100%	85
c. Serology	100%	11

d. Chest x-ray	100%	$	70
e. EKG	100%		48

4. Preoperative nursing care including
   a. Patient assessment including vital signs, brief relevant history and present complaint ... 100%
   b. History of allergies and drug sensitivities ... 100%
   c. Formulation of care plan based on assessment and objectives ... 100%
   d. Patient orientation to care and planned procedures ... 100%
   e. Implementation of appropriate cardiac care plan ... 100%
   f. Preoperative instruction and preparation ... 100%   315
   OR
5. Anesthesiologist's preoperative evaluation of patient with specification of risk level ... 100%

SURGICAL MANAGEMENT

6. Implantation of pacemaker ... 100%   157
   prep
7. X-ray to ascertain correct positioning of pacemaker ... 100%   750
   pacemaker
8. Threshold of pacemaker tested and recorded in room in which implantation is performed.
   Exception: Temporary pacemaker.

9. Pacemaker generator model recorded in room in which implantation is performed ... 100%
   Exception: Temporary pacemaker.

10. Type of electrode catheter recorded in room in which implantation is performed ... 100%
    Exception: Temporary pacemaker.

11. Report by operating surgeon on (a) preoperative diagnosis, (b) procedures performed and (c) description of tissues and findings, dictated or written immediately after surgery ... 100%

12. Management of complications
    a. Skin necrosis
       (1) Pacemaker repositioned ... 100%   390
       (2) Culture and sensitivity of skin lesion ... 100%   75
       (3) Antibiotic consistent with culture and sensitivity ... 100%
    b. Hematoma
       Aspiration of hematoma ... 100%   170
    c. Wound infection
       (1) Wound drained ... 100%   143
       (2) Culture and sensitivity of drainage ... 100%   75
       (3) Antibiotic consistent with culture and sensitivity ... 100%
       (4) In presence of gross infection, alternative pacing system implanted ... 100%   390
          Exception: Infection readily controlled.
    d. Pacemaker malfunction
       Pacemaker repositioned ... 100%   390
    e. Pacemaker failure
       Alternative pacing system implanted ... 100%   598

103

POSTOPERATIVE CARE

13. Anesthetist's postoperative evaluation of patient following transfer from Recovery Room   100%

14. EKG monitoring
    a. Constantly for at least 2 days postoperatively   100% $ 460
    b. Thereafter, daily EKG until discharge   100%   288

15. Patient at complete bed rest on back or left side for 24 hours postoperatively   100%

16. Postoperative nursing care
    a. Vital signs every 15 minutes until stable, then in accordance with postoperative care plan   100%
    b. Intravenous therapy and medications monitored and maintained   100%
    c. Daily charting of patient's condition and progress   100%
    d. Patient monitored for evidence of complications   100%

LENGTH OF STAY

17. Length of stay 6-10 days   100%   2,100-3,500
    Exceptions: (a) Early departure against medical advice;
    (b) presence of complications or other diagnoses such as cerebral vascular disease, peripheral vascular disease, chronic congestive heart failure or recent myocardial infarction justifying extension.

DISCHARGE STATUS

18. Patient discharged under the following conditions:
    a. Satisfactory functioning of pacemaker as reflected in EKG   100%
    b. Improvement in cardiac and general condition of patient   100%
    c. Patient and family instructed re (1) follow-up visit to physician, (2) any applicable dietary restrictions, (3) dosages and schedules of applicable medications and (4) need to avoid electrical hazards including proximity to microwave ovens   100%
    Exception: Instructions on transfer form.

SUGGESTED SAMPLE

Patients whose discharge diagnoses include any of the following conditions in association with a penetrating wound of the chest.

Broncho-pleural fistula	Moderate to massive pneumothorax
Empyema	Pulmonary distress
Fibrothorax	Septicemia

REVIEW

Criterion	Standard	Estimated Charge
JUSTIFICATION FOR EXTENDED STAY		
1. Presence of any of the conditions listed below following a penetrating wound of the chest	100%	
a. Broncho-pleural fistula		
b. Empyema		
c. Fibrothorax		
d. Moderate to massive pneumothorax		
e. Pulmonary distress		
f. Septicemia		
EMERGENCY ROOM CARE		
2. Emergency Room evaluation including documentation by the Emergency Room nurse of the following:		
a. Blood pressure	100%	$ 60 ER
b. Pulse and respiration	100%	
c. Specimens obtained for admission studies including		
(1) CBC	100%	
(2) Panel of 20 blood chemistries	100%	
(3) Urinalysis	100%	125
(4) Coagulation profile	100%	85
d. Portable chest x-ray	100%	40
3. Emergency Room management		
a. Physician notified by nurse immediately upon patient's arrival in Emergency Room	100%	
b. Physician's preliminary evaluation, describing chest wound, documented	100%	
c. Central venous pressure line inserted	100%	20
d. Nasogastric tube inserted	100%	20
e. Culture and sensitivity of wound ordered	100%	75
f. Prophylactic antibiotic administered	100%	
4. Patient admitted in presence of suspected or established penetration of chest wall or pleural cavity	100%	

SURGICAL MANAGEMENT

5. Thoracostomy performed in the presence of any one of the following conditions: 100% $1,797 OR

    307 anesthesia

   a. Respiratory distress

   b. Unstable vital signs   395 RR

   c. Bleeding in excess of 1,000 cc's into pleural cavity after insertion of chest tube   35 instruments

   d. Failure of lung to expand with chest tube

   e. Presence of broncho-pleural fistula

6. Endotracheal tube inserted before thoracostomy   100%   41
Exception: Thoracostomy not performed.

7. Patient's blood typed and cross matched for 6 units of blood   100%   50
Exception: Surgical repair not indicated.

8. Surgical repair and closure performed   100%   2,534 as in No. 5, above
Exception: Treatment other than closure and dressing not indicated.

9. Thoracotomy after thoracostomy   100%
Exception: Absence of pleural involvement.

10. Foley catheter in place for first 24 hours   100%   44
Exception: Surgical repair not indicated.

11. Report by operating surgeon of (a) preoperative diagnosis, (b) procedures performed and (c) condition of tissues and findings, dictated or written immediately after surgery   100%

    85 drain set

12 Management of complications   45

   a. Broncho-pleural fistula

     (1) Suction   100%   56

     (2) Thoracotomy with water seal drainage   100%   22 per day

     (3) Surgical repair in the absence of healing after 1 week of treatment   100%   2,534

   b. Empyema   85 drain set

     (1) Drainage   100%   40

     (2) Culture and sensitivity of drainage   100%   75

     (3) Antibiotic consistent with culture and sensitivity   100%

   c. Fibrothorax

     (1) Supportive care for 4-6 weeks, followed by   100%

     (2) Decortication   100%   2,534

   d. Moderate to massive pneumothorax   45-56

     Thoracotomy with water seal drainage   100%   22 per day

    85 drain set

   e. Pulmonary distress

     Assisted ventilation   100%   210 per 24 hours

   f. Septicemia

     (1) Culture and sensitivity   100%   75

     (2) Antibiotic consistent with culture and sensitivity   100%

     (3) In the event of septic shock, steroid within 12 hours after onset   100%
     Exception: Absence of septic shock.

POSTOPERATIVE CARE

13. Anesthetist's postoperative evaluation of patient following transfer
   from Recovery Room   100%
14. Postoperative nursing care including
   a. Vital signs every 15 minutes until stable, then per postoperative
      care plan   100%
   b. Pleural drainage system monitored and maintained   100%
   c. Intravenous therapy and medications monitored and maintained   100%
   d. Patient monitored for evidence of complications   100%

LENGTH OF STAY

15. Length of stay
   a. Following closure and dressing without surgical repair, 3-6 days   100% $1,050-2,100
   b. Following surgical repair, 7-11 days   100%   2,450-3,850

   Exceptions: (1) Early departure against medical advice;
   (2) complications or other diagnoses justifying extension.

DISCHARGE STATUS

16. Patient discharged under the following conditions:
   a. Temperature below 99.6 F for 36 hours before discharge   100%
   b. Chest x-ray showing absence of pneumonia or pneumothorax   100%
   c. Respiratory rate and quality within normal limits   100%
      *Record Analyst: Adult normal rate is 15-20 per minute.
      Normal quality refers to absence of wheezing, grunting or
      stridor. Find data in graphic chart and progress notes.*
   d. Patient and family instructed re (1) activity level, (2) any
      applicable medications and (3) follow-up visit to physician   100%
      Exception: Instructions on transfer form.

PERIPHERAL ARTERIAL EMBOLECTOMY
(Iliac, Femoral, Popliteal, Brachial or Subclavian)

SUGGESTED SAMPLE

Patients with a discharge diagnosis of peripheral arterial embolism whose hospital course was complicated by the need for amputation of an extremity or any part thereof, or whose hospital course was marked by cardiac arrhythmia, pulmonary disease, or thromboembolic disease remote from the anatomic area concerned.

REVIEW

Criterion	Standard	Estimated Charge
JUSTIFICATION FOR EXTENDED STAY		$ 25 supplies
1. The presence of at least one of the following conditions:	100%	8 kit
a. Postoperative complications such as		
(1) Need for amputation or reoperation (failure of embolectomy)		
(2) Need for treatment of cardiac disease		
(3) Need for treatment of coagulation defect		
(4) Pulmonary disease		
(5) Need for treatment of local or remote embolic or thrombotic phenomena		
(6) Remote organ failure		
b. Nonoperative complications such as		
(1) Cardiac disease		
(2) Pulmonary disease		
(3) Renal disease		
(4) Remote thromboembolic disease		
(5) Remote organ failure		
PREOPERATIVE STUDY AND CARE		
2. History with specific reference to:	100%	
a. Sudden onset of ischemia of an extremity accompanied by numbness and/or pain, with blanching or mottling of skin and/or loss of pulses		
b. Cardiac arrhythmia or failure		
c. Symptoms of cerebral, abdominal or renal embolization		
d. Hypertension		
e. Sensitivity to drugs or other allergens		
3. Documentation by physical examination of:		
a. Blanched or mottled appearance of an extremity or any part thereof	100%	
b. Absence of pulses in affected part	100%	
c. Lowered surface temperature of affected part	100%	

d.	Level of demarcation	100%	
e.	Status of cardiac arrhythmia or decompensation	100%	
f.	General physical examination with emphasis on vital organ status	100%	

4. Laboratory and other studies including:

a.	CBC, urinalysis and admission panel	100%	$ 125
b.	Coagulation profile	100%	85
c.	Serology	100%	11
d.	Chest x-ray	100%	70
e.	EKG	100%	48
f.	Arteriography of part concerned	0%	130

      Exception (Indication): Required to establish site.

5. Preoperative nursing care

a.	Patient assessment including vital signs, brief relevant history and present complaint	100%
b.	History of allergies and drug sensitivities	100%
c.	Formulation of care plan based on assessment and objectives	100%
d.	Patient orientation to care and planned procedures	100%
e.	Preoperative instruction in deep breathing, coughing and turning in bed following surgery	100%
f.	Preoperative preparation and medication	100%

6. Anesthesiologist's preoperative evaluation of operative and anesthesia risk — 100%

SURGICAL MANAGEMENT

1,290
OR
260
anesthesia
292
RR

7. Embolectomy by arteriotomy and closure thereof — 100%

8. Reestablishment of arterial flow with return of color and viability to extremity — 100%

    a. Specific description in operative report of any delay in or absence of return of viability — 100%

    b. Documentation of any need for ancillary surgical procedures at same sitting as embolectomy, or reoperation as indicated — 100%

9. Operative report containing (a) preoperative diagnosis; (b) description of operative findings; (c) description of surgical procedures; (d) type of anesthesia; (e) names of surgeon, all assistants and nurse personnel; (f) postoperative diagnosis; (g) condition of patient and pertinent anatomic parts upon leaving operating room and (h) sponge and instrument count — 100%

10. Management of complications

1,290
OR
260
anesthesia
292
RR

    a. Failure of embolectomy to restore circulation to extremity, as evidenced by persistence or recurrence of ischemic pallor or absence of pulses

        Surgical correction — 100%

    b. Pulmonary problem

      (1) In presence of suspicion of embolism,

         • Evaluation by means of diagnostic x-ray and lung scan — 100% — 75-350

         • Surgical intervention or balloon catheter as indicated and as feasible — 100%

• Oxygen as needed in respiratory distress	100%	$ 26 per 8 hours	
• Anti-coagulation as indicated	100%		

    (2) In presence of pneumonia,

• Evaluation by means of x-ray	100%	70
• Culture and sensitivity of sputum	100%	75
• Antibiotic consistent with sensitivity	100%	
• Oxygen as needed in respiratory distress	100%	26 per 8 hours

  c. Cardiac complications

    (1) In presence of congestive heart failure,

• Oxygen as needed	100%	26 per 8 hours
• Diuretics as indicated	100%	
• Low sodium diet	100%	
• Digitalis derivatives as indicated	100%	

       Exception: Presence of thyrotoxicosis.

• Patient positioned to minimize breathing difficulty	100%	

    (2) In presence of persistent arrhythmias,

• Anti-arrhythmic medication	100%	
• Cardioversion if indicated	100%	414 / 171 monitor
• Where arrhythmias persist, pacemaker implantation	100%	598

       Exception: Satisfactory response to conservative measures.

  d. Oliguria

Evaluation of renal function	100%	50

  e. Remote emboli

(1) Physical examination	100%	
(2) Evaluation by means of diagnostic x-rays and scans	100%	75-350

  f. Wound complications such as wound infection or dehiscence

(1) Culture and sensitivity of any drainage	100%	75
(2) Antibiotic consistent with sensitivity	100%	
(3) Conservative management of wound	100%	

       Exception: Failure of healing after appropriate trial and observation

POSTOPERATIVE MANAGEMENT

11. Postoperative evaluation by anesthetist following transfer from Recovery Room	100%	
12. Nursing note in Recovery Room		
a. Pulse and respiration determinations every 15 minutes until stable	100%	
b. Close monitoring for evidence of complications	100%	
c. Observation of extremity with special attention to color, presence of pulses and surface temperature	100%	
d. Accurate reporting of fluid input and output	100%	
e. Evidence of fulfillment of surgeon's postoperative orders	100%	
13. Documentation in record of dietician's consultation with patient	100%	

LENGTH OF STAY

14. Postoperative length of stay following embolectomy free of complications, 7-12 days   100% $2,450-4,200

    Exceptions: (a) Early departure against medical advice; (b) complications justifying extended stay.

DISCHARGE STATUS

15. Patient discharged under the following conditions:
    a. Circulation restored to extremity   100%
    b. Surgical wound healed   100%
    c. Cardiac medication ordered as indicated   100%
    d. Patient instructed re (1) medication dosage and schedule as applicable, (2) activity level and (3) follow-up visit to surgeon's office   100%
        Exception: Instructions on transfer form.

PODIATRIC SURGERY

SUGGESTED SAMPLE

Patients whose discharge diagnoses include any of the following conditions in association with podiatric surgery.

Hemorrhage	Painful postoperative swelling
Local infection	Wound slough

REVIEW

Criterion	Standard	Estimated Charge
JUSTIFICATION FOR EXTENDED STAY		$ 120 supplies
1. Presence of (a) hemorrhage, (b) local infection, (c) painful post-operative swelling or (d) wound slough following podiatric surgery	100%	8 kit
PREOPERATIVE CARE		
2. In the chart prior to surgery,		
a. Documentation of the presence of one of the following conditions:	100%	
(1) Hallux valgus with any of the following findings:		
(a) Exostosis of first metatarsal head		
(b) Displaced sesamoid		
(c) Contracted hallucis longus tendon		
(d) Exostosis of base of phalanx		
(e) Pain in first metatarsal joint		
(f) Bunions which interfere with walking or wearing shoes and have not responded to conservative treatment		
(2) Incurvated nail with any of the following findings:		
(a) Ingrown nail		
(b) Hypertrophied tissue		
(c) Subungual exostosis		
(3) Calcaneal spur with any of the following findings:		
(a) Calcaneal spur on plantar aspect of calcaneous		
(b) Planta fossa strain		
(c) Pain on plantar aspect of calcaneous		
b. Documentation of orthopedic consultation	100%	
Exception: Patient admitted by orthopedic surgeon.		
c. Documentation of medical consultation	100%	
Exception: Patient admitted by physician.		
d. History by physician	100%	
e. Physical examination report by physician	100%	
3. Laboratory and other studies performed prior to admission		
a. CBC, urinalysis and admission panel	100%	125
b. Coagulation profile	100%	85

    c. Fasting blood sugar   0% $ 11

        Exception (Indication):   Presence of diabetes or abnormal glucose test result.

    d. Chest x-ray within past 3 months with report in record   100%   70

    e. EKG   100%   48

        Exception: Patient under 40.

4. Preoperative nursing care including

    a. Patient assessment including vital signs, brief relevant history and present complaint   100%

    b. History of allergies and drug sensitivities   100%

    c. Formulation of care plan based on assessment and objectives   100%

    d. Patient orientation to care and planned procedures   100%

    e. Preoperative instructions suitable to anesthesia plan and operative procedure   100%

    f. Preoperative preparation and medication   100%

SURGICAL MANAGEMENT

5. One or more of the following procedures as indicated   100%   149 supplies

    a. Hallux valgus   35 instruments

        (1) Jones procedure for exostosis of head of first metatarsal and bursal sac   315 OR

        (2) Keller procedure for exostosis of base and head   210 anesthesia

        (3) Modified McBride sesamoid and exostosis

        (4) Lapides procedure

    b. Incurvated nail

        (1) Frost or modified procedure

        (2) Winnegrad partial ostectomy

        (3) Evulsion of nail and matrix

    c. Calcaneal spur

        (1) Partial ostectomy of calcaneous

        (2) Tendon release

6. Report by operating surgeon of (a) preoperative diagnoses, (b) procedures performed and (c) description of tissues and findings, dictated or written immediately after surgery   100%

7. Pathologist's report on any specimens submitted, consistent with Hospital's written procedures   100%   0

        Exception: Specimen submitted is on approved list of specimens exempt from microscopic examination.

8. Management of complications

    a. Hemorrhage   50 type

        (1) Patient's blood typed and cross matched for transfusion   100%   45 infusion

        (2) Transfusion as indicated by physician   100%   45-88 per unit

        (3) Re-closure as indicated   100%

    b. Local infection

        (1) Initially, administration of anti-staphylococcal agent   100%

        (2) Culture and sensitivity   100%   75

        (3) Antibiotic consistent with culture and sensitivity   100%

    c. Painful postoperative swelling

          Elevation of foot to 30 degree angle   100%

    d. Wound slough

      (1) Elevation of foot   100%

      (2) Removal of necrotic tissue with dressing changes   100%

POSTOPERATIVE CARE

9. Anesthetist's postoperative evaluation of patient following transfer
from Recovery Room   100%

10. Postoperative nursing care

    a. Vital signs every 15 minutes until stable, then per postoperative
nursing care plan   100%

    b. Intravenous therapy and medications monitored and maintained   100%

    c. Report on patient's tolerance of walking before discharge   100%

    d. Patient monitored for evidence of complications   100%

LENGTH OF STAY

11. Length of stay

    a. Hallux valgus, 5-6 days   100% $1,750-
                                                           2,100

    b. Incurvated nail, 4-7 days   100%   1,400-2,450

    c. Calcaneal spur, 5-8 days   100%   1,750-2,800

    Exceptions: (1) Early departure against medical advice;
(2) complications or other diagnoses justifying extension.

DISCHARGE STATUS

12. Patient discharged under the following conditions:

    a. Permitted limited walking with orthopedic shoes and crutches   100%   **42**
        Exceptions: (1) Orthopedic shoes not indicated for incurvated   including
nail; (2) crutches may not be required for hallux valgus or   bandages
incurvated nail.   postop boots
                                                                  cane

    b. Temperature below 99.6 F on day of discharge   100%

    c. All wounds healing with no evidence of uncontrolled infection   100%

    d. Complications absent   100%

    e. Patient and family instructed re (1) activity level, (2) use of
special support shoes and crutches as indicated, (3) any
applicable medications and (4) follow-up visit to physician   100%
        Exception: Instructions on transfer form.

POSTOPERATIVE WOUND INFECTION

SAMPLE

Patients whose discharge diagnoses include wound infections following surgery.

REVIEW

Criterion	Standard	Estimated Charge
INDICATION FOR INCLUSION IN THE STUDY		
1. Presence of a postoperative infection of skin or subcutaneous tissues manifested by the drainage of pus	100%	
LABORATORY STUDY		
2. Culture and sensitivity test	100%	$ 75
3. In the presence of any of the following findings, culture for presence of anaerobic bacteria:	100%	150
a. Foul smelling drainage		
b. Necrotic or gangrenous tissue		
c. Tissue gas		
d. Malignancy or other tissue destructive process		
e. Location of the infection in close proximity to a mucosal surface		
f. Infection in a patient who is, or who has been, receiving aminoglycoside antibiotics	100%	
Record Analyst: The aminoglycoside antibiotics include Gentamycin, Garamycin, Kanamycin, Kanarex, Tobramycin, Nebcin, Amikacin, Amikin, Neomycin, Paramycin, Humatin and Streptomycin. Ask your Review Committee or the Hospital's pharmacist for any additional information needed.		
4. Blood sugar level	100%	11
MANAGEMENT		
5. Incision and drainage of abscess	100%	52 supplies
6. Report by operating surgeon of (a) preoperative diagnosis, (b) procedures performed and (c) condition of tissues and findings, dictated or written immediately after surgery	100%	135 OR 50 anesthesia
7. Initially, administration of a broad spectrum antibiotic	100%	
8. Revision of antibiotic therapy in light of culture and sensitivity study	100%	
9. Management of complications		
Allergic reaction to anti-infective agents		
(1) Medications stopped	100%	
(2) Other anti-infective agent(s) substituted	100%	

10. Nursing care
    a. Maintenance and monitoring of intravenous therapy and medications   100%
    b. Monitoring and charting of fluid intake and output   100%
    c. Patient monitored for evidence of further complications   100%

LENGTH OF STAY

11. Length of stay assigned for principal diagnosis or procedure with complication of wound infection   100%

DISCHARGE STATUS WITH RESPECT TO WOUND INFECTION

12. Temperature below 99.4 F for 24 hours before discharge   100%
13. Evidence of resolution of wound infection   100%

    Record Analyst: Resolution will be reflected in decreased tenderness, pain, swelling or discharge. Find data in progress and nursing notes.

PROSTATECTOMY

SUGGESTED SAMPLE

Patients whose discharge diagnoses include any of the following in association with prostatectomy.

Fistula	Sepsis
Hemorrhage	Urinary retention
Renal failure	Wound infection

REVIEW

Criterion	Standard	Estimated Charge
JUSTIFICATION FOR EXTENDED STAY		$ 96 supplies
1. Presence of (a) fistula, (b) hemorrhage, (c) renal failure, (d) sepsis, (e) urinary retention or (f) wound infection following prostatectomy for benign prostatic hypertrophy	100%	8 kit
PREOPERATIVE STUDY AND CARE		
2. In the chart prior to surgery,		
a. Documentation of some combination of the following:	100%	
(1) Acute or chronic urinary retention with overflow		
(2) Hemorrhage of urinary tract origin		
(3) Intractable urinary tract infection		
(4) Azotemia		
(5) Presence of bladder calculi		
(6) Progressive signs or symptoms of obstruction such as (a) frequency, (b) hesitancy, (c) nocturia, (d) slow urinary stream or (e) dribbling		
b. History supporting preoperative diagnosis	100%	
c. Physical examination report including description of size, consistency and configuration of the prostate	100%	
3. Laboratory and other studies performed prior to admission, including		
a. CBC, urinalysis and admission panel	100%	125
b. Serology	100%	11
c. Coagulation profile	100%	85
d. Electrolytes	100%	25
e. Acid phosphatase level	100%	22
f. Urine culture and sensitivity	100%	75
g. Chest x-ray within past 3 months with report in record	100%	70
h. EKG	100%	48
Exception: Patient under 40.		
i. Intravenous pyelogram with post-voiding film	100%	125
4. Cystogram and ureterogram	100%	117
5. Cystoscopy	100%	83

6. Preoperative nursing care
   a. Patient assessment including vital signs, brief relevant history and present complaint 100%
   b. History of allergies and drug sensitivities 100%
   c. Formulation of care plan based on assessment and objectives 100%
   d. Patient orientation to care and planned procedures 100%
   e. Instruction in deep breathing, coughing and turning in bed following surgery 100%
   f. Preoperative preparation and medication 100%
7. Anesthesiologist's preoperative evaluation of patient with specification of ASA class and risk level 100%

SURGICAL MANAGEMENT

8. Procedure: One of the following as indicated .... 100% $1,112 OR
   a. Transurethral resection   213 anesthesia
   b. Suprapubic resection   225 RR
   c. Retropubic resection   22 instruments

9. Report by operating surgeon of (a) preoperative diagnosis, (b) procedures performed and (c) description of tissues and findings, dictated or written immediately after surgery 100%

10. Blood transfusion   50 type
    Exceptions (Indications):   (a) Operative blood loss exceeding   45 infusion
    500 cc's; (b) Hgb less than 10 gms %. .... 0%   45-88 per unit

11. Antibiotics to combat any pre-existing urinary tract infection 100%

12. Pathologist's report on tissue specimen supporting preoperative diagnosis 100%   115

13. Management of complications   1,112 OR
    a. Fistula   189 anesthesia
       (1) Catheter repositioned .... 100%   160 RR
       (2) Fistula excised and repaired .... 100%   22 instruments
    b. Hemorrhage   50 type
       (1) Blood replacement .... 100%   45 infusion
       (2) In presence of persistent bleeding, surgical exploration
           and packing .... 100%   45-88 per unit
    c. Renal failure
       (1) Administration of diuretics 100%
       (2) Peritoneal dialysis 100%   524
    d. Sepsis
       (1) Culture and sensitivity of blood 100%   75
       (2) Antibiotic consistent with culture and sensitivity 100%
    e. Urinary retention
       (1) Catheterization 100%   29
       (2) Re-evaluation of adequacy of recent resection 100%
       (3) In presence of inadequate resection, repeat resection 100%   1,483

f. Wound infection
   (1) Culture and sensitivity of wound   100% $ 75
   (2) Antibiotic consistent with culture and sensitivity   100%

POSTOPERATIVE CARE

14. Anesthetist's postoperative evaluation of patient following
transfer from Recovery Room   100%

15. Postoperative nursing care
  a. Vital signs every 15 minutes until stable, then hourly for 4
     hours, or per postoperative nursing care plan   100%
  b. Implementation of special Foley catheter care procedures   100%
  c. Measurement and charting of intake and output   100%
  d. Intravenous and drug therapies maintained and monitored   100%
  e. Patient monitored for evidence of complications   100%

LENGTH OF STAY

16. Length of stay
  a. Transurethral resection, 8-10 days   100%   2,800-3,500
  b. Suprapubic, retropubic or perineal resection, 12-16 days   100%   4,200-5,600
  Exceptions: (1) Early departure against medical advice;
  (2) complications or additional diagnoses justifying extension.

DISCHARGE STATUS

17. Patient discharged under the following conditions:
  a. Temperature below 99.6 F for 24 hours before discharge   100%
  b. Presence of adequate voiding   100%
  c. Presence of stable renal function   100%
  d. Wound healing   100%
  e. Absence of symptomatic infection   100%
  f. Absence of gross bleeding   100%
  g. Physical condition permitting care at home or in extended
     care facility   100%
  h. Patient and family instructed re (1) diet, (2) return to work,
     (3) activity level, (4) dosage and schedule of any medications,
     (5) any applicable treatment and (6) follow-up visit to
     physician   100%
  Exception: Instructions on transfer form.

SUGGESTED SAMPLE

Patients whose discharge diagnoses include intraocular infection, intrusion or extrusion of prosthetic implant, hemorrhagic or serous choroidal detachment or vitreous and/or subretinal hemorrhage in association with surgery for the repair of retinal detachment.

REVIEW

Criterion	Standard	Estimated Charge
JUSTIFICATION FOR EXTENDED STAY		$ 41 supplies
1. Presence of any of the following conditions in association with surgery for the repair of retinal detachment:	100%	8 kit
a. Increased intraocular pressure		
b. Intraocular infection		
c. Intrusion or extrusion of prosthetic implant		
d. Hemorrhagic or serous choroidal detachment		
e. Vitreous and/or subretinal hemorrhage		
PREOPERATIVE STUDY AND CARE		
2. In the chart before surgery for retinal repair,		
a. History with reference to loss of vision with floating opacities and/or light flashes with field loss consistent with diagnosis	100%	
b. Ophthalmoscopic examination with drawing of findings showing the presence of at least 1 of the following conditions:	100%	
(1) Retinal detachment upon opthalmoscopic examination		65 survey
(2) Retinal hole, tear or degenerative disease upon opthalmoscopic examination		
(3) Postoperative implant intrusion or extrusion and/or infection upon external examination or opthalmoscopy		
(4) Vitreous hemorrhage with diagnosis or suspicion of retinal detachment		
(5) Retinal elevation with diagnosis or suspicion of neoplasm		
3. Examinations including		
a. Visual field examination	100%	
b. Slit-lamp examination	100%	
c. Tonometric measurements	100%	
d. Visual acuity with and without correcting lens	100%	
Exception: Patient under 5 years of age.		
4. Laboratory and other studies including		
a. CBC, urinalysis and admission panel	100%	95
b. Chest x-ray within past 6 months with report in record	100%	70

5. Preoperative nursing care
   a. Patient assessment including vital signs, brief relevant history and present complaint — 100%
   b. History of allergies and drug sensitivities — 100%
   c. Formulation of nursing care plan based on assessment and objectives — 100%
   d. Patient orientation to care and planned procedures — 100%
   e. Preoperative preparation and instruction — 100%
6. Anesthesiologist's preoperative evaluation of patient with specification of ASA class and risk level — 100%
   Exception: Local anesthesia planned.

SURGICAL MANAGEMENT

$ 135
OR
10
instruments
19
medications
55
anesthesia

7. Repair of retina — 100%
8. Report by operating surgeon of (a) preoperative diagnosis, (b) procedures performed and (c) description of tissues and findings, dictated or written immediately after surgery — 100%
9. Management of complications
   a. Increased intraocular pressure
      (1)   In presence of angle closure, iridectomy — 100% — 219
      (2)   In presence of elevation not associated with closure, medical therapy — 100%
   b. Intraocular infection
      (1)   Culture and sensitivity — 100% — 75
      (2)   Antibiotic consistent with culture and sensitivity — 100%
      (3)   Removal of any foreign body present — 100% — 55 anesthesia
   c. Intrusion or extrusion of prosthetic implant
      Removal of implant — 100% — 219
   d. Hemorrhagic or serous choroidal detachment
      Bed rest and conservative management — 100%
   e. Vitreous and/or subretinal hemorrhage
      Bed rest and conservative management — 100%

POSTOPERATIVE CARE

10. Anesthetist's postoperative evaluation following transfer from Recovery Room — 100%
11. Postoperative nursing care including
    a. Pulse and respiration monitored every 15 minutes until stable, then per postoperative nursing care plan — 100%
    b. Positioning maintained — 100%
    c. Patient monitored for evidence of complications — 100%

LENGTH OF STAY

12. Length of stay 5-7 days — 100% — 1,750-2,450
    Exceptions: (a) Early departure against medical advice;
    (b) complications or other diagnoses justifying extension.

121

DISCHARGE STATUS

13. Patient discharged under the following conditions:
    a. Temperature below 99.6 F for 36 hours before discharge   100%
    b. Complications absent   100%
    c. Patient and family instructed re (1) activity level, including prohibition against strenuous activity or lifting of heavy objects, (2) dosage and schedule of any applicable medications, (3) eye care and (4) follow-up visit to physician   100%
    Exception: Instructions on transfer form.
    Record Analyst: The presence in the record of a copy of the surgeon's standard instructions, with an indication that the patient has received a copy, satisfies this requirement.

SAMPLE

Patients discharged following rhinoplasty.

REVIEW

Criterion	Standard	Estimated Charge
JUSTIFICATION FOR EXTENDED STAY		$ 107
1. Presence of (a) excessive postoperative swelling, (b) nasal hemorrhage or (c) wound infection	100%	
PREOPERATIVE STUDY AND CARE		
2. In the chart prior to surgery,		
a. History with specific reference to patient's reason for wishing to have surgery performed	100%	
b. Physical examination report with documentation of significant nasal and other findings	100%	
3. Photographs taken before admission, showing preoperative condition	100%	
4. Laboratory and other studies performed before admission, including		
a. CBC	100%	19
b. Urinalysis	100%	10
c. Chest x-ray within preceding 6 months, with report in record	100%	70
5. Preoperative nursing care including		
a. Patient assessment including vital signs, brief relevant history and patient's reason for surgery	100%	
b. History of allergies and drug sensitivities	100%	
c. Formulation of care plan based on assessment and objectives	100%	
d. Patient orientation and preoperative instruction	100%	
6. Anesthesiologist's preoperative evaluation of patient	100%	
Exception: Local anesthesia planned.		
SURGICAL MANAGEMENT		80 supplies
7. Report by operating surgeon of (a) preoperative diagnosis, (b) procedures performed and (c) description of tissues and findings, dictated or written immediately after surgery	100%	135 OR 55 anesthesia
8. Management of complications		19 medications
a. Excessive swelling		
(1) Head kept elevated	100%	
(2) Ice packs applied	100%	12.80[1]

---

[1] 4 @ 3.20 each, over 8-10 hours.

123

   b. Nasal hemorrhage
     (1) Evaluation of extent of bleeding   100%
     (2) Re-application of splint, followed by   100%
     (3) Re-packing   100%
   c. Wound infection
     (1) Culture and sensitivity   100% $ 75
     (2) Antibiotic consistent with culture and sensitivity   100%

POSTOPERATIVE CARE

9. Anesthetist's postoperative evaluation of patient following transfer from Recovery Room   100%

   Exception: Local anesthesia used.

10. Daily progress notes written   100%

11. Postoperative nursing care
   a. Pulse and respiration every 15 minutes until stable, then per postoperative care plan   100%
   b. Patient closely observed until fully alert and stable   100%
   c. Positioning requirements maintained with head elevated   100%
   d. Intravenous therapy and medications maintained and monitored   100%
   e. Patient monitored for evidence of complications   100%

LENGTH OF STAY

12. Length of stay 3 days   100%   1,050

   Exceptions: (a) Early departure against medical advice, (b) planned early departure, or (c) complications or other diagnoses justifying extension'

DISCHARGE STATUS

13. Patient discharged under the following conditions:
   a. Temperature below 99.6 F on day of discharge   100%
   b. Evidence of good wound healing with minimal drainage   100%
   c. Patient instructed re (1) activity level, (2) medications with dosages and schedules, (3) wound care and (4) follow-up visit to physician   100%

   Record Analyst: The presence in the record of a copy of the surgeon's standard instruction sheet covering at least these elements, with an indication that a copy was given to the patient, satisfies this requirement.

RHYTIDECTOMY

SUGGESTED SAMPLE

Patients discharged following rhytidectomy.

REVIEW

Criterion	Standard	Estimated Charge
INDICATIONS FOR RHYTIDECTOMY		$ 90 supplies
1. The presence of all of the following conditions:	100%	8 kit
a. Gradual redundancy of facial and neck tissues in a patient in good health		
b. Absence of chronic disease		
c. Absence of obesity		
d. Absence of any unrealistic expectations on the patient's part as to the effect or results of the surgery, documented by the patient's written preoperative statement describing his or her objectives and desires with respect to the planned procedures, recorded before admission		
e. Verbalized understanding on the patient's part as to the risks entailed in the procedures planned		
PREOPERATIVE STUDY AND CARE		
2. In the chart prior to surgery,		
a. Documentation of the presence of redundant tissue of face and neck	100%	
b. History including reference to etiology of condition and patient's need for plastic surgery to maintain satisfactory self-image	100%	
c. Physical examination report with documentation of indications for procedure	100%	
3. Photographs taken before admission, showing preoperative condition	100%	
4. Laboratory and other studies performed before admission, including		
a. CBC	100%	19
b. Urinalysis	100%	10
c. Chest x-ray within preceding 6 months, with report in record	100%	70
5. Preoperative nursing care including		
a. Patient assessment including vital signs, brief relevant history and patient's reason for surgery	100%	
b. History of allergies and drug sensitivities	100%	
c. Formulation of care plan based on assessment and objectives	100%	
d. Patient orientation and preoperative preparation	100%	
6. Preoperative evaluation by anesthesiologist with description of anesthesia plan in record	100%	

SURGICAL MANAGEMENT

7.	Rhytidectomy with flaps	100%	$ 85 supplies
8.	Application of padded face-lift dressing	100%	551 OR
			313 anesthesia
			19 medications
9.	Placement of cervical collar in operating room	100%	16
10.	Report by operating surgeon of (a) preoperative diagnosis, (b) procedures performed and (c) description of tissues and findings, dictated or written immediately after surgery	100%	15 dressing
11.	Pathologist's report on any specimens submitted	100%	
	Exception: Absence of specimens, or inclusion of such tissues on exempt list.		
12.	Management of complications	100%	
	Hemorrhage		
	Bleeders clamped	100%	

POSTOPERATIVE CARE

13	Postoperative evaluation by anesthetist following return to room	100%	
14.	Analgesics as needed for relief of pain	100%	3.20 per ice bag
15.	Removal of face-left dressing before discharge	100%	
16.	Postoperative nursing care		
	a. Patient observed closely until stable and alert	100%	
	b. Positioning requirements carried out	100%	
	c. Hair gently rinsed and dried before discharge	100%	

LENGTH OF STAY

17.	Length of stay, 24 hours maximum	100%	350
	Exception: Complications or other diagnoses justifying extension.		

DISCHARGE STATUS

18.	Patient discharged under the following conditions:	
	a. Wounds dry with no signs of complications	100%
	b. Patient's temperature below 99.4 F	100%
	c. Patient instructed re (1) facial care, (2) no jogging, strenuous exercise or lifting of heavy objects, (3) continued wearing of cervical collar, (4) hair to be gently shampooed in shower after 2-3 days and (5) follow-up visit to surgeon in 3-4 days	100%

Record Analyst: The presence in the record of a copy of the surgeon's standard instruction sheet covering at least these elements, with an indication that a copy was given to the patient, satisfies this requirement.

STRABISMUS, SURGICAL CORRECTION

SAMPLE

Patients discharged following the surgical correction of strabismus.

REVIEW

Criterion	Standard	Estimated Charge
JUSTIFICATION FOR EXTENDED STAY		$ 43 supplies
1. The presence of wound infection or of wound or suture separation following surgery for the correction of strabismus	100%	8 kit
PREOPERATIVE STUDY AND CARE		
2. In the chart prior to surgery,		
a. History with reference to the ocular problem	100%	
b. Reports of routine physical examination and of ocular examinations including reference to the presence of any of the following conditions as an indication for surgery:	100%	
(1) Visual axis deviation		
(2) Diagnosis or suspicion of strabismus secondary to intraocular, intraorbital or intracranial lesion		
(3) Radiologic demonstration of intraocular, intraorbital or intracranial lesion		
c. Reports of ocular studies including the following:	100%	
(1) Motility examination including cardinal excursions		
(2) Measurement and documentation of deviation		
(3) Cycloplegic refraction findings		
(4) Opthalmoscopic examination		
(5) Visual acuity with and without correcting lens		
Exception: Patient under 5 years of age.		
3. Laboratory and other studies performed prior to admission, including		
a. CBC, urinalysis and admission panel of 6 studies	100%	81
b. Chest x-ray	100%	70
4. Preoperative nursing care including		
a. Patient assessment including vital signs, brief relevant history and patient's or parent's reason for surgery	100%	
b. History of allergies and drug sensitivities	100%	
c. Formulation of care plan based on assessment and objectives	100%	
d. Patient orientation to surroundings and planned care	100%	
e. Preoperative instruction and preparation	100%	
5. Anesthesiologist's preoperative evaluation of patient	100%	
Exception: Local anesthesia planned.		

SURGICAL MANAGEMENT

$ 135
OR
55
anesthesia
19
medications
22
instruments

6. Surgical correction by means of resection, recession, myomectomy or tuck as indicated ... 100%

7. Report by operating surgeon of (a) preoperative diagnosis, (b) procedures performed and (c) description of tissues and findings, dictated or written immediately after surgery ... 100%

8. Management of complications
    a. Wound infection
        (1) Culture and sensitivity ... 100% ... 75
        (2) Appropriate antibiotic ... 100%
    b. Wound or suture separation
        Surgical repair of wound ... 100% ... 231

POSTOPERATIVE CARE

9. Anesthetist's postoperative evaluation of patient following transfer from Recovery Room ... 100%
    Exception: Use of local anesthesia.

10. Postoperative nursing care including
    a. Nursing Service to instruct Hospital's telephone operators not to route any calls to patient's phone until further notice ... 100%
        Exception: Parent, nurse or sitter present in room at all times.
    b. Pulse and respiration every 15 minutes until stable, then per postoperative care plan ... 100%
    c. Maintenance of any positioning requirements ... 100%
    d. Patient monitored for evidence of complications ... 100%

LENGTH OF STAY

11. Length of stay 2 days ... 100% ... 802[1]
    Exceptions: (a) Early departure against medical advice; (b) complications or other diagnoses justifying extension.

DISCHARGE STATUS

12. Patient discharged under the following conditions:
    a. Temperature below 100 F on day of discharge ... 100%
    b. Complications absent ... 100%
    c. Patient and family instructed re (1) eye care and hygiene, (2) activity level including prohibition against lifting of heavy objects, (3) dosage and schedule of any medications and (4) follow-up visit to physician ... 100%
        Exception: Instructions on transfer form.
        Record Analyst: The presence in the record of a copy of the surgeon's standard instructions covering at least these elements, with an indication that the patient or his parent has received a copy, satisfies this requirement.

---

[1] Assuming pediatric admission.

THYROIDECTOMY

SUGGESTED SAMPLE

Patients whose discharge diagnoses include any of the following conditions in association with thyroidectomy

Bilateral recurrent laryngeal nerve injury	Tetany
Persistent hypothyroidism	Thyroid storm
Postoperative bleeding	

REVIEW

Criterion	Standard	Estimated Charge
JUSTIFICATION FOR EXTENDED STAY		$ 117 supplies
1. Presence of any of the following conditions following thyroidectomy:	100%	8 kit
a. Bilateral recurrent laryngeal nerve injury		
b. Persistent hypothyroidism		
c. Tetany		
d. Thyroid storm		
PREOPERATIVE STUDY AND CARE		
2. In the chart prior to surgery,		
a. Documentation of the presence of any of the following:	100%	
(1) Diffuse goiter producing dyspnea, hoarseness, cough, dysphagia or disfigurement		
(2) Intrathoracic goiter		
(3) Metabolic syndrome with hyperthyroidism		
(4) Solitary firm non-functioning thyroid nocule		
b. History	100%	
c. Physical examination with specific reference to thyroid and cardiac status and to the presence or absence of exophthalmos	100%	
3. Laboratory and other studies performed prior to admission		
a. CBC, urinalysis and admission panel of 20 studies	100%	125
b. Coagulation profile	100%	85
c. Serology	100%	11
d. Blood cholesterol level	100%	24
e. Thyroid function tests including		
(1) Protein-bound iodine	100%	61
(2) Resin uptake	100%	43
(3) 24-hour radio-iodine uptake	100%	94
f. Thyroid scan (1-131) documented in record	100%	380
g. Chest x-ray	100%	70
h. EKG	100%	48
i. Blood typed and cross-matched for transfusion	100%	50

129

4. Preoperative nursing care
   a. Patient assessment including vital signs, brief relevant history and present complaint 100%
   b. History of allergies and drug sensitivities 100%
   c. Formulation of care plan based on assessment and objectives 100%
   d. Patient orientation to care and planned procedures 100%
   e. Preoperative instruction in deep breathing, coughing and turning in bed following surgery 100%
   f. Preoperative preparation and medication 100%
5. Preoperative control of thyrotoxicosis with propylthiouracil and Lugol's solution 100%
   Exception: Absence of thyrotoxicosis.
6. Anesthesiologist's preoperative evaluation of patient with specification of ASA class and risk level 100%

SURGICAL MANAGEMENT

		supplies
7. Subtotal thyroidectomy	100%	$ 930 OR
8. Report by operating surgeon of (a) preoperative diagnosis, (b) procedures performed and (c) description of tissues and findings, dictated or written immediately after surgery	100%	213 anesthesia / 22 instruments
9. Pathologist's report in record, confirming diagnosis	100%	345 RR
10. Management of complications		115 pathologist
a. Bilateral recurrent laryngeal nerve injury		
Tracheotomy	100%	74
b. Persistent hypothyroidism		
Administration of dessicated thyroid	100%	
c. Postoperative bleeding		
(1) If detected early, reopening of incision and control of bleeding under intratracheal anesthesia in operating room, followed by tracheotomy	100%	135 OR / 74
		213 anesthesia
(2) In emergency, in presence of imminent tracheal obstruction, immediate opening of incision and evacuation of clot, followed by tracheotomy	100%	345 RR / 74
d. Tetany		
(1) Intravenous calcium gluconate	100%	
(2) Administration of oral calcium	100%	
e. Thyroid storm		
(1) Sedation	100%	
(2) Cooling of patient	100%	137
(3) Maintenance of high fluid intake	100%	
(4) Administration of digitalis	100%	
(5) Administration of intravenous sodium iodide and/or cortisone	100%	

Record Analyst: Thyroid storm is reflected in fever, rapid pulse, restlessness, cardiac signs and in uncontrolled delirium. Find data in nursing notes and progress notes.

ICU, 2 days: 1,540

POSTOPERATIVE CARE

11. Anesthetist's postoperative evaluation of patient following transfer from Recovery Room — 100%

12. Postoperative nursing care including
    a. Pulse and respiration every 15 minutes until stable, then per postoperative nursing care plan — 100%
    b. Fluid intake and output monitored — 100%
       Exception: Monitoring not ordered.
    c. Intravenous therapy and medications monitored and maintained — 100%
    d. Documentation of patient's tolerance for walking before discharge — 100%
    e. Patient monitored for evidence of complications — 100%

LENGTH OF STAY

13. Length of stay
    a. Preoperative, 1 day — 100% $ 350
    b. Postoperative, 4-5 days — 100%   1,400-1,750
       Exceptions: (1) Early departure against medical advice; (2) complications or other diagnoses justifying extension.

DISCHARGE STATUS

14. Patient discharged under the following conditions:
    a. Temperature below 99.4 F for 36 hours before discharge — 100%
    b. Wound healing satisfactorily — 100%
    c. Physiologic imbalance corrected and condition stable — 100%
    d. Patient and family instructed re (1) activity level, (2) dosage and schedule of medications if applicable, (3) wound care and (4) follow-up visit to physician — 100%
       Exception: Instructions on transfer form.

TONSILLECTOMY AND ADENOIDECTOMY

SAMPLE

Patients discharged following tonsillectomy with or without adenoidectomy.

REVIEW

Criterion	Standard	Estimated Charge
JUSTIFICATION FOR EXTENDED STAY		$ 107 supplies
1. Presence of postoperative infection or postoperative bleeding	100%	8 kit
PREOPERATIVE STUDY AND CARE		
2. In the chart prior to surgery,		
a. Documentation of the presence of one or more of the following sets of conditions in a patient over 5 years of age	100%	
(1) Four or more documented attacks of tonsillitis in a year		
(2) At least 2 throat cultures positive for streptococcus		
(3) Severe recurrent otitis media of the catarrhal type with decrease in hearing		
(4) Severely enlarged adenoids with posterior nasal obstruction		
(5) Recurrent rhinosinusitis		
b. History	100%	
c. Physical examination report with specific reference to condition of tonsils	100%	
3. Laboratory and other studies performed prior to admission		
a. CBC and urinalysis	100%	29
b. Coagulation profile	100%	85
c. Chest x-ray within past month with report in record	100%	70
4. Preoperative nursing care including		
a. Patient assessment including vital signs, brief relevant history and present complaint	100%	
b. History of allergies and drug sensitivities	100%	
c. Formulation of care plan based on assessment and objectives	100%	
d. Patient orientation to surroundings and planned procedures	100%	
e. Preoperative instructions consistent with anesthesia plan	100%	
f. Preoperative preparation and medication	100%	
5. Anesthesiologist's preoperative evaluation of patient with specification of ASA class and risk level	100%	

SURGICAL MANAGEMENT

6.	Tonsillectomy or tonsillectomy with adenoidectomy	100%	
7.	Report by operating surgeon of (a) preoperative diagnosis, (b) procedures performed and (c) description of tissues and findings, dictated or written immediately after surgery	100%	

$ 80
supplies
135
OR
165
anesthesia
160
RR
12
instruments

8. Pathologist's report confirming presence of hypertrophied tonsils
   and, where applicable, of adenoids   100%   23
9. Management of complications
   a. Postoperative infection
      (1) Culture and sensitivity   100%   75
      (2) Antibiotic consistent with culture and sensitivity   100%
   b. Postoperative bleeding
      (1) Patient's blood typed and cross matched for transfusion   100%   50
      (2) Coagulation profile reviewed and repeated   100%   64
      (3) Patient transfused   100%   45 infusion
          Exception: Blood loss estimated at less than 500 cc's.   45-88 per unit

POSTOPERATIVE CARE

10. Anesthetist's postoperative evaluation of patient following transfer
    from Recovery Room   100%
11. Postoperative nursing care
    a. Pulse and respiration every 15 minutes until stable, then per
       postoperative nursing care plan   100%
    b. Intravenous therapy and medications monitored and
       maintained   100%
    c. Documentation of patient's tolerance for walking before
       discharge   100%
    d. Patient monitored for evidence of complications   100%

LENGTH OF STAY

12. Length of stay 2 days   100%   700
    Exception: Complications or other diagnoses justifying extension.

DISCHARGE STATUS

13. Patient discharged under the following conditions:
    a. Temperature below 100 F for at least 24 hours before discharge   100%
    b. Patient and family instructed re (1) soft diet, (2) oral hygiene
       and need to watch for bleeding, (3) limited activity with
       return to school in one week and (4) follow-up visit to
       physician   100%
       Exception: Instructions on transfer form.
       *Record Analyst: The presence in the record of the surgeon's
       standard discharge instructions covering at least these elements,
       with an indication that a copy has been received by the
       patient or his parent, satisfies this requirement.*

GYNECOLOGY AND OBSTETRICS

ABORTION, FIRST TRIMESTER

SUGGESTED SAMPLE

Patients discharged following first trimester abortion associated with extended stay resulting from the presence of cervical laceration, hemorrhage or infection.

REVIEW

Criterion	Standard	Estimated Charge
JUSTIFICATION FOR EXTENDED STAY		$ 42 supplies
1. Presence of any of the following in association with first trimester abortion:	100%	
a. Cervical laceration		
b. Hemorrhage		
c. Infection		
PREOPERATIVE STUDY AND CARE		
2. In the chart prior to surgery,		
a. History including reference to each of the following:	100%	
(1) Pregnancy of less than 12 weeks' duration		
(2) Referral of the patient by a physician who has performed a general evaluation		
(3) Record of any previous abortions		
(4) Record of any previous pelvic surgery		
(5) Record of any allergies or drug sensitivities		
b. Report of complete physical examination including pelvic examination	100%	
3. Laboratory and other studies including		
a. CBC with Hgb at least 10 gms % and Hct at least 30%	100%	19
b. Urinalysis	100%	10
c. Vital signs within normal limits	100%	
d. White blood count no higher than 14,000	100%	
e. Chest x-ray within past 3 months, with report in record	100%	70
f. EKG	100%	
g. Coagulation profile	100%	85
h. Social worker's evaluation of patient	100%	
4. Preoperative nursing care		
Physical and psychological preparation of the patient for surgery, including preoperative instruction in deep breathing, coughing and turning in bed after surgery	100%	
5. Anesthesiologist's preoperative evaluation of patient with statement of anesthetic plan	100%	
MANAGEMENT		12 supplies
6. Bimanual pelvic examination under anesthesia	100%	
7. Suction procedure	100%	123

8. Dilatation and extraction   0% $ 123

    Exceptions (Indications): (a) Presence of uterine abnormalities, (b) presence of high degree of probability that the pregnancy may be of longer duration than 13 weeks with hardening of fetal bones.

50
anesthesia

109
RR

9. Report by operating surgeon of (a) preoperative diagnosis, (b) procedures performed and (c) description of tissues and findings, dictated or written immediately after surgery   100%

10. Pathologist's report supporting preoperative diagnosis   100%   23

11. Management of complications

    a. Cervical laceration with bleeding   147
OR

       (1) Examination to determine size of lesion   100%   55
anesthesia

36
RR

       (2) Cervical suture   100%

          Exception: Presence of a large lesion with bleeding from a large vessel.

       (3) Immediate laparotomy to repair bleeding vessel   100%   616

          Exception: Presence of small cervical lesion reparable from below.

165
anesthesia

150
RR

       (4) Transfusion   100%   50
type

          Exception: Blood loss less than 250 cc.

45
infusion

45-88
per unit

    b. Hemorrhage resulting from retention of products of conception   123

50
anesthesia

       (1) Complete removal of products of conception   100%   50
type

       (2) Transfusion   100%   45
infusion

    c. Infection   45-88
per unit

109
RR

       (1) Search for and removal of any foreign bodies or retained products of conception   100%   173

       (2) Culture and sensitivity followed by appropriate antibiotic   100%   75

       (3) Uterotonics as indicated   100%

       (4) Intravenous fluids in presence of dehydration   100%   20

POSTOPERATIVE CARE

12. Anesthetist's postoperative evaluation of patient after discharge from Recovery Room   100%

13. Postoperative nursing care

    a. Monitoring of vital signs every 15 minutes until stable, then hourly for 4 hours   100%

    b. Observation of patient for evidence of bleeding or other complications   100%

LENGTH OF STAY

14. Length of stay
    a. Prior to abortion, maximum of 1 day   100% $ 350
    b. Postoperative
       (1) Cervical laceration, 4-6 days   100%   1400-2100
       (2) Hemorrhage, 4-6 days   100%   1400-2100
       (3) Infection, 4-6 days   100%   1400-2100
       (4) In the absence of complications, 1 day maximum   100%   350

DISCHARGE STATUS

15. Patient discharged under the following conditions: 3
                                                                                        supplies
    a. Vaginal bleeding under control
    b. Temperature below 99.4 F
    c. Complications absent
    d. Patient instructed re (1) personal hygiene, (2) level of activity,
       including sexual activity and (3) follow-up visit to physician   100%

SUGGESTED SAMPLE

Patients exhibiting any of the following conditions in association with abdominal hysterectomy.

Hematoma	Pulmonary embolism
Ligature of ureters	Rectovaginal fistula
Pelvic abscess	Small bowel fistula
Pelvic thrombophlebitis	Vesicovaginal fistula
Postoperative hemorrhage	Wound dehiscence

REVIEW

Criterion	Standard	Estimated Charge
JUSTIFICATION FOR EXTENDED STAY		$ 82 supplies
1. Presence of any of the following conditions following abdominal hysterectomy:	100%	8 kit
(a) Hematoma, (b) ligature of ureters, (c) pelvic abscess, (d) pelvic thrombophlebitis, (e) postoperative hemorrhage, (f) pulmonary embolism, (g) rectovaginal fistula, (h) small bowel fistula, (i) vesicovaginal fistula or (j) wound dehiscence		
PREOPERATIVE STUDY AND CARE		
2. In the chart prior to surgery,		
a. Documentation of the presence of any of the following conditions:	100%	
(1) Bleeding uterine fibroids		
(2) Fibroids larger than 12 weeks' pregnancy in patient over 35		
(3) Tubo-ovarian abscesses or other infection		
(4) Carcinoma in situ of the cervix		
(5) Endometrial carcinoma Stage 1A limited to endometrium		
(6) Endometriosis		
(7) Hysterectomy planned in conjunction with bilateral ovariectomy		
(8) Hysterectomy to be performed incidentally to other surgery for pelvic neoplasms		
b. History with reference to any previous pelvic surgery	100%	
c. Physical examination report including pelvic examination shortly before or after admission	100%	
3. Laboratory and other studies performed before admission		
a. CBC, urinalysis and admission panel of 20 studies	100%	125
b. Coagulation profile	100%	85
c. Serology	100%	11
d. Chest x-ray	100%	70

e. EKG	100%	$ 48
Exception: Patient under 40.		
f. Negative pregnancy test	100%	32
Exception: Patient over 50.		
4. Preoperative irradiation	0%	

Exceptions: (a) Presence of advanced endometrial carcinoma greater than Stage 1A or (b) presence of a uterus that can be sounded to a depth greater than 10 cms.

5. Preoperative nursing care including

a. Patient assessment including vital signs, brief relevant history and present complaint	100%	
b. History of allergies and drug sensitivities	100%	
c. Formulation of nursing care plan	100%	
d. Patient orientation to care and planned procedures	100%	
e. Preoperative instruction in deep breathing, coughing and turning in bed following surgery	100%	
f. Preoperative preparation and medication	100%	
6. Anesthesiologist's preoperative evaluation of patient with specification of ASA class and risk level	100%	

SURGICAL MANAGEMENT

7. Dilatation and curettage before hysterectomy	100%	61 supplies
Exception: Absence of bleeding.		535 OR
		236 anesthesia
		32 instruments
		300 RR
8. Abdominal hysterectomy	100%	100 drain set
9. Report by operating surgeon of (a) preoperative diagnosis, (b) procedures performed and (c) description of tissues and findings, dictated or written immediately after surgery	100%	
10. Pathologist's report supporting preoperative diagnosis	100%	115
11. Management of complications		
a. Hematoma		52
(1) Drainage of hematoma	100%	55 anesthesia
		11 instruments
(2) Culture and sensitivity of drainage	100%	75
(3) Antibiotic consistent with culture and sensitivity	100%	
b. Ligature of ureters		
(1) Release of ligation	100%	535 OR
		11 instruments
		236 anesthesia
		187 RR
(2) Intravenous pyelogram	100%	225

140

	(3)	Retrograde catheterization	100%	16
	(4)	Resection and anastomosis of portion of ureter as indicated	100%	
c.	Pelvic abscess			$ 135 OR
	(1)	Drainage by posterior colpotomy	100%	11 instruments 55 anesthesia
	(2)	Culture and sensitivity of drainage	100%	75-150
	(3)	Antibiotic consistent with culture and sensitivity	100%	
d.	Pelvic thrombophlebitis			
	(1)	Culture and sensitivity of blood	100%	75
	(2)	Antibiotic consistent with culture and sensitivity	100%	
	(3)	Anticoagulant therapy	100%	
e.	Postoperative hemorrhage			535 OR
	(1)	Ligation of vessel	100%	11 instruments
	(2)	Vaginal packing	100%	14 pack
	(3)	Transfusion	100%	50 type 45 infusion 45-88 per unit
f.	Pulmonary embolism			
	(1)	Lung scan to confirm	100%	270
	(2)	Anticoagulant therapy	100%	
	(3)	Complete bed rest	100%	
g.	Rectovaginal fistula			535 OR
		Surgical repair when abdominal wound has healed	100%	236 anesthesia 11 instruments 190 RR
h.	Small bowel fistula			535 OR
	(1)	Prophylactic antibiotic with culture and sensitivity ordered	100%	236 anesthesia
	(2)	Immediate surgical repair	100%	11 instruments
	(3)	Any ileus decompressed	100%	190 RR
i.	Vesicovaginal fistula			535 OR
	(1)	Conservative care until completion of healing, followed by	100%	236 anesthesia
	(2)	Dissection of anterior vaginal wall and closure of tract	100%	11 instruments 190 RR
j.	Wound dehiscence			135 OR
	(1)	Repair of wound	100%	55 anesthesia
	(2)	Prophylactic antibiotic with culture and sensitivity ordered	100%	11 instrument

POSTOPERATIVE CARE

12. Postoperative evaluation by anesthetist following transfer from Recovery Room   100%

13. Postoperative nursing care
    a. Vital signs every 15 minutes until stable, then hourly for 4 hours or per postoperative nursing care plan   100%
    b. Monitoring of intravenous therapy, medications and intake and output   100%
    c. Patient encouraged to breathe deeply, cough and turn in bed   100%
    d. Patient monitored for evidence of complications   100%

LENGTH OF STAY

14. Length of stay
    a. Preoperative, 1 day maximum   100% $ 350
    b. Total length of stay
       (1) In absence of malignancy, 9 days maximum   100%   3,150
       (2) In presence of malignancy, 18 days maximum   100%   6,300

    Exceptions: (1) Early departure against medical advice; (2) complications or other diagnoses justifying extension.

DISCHARGE STATUS

15. Patient discharged under the following conditions:
    a. Temperature below 99.6 F for at least 24 hours before discharge   100%
    b. Complications absent   100%
    c. Minimal vaginal discharge   100%
    d. Patient able to void spontaneously   100%
    e. Normal bowel function established with 1 normal stool during the 24 hours before discharge   100%
    f. Patient instructed re (1) bathing and personal hygiene, (2) wound care, (3) level of activity including sexual activity, (4) medication and (5) follow-up visit to physician.
       Exception: Instructions on transfer form.

SAMPLE

Insulin-dependent obstetrical patients who have been discharged from the hospital following a routine or non-routine admission for the evaluation and management of diabetes during pregnancy.

REVIEW

Criterion	Standard	Estimated Charge
INITIAL HOSPITALIZATION		
INDICATION FOR ADMISSION		$ 8 kit
1. Need to assess the health status of a pregnant patient who is already receiving insulin or who is to begin insulin treatment	100%	
EVALUATION		
2. History	100%	
3. Physical examination	100%	
4. Laboratory studies including		
a. CBC with differential	100%	35
b. Admission panel of 20 blood chemistries	100%	86
c. T_3 Resin Uptake	100%	43
d. Thyroxine (T_4)	100%	45
e. Hemoglobin A_{1C}	100%	26
f. Free thyroxin index (FTI)	100%	45
g. Urinalysis	100%	11
h. Urine albumin	100%	3
i. Urine culture and sensitivity	100%	75
j. On the first and last full hospital days,		
(1) Urine protein	100%	199
(2) Creatinine clearance	100%	54
(3) Urine glucose	100%	14
k. Retinal photographs in Class D and Class F patients	100%	26
Exception: Absence of diabetic retinopathy.		
MANAGEMENT AND IMPLEMENTATION OF DIABETIC CONTROL		
5. Dietetic management plan followed		
a. 32 Kcal/kg of ideal body weight up to 16 weeks	100%	35
b. 38 Kcal/kg of ideal body weight from 16 weeks to term	100%	
c. Distribution of intake to be $\frac{2}{7}$, $\frac{2}{7}$, $\frac{2}{7}$ and $\frac{1}{7}$, with meals at 0800, 1300, 1800 and 2200 hours	100%	
6. Blood sugar measurements		
a. First and last full hospital days, plasma glucose profile pre-meal, 1 hour after each meal and 2 hours after each meal	100%	54
b. Interim days, pre-meal plasma glucose	100%	27

    c. Patient to measure venous or capillary blood samples obtained at the same times with BG Chemstrips or blood glucose meter   100%

7. Pre-meal testing of urine for glucose and ketones   100%

8. Insulin treatment
    a. Patient classified as Type I or Type II diabetic   100%
    b. Type I to receive regular insulin ½ hour before each meal and Ultra-Lente insulin ½ hour before breakfast and/or supper   100%
    c. Type II to receive regular insulin ½ hour before breakfast and supper, and Ultra-Lente insulin ½ hour before breakfast and/or supper   100%

PATIENT EDUCATION

9. Documentation in the medical record of the instructional program provided by the dietician to the patient and her significant others   100%

DISCHARGE STATUS

10. Patient discharged under the following conditions:
    a. Complications absent   100%
    b. Diabetes under control   100%
    c. Patient and family instructed re (1) diet, (2) activity level and (3) necessity to follow prescribed schedule of visits to physician's office or outpatient clinic   100%

DILATATION AND CURETTAGE

SUGGESTED SAMPLE

Patients whose discharge diagnoses include transfusion reaction, uterine infection or uterine perforation following dilatation and curettage for dysfunctional uterine bleeding.

REVIEW

Criterion	Standard	Estimated Charge
JUSTIFICATION FOR EXTENDED STAY		$ 42 supplies
1. Presence of (a) transfusion reaction, (b) uterine infection or (c) uterine perforation following dilatation and curettage for dysfunctional uterine bleeding	100%	8 kit
PREOPERATIVE STUDY AND CARE		
2. In the chart prior to surgery,		
a. Documentation of the presence of at least one of the following conditions:	100%	
(1) An acute episode of bleeding or of hemorrhage		
(2) Chronic uterine abnormalities with anemia		
(3) Abnormal uterine bleeding of over 3 months' duration		
b. History with specific reference to menstrual and endocrine histories, endocrine therapy if any, possible pregnancy or pelvic infection	100%	
3. Laboratory and other studies performed prior to admission		
a. CBC, urinalysis and admission panel of 6 studies	100%	52
b. Serology	100%	11
c. Negative pregnancy test	100%	32
Exception: Patient over 50.		
d. Pap smear within past year with report in record	100%	23
e. Chest x-ray within past 6 months with report in record	100%	70
4. Preoperative nursing care including		
a. Patient assessment including vital signs, brief relevant history and present complaint	100%	
b. History of allergies and drug sensitivities	100%	
c. Formulation of care plan based on assessment and objectives	100%	
d. Patient orientation to care and nursing procedures	100%	
e. Documentation of any pain or bleeding noted	100%	
f. Patient instructed in deep breathing, coughing and turning in bed after surgery	100%	
g. Preoperative preparation and medication	100%	
5. Anesthesiologist's preoperative evaluation of patient and note on anesthesia plan	100%	

SURGICAL MANAGEMENT

6. Dilatation and curettage	100%	$ 256
		50 type
7. Blood transfusion	0%	45 infusion
Exception: Hgb below 10 gms % or systolic blood pressure below 100 mm Hg.		45-88 per unit
8. Report by operating surgeon of (a) preoperative diagnosis, (b) procedures performed and (c) description of tissues and findings, dictated or written immediately after surgery	100%	
9. Pathologist's report consistent with preoperative diagnosis	100%	
10. Management of complications		
a. Transfusion reaction		
(1) Transfusion stopped	100%	
(2) Patient's blood re-typed and cross matched	100%	50
(3) Antihistamine administered	100%	
b. Uterine infection		
(1) Culture and sensitivity	100%	75
(2) Antibiotic consistent with culture and sensitivity	100%	
c. Uterine perforation		
(1) Observation and conservative management	100%	
(2) In presence of evidence of infection, such as elevated temperature, culture and sensitivity	100%	75
(3) In presence of positive culture, antibiotic consistent with culture and sensitivity	100%	

POSTOPERATIVE CARE

11. Anesthetist's postoperative evaluation of patient following transfer from Recovery Room	100%	
12. Postoperative nursing care including		
a. Vital signs every 15 minutes until stable, then per postoperative nursing care plan	100%	
b. Patient monitored for evidence of complications	100%	

LENGTH OF STAY

13. Length of stay 2 days including 1 day preoperative	100%	700
Exception: Presence of complications or other diagnoses justifying extension.		

DISCHARGE STATUS

14. Patient discharged under the following conditions:		
a. Temperature below 99.6 F on day of discharge	100%	
b. Hgb equal to or greater than 10 gms %	100%	
c. Patient instructed re (1) bathing and personal hygiene and (2) follow-up visit to physician	100%	

   Exception: Instructions on transfer form.

Record Analyst: The presence in the record of the surgeon's standard discharge instructions covering at least these elements, with an indication that the patient has received a copy, satisfies this requirement.

146

SAMPLE

Patients discharged with the diagnosis of ectopic pregnancy.

REVIEW

Criterion	Standard	Estimated Charge
INDICATIONS FOR ADMISSION TO THE HOSPITAL		$ 42 supplies
1. In a patient who is 2 to 3 weeks past a skipped menstrual period, the presence of any of the following:	100%	8 kit
a. Spotting and cramping pain		
b. Sudden severe pain accompanied by blood loss		
c. Signs of shock		
d. Severe peritoneal irritation		
PREOPERATIVE STUDY AND CARE		
2. In the chart prior to surgery,		
a. Documentation of a history of a menstrual period skipped for from 2 to 3 weeks, symptoms of pregnancy, and any of the following conditions:	100%	139
(1) Spotting accompanied by cramping pain		
(2) Sudden severe pain accompanied by blood loss		
(3) Signs of shock		
(4) Severe peritoneal irritation		
b. Physical examination	100%	
3. Laboratory and other studies performed prior to surgery		
a. Pregnancy test	100%	32
b. Colpocentesis in search of free blood	100%	85
c. Laparoscopy performed in hospital	100%	60
d. Ultrasound examination	100%	13
Exception: History of skipped period less than 5 weeks.		
e. CBC, urinalysis and admission panel of 20 studies	100%	125
f. Serology	100%	11
g. Chest x-ray within past 3 months with report in record	100%	70
4. Preoperative nursing care including		
a. Patient assessment including vital signs, brief relevant history and present complaint	100%	
b. History of allergies and drug sensitivities	100%	
c. Formulation of care plan based on assessment and objective	100%	
d. Patient orientation to care and nursing procedures	100%	
e. Documentation of any pain and bleeding noted	100%	
f. Patient instructed in deep breathing, coughing and turning in bed after surgery	100%	
g. Preoperative preparation and medication	100%	

5. Anesthesiologist's preoperative evaluation of patient with ASA class and level of risk — 100%

6. Patient's blood typed and cross matched — 100% — $ 50

SURGICAL MANAGEMENT

7. In tubal pregnancy of less than 4 weeks' duration,
   a. Removal of products of conception — 100%
   b. Primary repair of tube — 100%

   60 supplies
   500 OR
   212 anesthesia
   22 instruments
   160 RR

8. In tubal pregnancy of 4 or more weeks' duration,
   a. Removal of products of conception — 100%
   b. Secondary repair of tube after healing from removal of products of conception, with plan for repair documented in record — 100%

   500 OR
   212 anesthesia
   22 instruments
   160 RR

9. In the presence of shock, salpingectomy — 100%
   Exception: Absence of shock.

   500 OR
   212 anesthesia
   22 instruments
   160 RR

10. Blood transfusion — 0%
    Exceptions: (a) Hgb below 10 gms %, (b) systolic blood pressure below 100 mm Hg, or (c) surgical blood loss in excess of 500 cc's.

    45 infusion
    45-88 per unit

11. Report by operating surgeon of (a) preoperative diagnosis, (b) procedures performed and (c) description of tissues and findings, dictated or written immediately after surgery — 100%

12. Pathologist's report on specimen consistent with preoperative diagnosis — 100%

    60

13. Management of complications
    Hemorrhage and shock
    (1) Patient transfused — 100%
    (2) Surgical intervention, with bleeders clamped — 100%

    45 infusion
    45-88 per unit
    135 OR
    142 anesthesia

POSTOPERATIVE CARE

14. Anesthetist's postoperative evaluation of patient following transfer from Recovery Room — 100%

15. Postoperative nursing care including
    a. Vital signs every 15 minutes until stable, then per postoperative nursing care plan — 100%
    b. Patient monitored for evidence of complications — 100%
    c. Intravenous therapy monitored and maintained — 100%
    d. Intake and output charted — 100%

16. Patient encouraged to breathe deeply, cough and turn in bed following surgery — 100%

148

LENGTH OF STAY

17. Length of stay depending upon surgical procedure:
    a. Following removal of products of conception and primary
       repair of tube, 2-3 days   100% $700-1,050
    b. Following removal of products of conception with planned
       secondary repair of tube, 4-5 days   100%   1,400-1,750
    c. Following salpingectomy, 1 week   100%   2,450

    Exceptions: (1) Early departure against medical advice;
    (2) complications or other diagnoses justifying extension.

DISCHARGE STATUS

18. Patient discharged under the following conditions:
    a. Temperature below 99.6 F on day of discharge   100%
    b. Patient ambulatory
    c. Pain absent or minimal
    d. Complications absent
    e. Patient instructed re (1) abstinence from sexual activity
       pending scheduled follow-up visit; (2) no use of douches
       pending scheduled follow-up visit; (3) follow-up visit to
       physician within from 3 to 4 weeks following discharge   100%

    Exception: Instructions on transfer form.

PRE-ECLAMPSIA AND ECLAMPSIA

SUGGESTED SAMPLE

Patients whose discharge diagnoses include pre-eclampsia, eclampsia or toxemia of pregnancy.

REVIEW

Criterion	Standard	Estimated Charge
INDICATIONS FOR ADMISSION		$ 117 supplies
1. Presence in a pregnant patient of any of the following conditions or combinations of conditions:	100%	8 kit
a. Diastolic blood pressure of 110 mm Hg or above		
b. Systolic blood pressure of 160 mm Hg or above		
c. Oliguria of less than 400 ml per 24 hours		
d. Proteinuria of 5 gms per 24 hours in conjunction with any of the above		14
e. Hyperreflexia in conjunction with any of the above		
INVESTIGATION		
2. Laboratory studies including		
a. CBC	100%	19
b. Urinalysis	100%	10
c. Serial hematocrit levels	100%	19
d. Blood urea nitrogen level	100%	19
e. Serial uric acid level	100%	24
f. Measurement of urinary estriol 3 times a week	100%	256 per week
MANAGEMENT		
3. Bed rest	100%	
4. Low sodium diet	100%	
5. Diuretics	100%	
6. Sedation with phenobarbitol	100%	
7. Nursing care including		
a. Monitoring of blood pressure every 6 hours	100%	
b. Daily monitoring of urine albumin	100%	
8. Prevention and control of convulsions with magnesium sulfate	100%	
Exception: Absence of evidence of central nervous system involvement.		
9. Induction or Caesarian section	0%	107 or 500
Exceptions (Indications): (a) Failure of conservative measures to control pre-eclamptic condition effectively, or (b) presence of continuing maternal and intrauterine fetal risk.		

10. Management of complications
    a. Generalized convulsions
       (1) Magnesium sulfate 100%
       (2) Phenobarbitol sedation and observation for 24 hours ... 100%
       (3) Induction of labor .... 100% $ 107
    b. Premature labor
       (1) Magnesium sulfate 100%
       (2) Antihypertensive medication 100%
    c. Diplopia
       (1) Antihypertensive medication 100%
       (2) Sedation 100%
       (3) Bed rest 100%
       (4) Diuretics 100%
       (5) Low sodium diet 100%
    d. Hemorrhagic retinitis or retinal detachment
       Induction of labor 100%   107
    e. Hypofibrinogenemia
       (1) Determination of fibrinogen level 100%   14
       (2) Whole blood and fibrinogen transfusion 100%   50
                                                                             type
                                                                             45
                                                                             infusion
                                                                             45-88
                                                                             per unit

LENGTH OF STAY

11. For control of pre-eclampsia or eclampsia, 7-8 days 100% 2,450-2,800

DISCHARGE STATUS

12. Patient discharged under the following conditions:
    a. Arterial blood pressure no higher than 140 systolic and
       90 diastolic 100%
    b. Absence of proteinuria 100%   14
    c. Absence of edema 100%
    d. Absence of complications of pre-eclampsia or toxemia 100%
    e. Patient and family instructed re (a) schedule and dosage of
       medications as applicable, (b) diet as applicable and
       (c) follow-up visit to physician 100%   35
       Exception: Instructions on transfer form.

PRIMARY CAESARIAN SECTION

SUGGESTED SAMPLE

Patients whose discharge diagnoses include anemia, infection or phlebitis following caesarian section.

REVIEW

Criterion	Standard	Estimated Charge
JUSTIFICATION FOR EXTENDED STAY		$ 120 supplies 8 kit
1. Presence of any of the following after delivery by caesarian section	100%	
a. Anemia with Hgb below 9 gms %		19 CBC
b. Infection with temperature over 101.4 F for 48 hours		
c. Phlebitis		
PREOPERATIVE STUDY AND CARE		
2. In the chart prior to surgery, History and physical examination report showing the presence of any of the following indications for surgery:	100%	
a. Demonstrated fetopelvic disproportion, definite or borderline, by pelvimetry		
b. Placenta praevia or abruptio placentae		
c. Fetal distress		
d. Prolapsed cord		
e. Malpresentation		
f. Uterine inertia		
g. Failure of forceps		
h. Medical complications such as eclampsia, pre-eclampsia, diabetes, hemolytic diseases or cardiac problems		
3. Laboratory studies including		
a. Customary preoperative tests including CBC, urinalysis and and admission panel of 20 studies	100%	125
b. Coagulation profile	100%	85
c. Serology report in record	100%	11
General Exception to Criteria 3, 3b and 3c: Emergency surgery mandatory before procedures can be performed.		
4. Preoperative nursing care		
a. Patient assessment including vital signs and report of labor status	100%	
b. History of allergies and drug sensitivities	100%	
c. Patient orientation to surroundings and nursing procedures	100%	
d. Formulation of initial care plan based on assessment	100%	
e. Preoperative preparation and medication	100%	
5. Anesthesiologist's preoperative evaluation of patient	100%	

SURGICAL MANAGEMENT

		$ 62 supplies

6. Low transverse caesarian section — 100% — 500 OR / 165 anesthesia / 187 RR / 12 instruments

   Exceptions: (a) planned tubal excision and division, or
   (b) planned hysterectomy.

7. Report by operating surgeon of (a) preoperative diagnosis,
   (b) procedures performed and (c) description of tissues and
   findings, dictated or written immediately after surgery — 100%

8. Management of complications
   a. Anemia with Hgb below 9 gms % following delivery
      (1) Serial hemoglobin determinations — 100% — 56
      (2) Patient's blood typed and cross matched for transfusion — 100% — 50
      (3) Blood transfusion as indicated — 100% — 45 infusion / 45-88 per unit

   b. Infection
      (1) Culture and sensitivity of blood, urine, lochia or drainage — 100% — 75
      (2) Complete blood count (CBC) — 100% — 19
      (3) Antibiotic consistent with culture and sensitivity — 100%

   c. Phlebitis
      (1) Location determined — 100%
      (2) Coagulation profile repeated — 100% — 64
      (3) Anticoagulant therapy instituted — 100%
      (4) Analgesics administered — 100%
      (5) Heat applied to affected part — 100% — 9
      (6) Affected part elevated — 100%

POSTOPERATIVE CARE

9. Anesthetist's postoperative evaluation of patient following
   transfer from Recovery Room — 100%

10. Postoperative nursing care
    a. Vital signs every 15 minutes until stable, then hourly for
       4 hours, then per postoperative care plan — 100%
    b. Intravenous and drug therapies monitored and maintained — 100%
    c. Patient encouraged to breathe deeply, cough and turn in bed — 100%
    d. Foley catheter care maintained — 100%

       Exception: Foley catheter not in use.

    e. Patient monitored for evidence of complications — 100%

LENGTH OF STAY

11. Length of stay 6-7 days — 100% — 2,100-2,450

    Exceptions: (a) Early departure against medical advice; (b) early
    departure for valid socio-economic reasons; (c) complications or
    other diagnoses justifying extension.

DISCHARGE STATUS

12. Patient discharged under the following conditions:
    a. Temperature below 100 F for at least 24 hours before
       discharge   100%
    b. Incision dry and healing   100%
    c. Patient tolerating general diet   100%
       Exception: Presence of other condition requiring modified diet.
    d. Absence of complications   100%
    e. Patient instructed re (1) activity level including sexual activity,
       (2) bathing and personal hygiene, (3) specifics of breast and
       incision care and (4) scheduling of follow-up visit to physician   100%
    f. Patient instructed re (1) feeding of infant, (2) bathing and care
       of infant and (3) follow-up visit to pediatrician   100% $ 50
       Exception: Mother not planning to take infant home, but to
       relinquish for foster care or adoption.

SUGGESTED SAMPLE

Patients whose discharge diagnoses include any of the following complications following sterilization.

Anesthesia-related complications
Hemorrhage
Pelvic thrombophlebitis

Pulmonary embolism
Sepsis
Wound infection

REVIEW

Criterion	Standard	Estimated Charge
JUSTIFICATION FOR EXTENDED STAY		$ 72 supplies
1. Presence of any of the following conditions in association with sterilization:	100%	8 kit
a. Anesthesia-related complications		
b. Hemorrhage		
c. Pelvic thrombophlebitis		
d. Pulmonary embolism		
e. Sepsis		
f. Wound infection		
PREOPERATIVE STUDY AND CARE		
2. In the chart prior to surgery,		
a. History showing absence of contraindications to elective surgery	100%	
b. Physical examination report showing absence of contraindications to elective surgery	100%	
c. Documentation of informed consent	100%	
3. Laboratory and other studies including		
a. CBC, urinalysis and admission panel of 6 studies	100%	52
b. Report on cervical cytology study within past year	100%	11
c. Serology	100%	11
d. Chest x-ray within the past month with report in record	100%	70
e. Negative pregnancy test	100%	32
Exception: Procedure performed less than 1 month following delivery.		
4. Preoperative nursing care		
a. Patient assessment including vital signs and brief relevant history	100%	
b. History of allergies and drug sensitivities	100%	
c. Formulation of nursing care plan based on assessment	100%	
d. Patient orientation to surroundings and nursing procedures	100%	
e. Preoperative instruction in deep breathing, coughing and turning in bed following surgery	100%	
f. Preoperative preparation and medication	100%	

MANAGEMENT

5. Either of the following procedures: 100% $ 600
   OR
   a. Excision and division   165 anesthesia

   Contraindications: History of extensive pelvic surgery or pathology contributing to the presence of adhesions.   150 RR   22 instruments

   (1) Report by operating surgeon on (a) preoperative diagnosis, (b) procedures performed including division of tubes and removal of segments of tubes and (c) description of tissues and findings, dictated or written immediately after surgery   100%

   (2) Pathologist's report on tubal tissue specimens in record   100%   23

   b. Laparoscopy and tubal cautery   600 OR   165 anesthesia

   (1) Report by operating surgeon on (a) preoperative diagnosis, (b) procedures performed and (c) description of tissues and findings, dictated or written immediately after surgery   100%   150 RR   22 instruments

   (2) Pathologist's report on tubal tissue specimens in record   100%   23

6. Management of complications

   a. Anesthesia-related complications

   (1) Respiratory complications

      (a) Patent airway established and maintained   100%   70

      (b) Adequate ventilation maintained   100%

   (2) Cardiovascular complications

      (a) Prompt recognition of a patient in shock or with chest pain   100%

      (b) Implementation of cardiac emergency plan with administration of oxygen, fluids and vasopressors   100%   125

   b. Hemorrhage

   (1) Patient's blood typed and cross matched for transfusion   100%   50

   (2) Transfusion performed   100%   45 infusion   45-88 per unit

   (3) Coagulation profile obtained   100%   64

   (4) Electrolyte levels determined   100%   25

   (5) Intake and output monitored   100%

   c. Pelvic thrombophlebitis

   (1) Anticoagulant therapy instituted   100%

   (2) Intravenous fluids   100%   20

   (3) Electrolyte levels determined   100%   25

   (4) Intake and output monitored   100%

   d. Pulmonary embolism

   (1) Confirmation by lung scan   100%   270

   (2) Oxygen administered   100%   26

   (3) Chest x-ray for evaluation   100%   70

   (4) Intravenous fluids   100%   20

(5) Electrolyte levels determined	100%	$ 25
(6) Intake and output monitored	100%	
(7) Anticoagulant therapy instituted	100%	

e. Sepsis

(1) Chest x-ray for evaluation	100%	70
(2) Culture and sensitivity of blood	100%	75
(3) Antibiotic consistent with culture and sensitivity	100%	
(4) Intravenous fluids	100%	20
(5) Electrolyte levels determined	100%	25
(6) Intake and output monitored	100%	

f. Wound infection

(1) Culture and sensitivity of wound	100%	75
(2) Antibiotic consistent with culture and sensitivity	100%	

POSTOPERATIVE CARE

7. Anesthetist's postoperative evaluation of patient following transfer from Recovery Room	100%	
8. Postoperative nursing care		
a. Vital signs every 15 minutes until stable, then per postoperative nursing care plan	100%	
b. Patient encouraged to breathe deeply, cough and turn in bed	100%	
c. Intravenous therapy maintained and monitored	100%	

Exception: Absence of intravenous therapy, as in laparoscopy and cautery without complications.

LENGTH OF STAY

9. Length of stay		
a. In excision and division following delivery, maximum of 2 days beyond days assigned for labor and delivery	100%	700
b. Where patient admitted for excision and division only, 3-4 days	100%	1,050-1,400
c. For laparoscopy and tubal cautery only, 8 hours to 2 days	100%	0-700

Exception: Presence of complications or other diagnoses justifying extension.

DISCHARGE STATUS

10. Patient discharged under the following conditions:		
a. Vital signs stable with temperature below 99.6 F	100%	
b. Patient instructed re (1) level of activity including sexual activity, (2) wound care and (3) follow-up visit to physician	100%	

Exception: Instructions on transfer form.

SUGGESTED SAMPLE

Patients whose discharge diagnoses include any of the following conditions in association with vaginal hysterectomy.

Hematoma	Pulmonary embolism
Ligature of ureters	Rectovaginal fistula
Parametritis	Recurrent cystitis
Pelvic abscess	Separation of vaginal repair
Pelvic thrombophlebitis	Small bowel fistula
Postoperative hemorrhage	Vesicovaginal fistula

REVIEW

Criterion	Standard	Estimated Charge
JUSTIFICATION FOR EXTENDED STAY		$ 120 supplies 8 kit
1. Presence of any of the following conditions following vaginal hysterectomy:	100%	
(a) Hematoma, (b) ligature of ureters, (c) parametritis, (d) pelvic abscess, (e) pelvic thrombophlebitis, (f) postoperative hemorrhage, (g) pulmonary embolism, (h) rectovaginal fistula, (i) recurrent cystitis, (j) separation of vaginal repair, (k) small bowel fistula, or (l) vesicovaginal fistula		
PREOPERATIVE STUDY AND CARE		
2. In the chart prior to surgery,		
a. Documentation of the presence of uterine prolapse with cystocele or rectocele, with cervix at or below ischeal spine	100%	
b. History with specific reference to any previous pelvic surgery	100%	
c. Physical examination report including pelvic examination performed shortly before or after admission	100%	
3. Laboratory and other studies performed prior to admission		
a. CBC, urinalysis and admission panel	100%	125
b. Coagulation profile	100%	85
c. Serology	100%	11
d. Chest x-ray	100%	70
e. EKG	100%	48
Exception: Patient under 40.		
f. Negative pregnancy test	100%	32
Exception: Patient over 50.		
g. Report on cervical cytology study within past year	100%	11
4. Preoperative nursing care		
a. Patient assessment including vital signs, brief relevant history and present complaint	100%	
b. History of allergies and drug sensitivities	100%	
c. Formulation of nursing care plan based on assessment	100%	

d. Patient orientation to surroundings and nursing procedures	100%	
e. Preoperative instruction in deep breathing, coughing and turning in bed following surgery	100%	
f. Preoperative preparation and medication	100%	
5. Anesthesiologist's preoperative evaluation of patient, with specification of ASA class and risk level	100%	

SURGICAL MANAGEMENT

6. Vaginal hysterectomy	100%	$ 535 OR
7. Report by operating surgeon on (a) preoperative diagnosis, (b) procedures performed and (c) description of tissues and findings, dictated or written immediately after surgery	100%	236 anesthesia 32 instruments 300 RR
8. Pathologist's report on tissue specimen	100%	60 pathologist
9. Management of complications		
a. Hematoma		55 anesthesia
(1) Drainage of hematoma	100%	52
(2) Culture and sensitivity of drainage	100%	75
(3) Antibiotic consistent with culture and sensitivity	100%	
b. Ligature of ureters		535 OR
(1) Release of ligation	100%	236 anesthesia
(2) Intravenous pyelogram	100%	225
(3) Retrograde catheterization	100%	16
(4) Resection and anastomosis of portion of ureter as indicated	100%	11 instruments 187 RR
c. Parametritis		
(1) Culture and sensitivity	100%	75
(2) Antibiotic consistent with culture and sensitivity	100%	
d. Pelvic abscess		55 anesthesia
(1) Drainage of abscess	100%	52
(2) Culture and sensitivity of drainage	100%	75
(3) Antibiotic consistent with culture and sensitivity	100%	
e. Pelvic thrombophlebitis		
(1) Culture and sensitivity of blood	100%	75
(2) Antibiotic consistent with culture and sensitivity	100%	
(3) Anticoagulant therapy	100%	
f. Pulmonary embolism		
(1) Confirmation by lung scan	100%	270
(2) Anticoagulant therapy	100%	
(3) Complete bed rest	100%	

g.	Rectovaginal fistula		$ 535 OR
	Surgical repair when vaginal repair is completely healed	100%	236 anesthesia
			187 RR
			22 instruments
h.	Recurrent cystitis		
	(1) Urine culture and sensitivity	100%	75
	(2) Antibiotic consistent with culture and sensitivity	100%	
i.	Separation of vaginal repair		55 anesthesia
	Incision resutured	100%	135 OR
j.	Small bowel fistula		
	(1) Prophylactic antibiotic, with culture and sensitivity ordered	100%	150
	(2) Immediate surgical repair	100%	535 OR
	(3) Any ileus decompressed	100%	236 anesthesia
			300 RR
			32 instruments
k.	Vesicovaginal fistula		
	(1) Conservative care until completion of healing, followed by	100%	535 OR
	(2) Dissection of anterior vaginal wall and closure of tract	100%	236 anesthesia
			300 RR
			32 instruments

POSTOPERATIVE CARE

10. Anesthetist's postoperative evaluation of patient following transfer from Recovery Room — 100%

11. Postoperative nursing care
    a. Pulse and respiration every 15 minutes until stable, then per postoperative nursing care plan — 100%
    b. Intravenous therapy and medications monitored and maintained — 100%
    c. Intake and output monitored and charted — 100%
    d. Patient encouraged to breathe deeply, cough and turn in bed — 100%
    e. Condition of wound documented at time of dressing change — 100%
    f. Patient monitored for evidence of complications — 100%

LENGTH OF STAY

12. Length of stay 6-8 days — 100% — 2,100-2,800
    Exceptions: (a) Early departure against medical advice;
    (b) complications or other diagnoses justifying extension.

DISCHARGE STATUS

13. Patient discharged under the following conditions:
    a. Temperature below 99.6 F for at least 24 hours before discharge   100%
    b. Patient able to void spontaneously   100%
    c. Normal bowel function established   100%
    d. Vaginal discharge minimal   100%
    e. Complications absent   100%
    f. Patient instructed re (1) bathing and personal hygiene,
       (2) wound care, (3) level of activity including sexual activity
       and (4) follow-up visit to physician   100%

    Exception: Instructions on transfer form.

PEDIATRICS

GASTROENTERITIS IN THE PEDIATRIC PATIENT

SUGGESTED SAMPLE

Patients under the age of sixteen whose discharge diagnoses include febrile convulsions, severe dehydration, acidosis or alkalosis in association with gastroenteritis.

REVIEW

Criterion	Standard	Estimated Charge
JUSTIFICATION FOR EXTENDED STAY		
1. Presence of (a) febrile convulsions, (b) dehydration with severe electrolyte imbalance, (c) acidosis or (d) alkalosis	100%	
DIAGNOSTIC STUDY		
2. History with reference to symptomatology	100%	
3. Physical examination report	100%	
4. Laboratory and other studies including		
a. CBC, urinalysis and admission panel	100%	$ 125
b. Stool culture	100%	4
c. Serum electrolytes	100%	25
Exception: Patient admitted primarily because of need for monitoring of progress, because of parental inability to provide proper care, or on the basis of some condition other than vomiting and diarrhea justifying admission.		
d. Lumbar puncture	0%	15 test 38.50 procedure
Exception (Indication): Suspicion of meningitis.		
MANAGEMENT		
5. Nursing care		
a. Patient assessment including vital signs, brief relevant history, present complaint and weight	100%	
b. History of allergies and drug sensitivities	100%	
c. Formulation of nursing care plan based on assessment and clinical objectives	100%	
d. Patient orientation to surroundings and nursing procedures	100%	
e. Intravenous and drug therapies maintained and monitored	100%	
f. Patient monitored for evidence of complications	100%	
6. Intravenous fluids administered	100%	20
Exception: Absence of dehydration.		
7. Modified diet ordered	100%	
8. Administration of antibiotics	0%	
Exceptions: Established presence of (a) Shigellosis, (b) Salmonella, or (c) associated infections that warrant the use of antibiotics.		

9. Cutdown for administration of intravenous fluids	0%	$ 25

Exceptions (Indications):
a. Peripheral venous route has been tried without success
b. Patient in shock with collapsed veins
c. Site of venipuncture unsuitable for intravenous administration

10. Management of complications

a. Febrile convulsions		
(1) Measures taken to reduce body temperature	100%	
(2) Culture and sensitivity of blood	100%	75
(3) Antibiotic consistent with sensitivity	100%	
b. Dehydration with severe electrolyte imbalance		
(1) Determination of electrolyte levels	100%	25
(2) Maintenance of intravenous fluids	100%	20
c. Acidosis		
In presence of blood pH below 7.35 on laboratory report,		
(1) Physician to be notified immediately	100%	
(2) Any diarrhea to be reported to physician every 8 hours	100%	
(3) Intravenous fluids to be maintained	100%	20
(4) Medications to be maintained	100%	
d. Alkalosis		
In presence of blood pH above 7.45 on laboratory report,		
(1) Physician to be notified immediately	100%	
(2) Intravenous fluids to be maintained	100%	20
(3) Medications to be maintained	100%	

Record Analyst: Note any reports of intractable, copious vomiting in nursing narrative notes.

LENGTH OF STAY

11. Length of stay 3-5 days	100%	1,125-1,875

Exceptions: (a) Early departure against medical advice;
(b) complications or other diagnoses justifying extension.

DISCHARGE STATUS

12. Patient discharged under the following conditions:

a. Temperature below 100 F for 24 hours before discharge	100%	
b. Patient retaining liquids	100%	
c. Activity level normal or near normal for age for 24 hours before discharge *(See nursing notes.)*	100%	
d. Discharge weight stable, either greater than admission weight or no longer declining	100%	
e. Dietician's conference with parent concerning post-discharge dietary management documented	100%	
f. Parents instructed re (1) diet, (2) dosages and schedules of applicable medications and (3) follow-up visit to physician	100%	

Exception: Instructions on transfer form.

NEWBORN NURSERY

SAMPLE

Newborn infants born in this hospital or transferred to this hospital on the first day of life.

REVIEW

Criterion	Standard	Estimated Charge
JUSTIFICATION FOR EXTENDED STAY		
1. Presence of any of the following conditions:	100%	
a. Hyperbilirubinemia with cord blood value over 2 mg/dl	100%	
b. Immaturity	100%	
c. Respiratory distress syndrome	100%	
NEONATAL STUDY AND CARE		
2. Documentation of the following findings and measures:		
a. Birth weight at least 5 pounds (2.268 gms.)	100%	
b. 6 minute Apgar score at least 8	100%	
c. Eye prophylaxis performed in delivery room	100%	$9.75
d. Dextrostick test normal	100%	
e. Vitamin K (1 mg intramuscular) administered	100%	
f. Serology negative	100%	11
g. Record of		
(1) Head circumference	100%	
(2) Body length	100%	
h. Coombs test for hemolytic anemia	0%	14
Exception (Indication): Mother Rh negative and father Rh positive.		
i. Identification procedures including footprint and wrist band		
SPECIAL PROCEDURES		
3. PKU value normal	100%	5
Record Analyst: (a) Where infant is receiving formula, test is performed more than 1 day after formula is started. (b) Where infant is breast fed, test is performed after 4th day of life.		
4. Where circumcision is to be performed, procedure documented within 3 days after birth	100%	49
Exceptions: (a) Circumcision not planned, or (b) female infant.		
5. Management of medical complications		
a. Hyperbilirubinemia		
(1) Phototherapy exposure	100%	150
(2) Bilirubin levels checked during phototherapy course	100%	24
(3) Infant's eyes protected during phototherapy treatments	100%	
(4) Body temperature monitored	100%	
(5) Average decrease of bilirubin amounting to 3 to 4 mgs of serum indirect bilirubin in 8 to 12 hours	100%	24

b. Immaturity

    (1) Infant placed in incubator with temperature maintained at 88-89 F   100% $ 556 per day

    (2) In presence of respiratory distress, oxygen at concentration below 40% in a noncyanotic infant   100%   26

        Exception: Absence of respiratory distress.

    (3) In presence of respiratory distress, parenteral fluids administered through umbilical vein   100%   20

        Exception: Absence of respiratory distress.

c. Respiratory distress syndrome

    (1) Infant placed in Isolette   100%   556 per day

    (2) Head positioned in slight hyperextension   100%

    (3) Airway clear   100%

    (4) Ambient oxygen concentration below 40%   100%   26

        Exception: Presence of cyanosis.

    (5) Frequent monitoring of blood gases   100%   70

    (6) In presence of respiratory acidosis, assisted ventilation   100%   280 per 24 hours

        Exception: Absence of respiratory acidosis.

    (7) In presence of metabolic acidosis, parenteral fluids administered through umbilical vein   100%   20

        Exception: Absence of metabolic acidosis.

6. Management of social complications

  a. Unavailability of suitable home or inability of parent(s) to provide proper care for infant

    (1) Early Social Service contact with mother and significant others to evaluate home conditions and ability of mother to care for infant   100%

    (2) Where indicated, arrangements made with community agency to bring about appropriate placement or referral for foster care   100%

    (3) Documentation in record of follow-up by telephone or other means following discharge from hospital   100%

  b. Maternal complications requiring extended hospital stay

    (1) Social Service assessment of ability of other family members to provide temporary care for infant   100%

    (2) Social Service assistance to family in obtaining services of community agencies providing temporary homemakers, visiting nurses or other help as needed to permit infant to be cared for in home   100%

        Exception: Family self-sufficient.

LENGTH OF STAY

In Absence of Complications

7. Length of stay

  a. Delivered by Caesarian section

Single term hospital delivery	6-7 days	100%	960-1,120
Single pre-term hospital delivery	6-8 days	100%	3,336-4,448
Twin or multiple hospital delivery[1]	6-8 days	100%	1,920-2,560

---

[1] Estimates based on assumption of twin births.

b. Delivered in hospital, other than by Caesarian section

Single term delivery	3-4 days	100%	$480-640
Single pre-term delivery	5-12 days	100%	2,800-5,600
Twin or multiple term delivery	4-6 days	100%	640-960

c. Delivered outside the hospital

Single or multiple term delivery	3-4 days	100%	480-640
Single or multiple pre-term delivery	6-15 days	100%	3,360-6,720

Exception: Complicating factors other than, or in addition to, immaturity, justifying extension.

Record Analyst: In determining the length of stay, the day of the mother's admission usually is not counted. Review this matter with your Committee so that your criteria will conform to local policy.

DISCHARGE STATUS

8. Infant discharged under the following conditions:

   a. Infant afebrile on day of discharge   100%

   Record Analyst: Obtain acceptable temperature level from your Committee.

   b. Weight gain or loss documented   100%

   c. Presence of good sucking reflex documented   100%

   d. Vomiting absent   100%

   e. Complications absent   100%

   f. Mother instructed re (1) feeding, (2) bathing and hygiene, (3) significance of and response to crying and (4) follow-up visit to pediatrician   100%

   Exception: Infant to be placed for foster care or adoption directly from hospital.

PNEUMONITIS IN THE PEDIATRIC PATIENT

SUGGESTED SAMPLE

Patients under the age of sixteen whose discharge diagnoses include atelectasis, pleural effusion, empyema, lung abscess, septicemia or an adverse reaction to a therapeutic drug in association with pneumonitis.

REVIEW

Criterion	Standard	Estimated Charge
JUSTIFICATION FOR EXTENDED STAY		
1. Presence of (a) atelectasis, (b) pleural effusion, (c) empyema or lung abscess, (d) septicemia or (e) an adverse reaction to a therapeutic drug in association with pneumonitis	100%	
DIAGNOSTIC STUDY		
2. History with reference to symptomatology	100%	
3. Physical examination including reference to any respiratory distress	100%	

Record Analyst: Respiratory distress will be reflected in (a) cyanosis, (b) respiratory rate greater than 30 per minute, or (c) grunting. Find references in physical examination report, nursing notes, graphic chart and progress notes.

Criterion	Standard	Estimated Charge
4. Laboratory and other studies		
a. CBC, urinalysis and admission panel	100%	$ 125
b. White blood count differential	100%	35
c. Skin test for tuberculosis	100%	
d. Chest x-ray taken subsequent to date of onset or at admission	100%	70
e. Bronchoscopy	0%	190

Exception: Presence of lobar pneumonia unresolved after 1 week of treatment.

Criterion	Standard	Estimated Charge
5. Nursing care		
a. Patient assessment including vital signs, weight, brief relevant history and present complaint	100%	
b. History of allergies and drug sensitivities	100%	
c. Formulation of nursing care plan based on assessment and clinical objectives	100%	
d. Patient orientation to surroundings and nursing procedures	100%	

Exception: Patient under 3 years of age.

MANAGEMENT

Criterion	Standard	Estimated Charge
6. Culture and sensitivity	100%	75
7. Antibiotic consistent with culture and sensitivity	100%	
8. Treatment with either	0%	
a. Chloramphenicol or		
b. Tetracycline		

Exception: Absence of any other appropriate anti-infective agent.
Record Analyst: Note reduced dosage and special schedules for children.

9. Nursing care
   a. Charting of pulse, respiration, temperature and medications on each shift — 100%
   b. Patient monitored for evidence of complications — 100%

10. Management of complications
    a. Atelectasis
       (1) Oxygenation maintained — 100%
       (2) Blood gases monitored — 100% — $ 70
       (3) Respirations and temperature every 4 hours or per nursing care plan — 100%
       (4) Chest x-ray at onset — 100% — 70
       (5) Serial chest x-rays — 100% — 140
       (6) Antibiotics consistent with culture and sensitivity — 100%
       (7) Inhalation therapy — 100% — 22
       (8) Bed rest maintained — 100%
    b. Empyema or lung abscess
       (1) Culture and sensitivity — 100% — 75
       (2) Antibiotic consistent with culture and sensitivity — 100%
       (3) Respirations and temperature every 4 hours or per nursing care plan — 100%
       (4) Bed rest maintained — 100%
    c. Pleural effusion
       Needle drainage of effusion — 100% — 90
    d. Septicemia
       (1) Culture and sensitivity of blood — 100% — 75
       (2) Antibiotic consistent with culture and sensitivity — 100%
       (3) Bed rest — 100%
    e. Adverse reaction to therapeutic drug
       Discontinuation of drug in use and substitution of alternative medication — 100%

LENGTH OF STAY

11. Length of stay
    a. In absence of complications, 5-8 days — 100% — 1,875-3,000
    b. In presence of adverse reaction to therapeutic drug, 1 day beyond assigned length of stay — 100% — 2,250-3,375
    c. In presence of any of the complications listed above under Criterion 10, 8-9 days — 100% — 3,000-3,375

DISCHARGE STATUS

12. Patient discharged under the following conditions:
    a. Temperature below 99.6 F for at least 24 hours before discharge — 100%
    b. Absence of respiratory distress — 100%
    c. Clearing of, or marked improvement in, radiological evidence of infiltrate — 100%
    d. Parent(s) instructed re (1) activity level, (2) diet, (3) dosages and schedule of applicable medications and (4) follow-up visit to physician — 100%
       Exception: Instructions on transfer form.

170

PSYCHIATRY

SUGGESTED SAMPLE

Patients who have been admitted to the hospital primarily for the treatment of anorexia nervosa.

REVIEW

Criterion	Standard	Estimated Charge
JUSTIFICATION FOR DIAGNOSIS		
1. In a patient whose body weight is less than 80% of the estimated ideal weight for the patient's sex, age and body type,		
a. The absence of all of the following conditions:	100%	
(1) Any demonstrable mechanical or functional impediment to the ingestion, digestion and absorption of food		
(2) Disorders of toxic or organic origin that might interfere with adequate nutrition		
(3) Simmonds' disease or pituitary cachexia		
(4) Acute pituitary necrosis		
(5) Tuberculosis		
(6) Environmental circumstances contributing to starvation		
in conjunction with		
b. The presence of a combination of any of the following:	100%	
(1) Low blood pressure		
(2) Bradycardia		
(3) Lanugo hair		
(4) Low blood sugar		
(5) Loss of hair from scalp		
(6) Amenorrhea		
(7) Acrocyanosis		
(8) Carotenemia		
and		
c. The presence of		
(1) Low follicle stimulating hormone titer	100%	
(2) Low luteinizing hormone titer	100%	
(3) Intense fear of becoming obese	100%	
(4) Disturbance of body image, with the patient feeling that he or she is fat	100%	
JUSTIFICATION FOR ADMISSION		
2. Severe malnutrition with		
a. Electrolyte imbalance	100%	
b. Inability to improve the patient's nutritional status on an outpatient basis	100%	
c. Body weight less than 80% of the patient's ideal weight	100%	

DIAGNOSTIC STUDY

3. In the chart,
   a. Brief relevant history including history of any treatment for anorexia — 100%
   b. Physical examination report — 100%
   c. Admission note by attending physician — 100% — $ 60
4. Laboratory and other studies including
   a. CBC, urinalysis and admission panel of 20 blood chemistry measures — 100% — 125
   b. Electrolyte levels — 100% — 25
   c. Blood sugar level — 100% — 10
   d. Thyroid studies including T3, T4 and thyroid stimulating hormone — 100% — 196
   e. Follicle stimulating hormone — 100% — 69
   f. Luteinizing hormone — 100% — 69
   g. Skull survey and CT scan of skull — 100% — 328
   h. Trace measure of zinc — 100% — 29
   i. Trace measure of magnesium — 100% — 29
5. In the chart within 72 hours after admission,
   a. Psychiatric assessment — 100%
   b. Comprehensive treatment plan including specification of modalities to be employed — 100%

MANAGEMENT

6. Patient given high carbohydrate, high fat diet including
   a. Modified diet menus including solid food — 100% — 35
   b. Liquid food supplements as needed by the patient who resists solid foods — 100%
   c. Peripheral or central hyperalimentation in addition to solid food as needed to maintain daily intake of 4,000 to 5,000 calories — 100% — 90 per day

   Exception: Desired daily intake maintained orally.
7. Medications as indicated — 100%
8. Documented implementation of psychiatric treatment plan, including
   a. Daily psychotherapeutic interviews with patient — 100% — 224 per week
   b. Psychotherapeutic sessions with patient's parents and other members of the household — 100% — 60 per week
   c. Milieu therapy directed toward objectives of building patient's sense of worth and independence and of her acceptance of weight gain without guilt or depression — 100%
   d. Application of appropriate reward system — 100%
   e. Observation and charting of any failure to continue weight gain following visits by relatives or others — 100%
   f. Assistance to patient in meeting developmental requirements appropriate to age in such areas as schooling, recreational activities and social interaction — 100%

173

g. Monitoring of progress as reflected in physician's progress notes written at least 3 times a week — 100%

h. Periodic reassessment with documentation of any resulting revisions in treatment plan — 100%

9. Nursing care including

   a. At admission,

     (1) Patient assessment including vital signs, brief relevant history, weight and patient's statement of reason for admission to hospital — 100%

     (2) History of allergies and drug sensitivities — 100%

     (3) Patient orientation to surroundings and planned nursing procedures — 100%

     (4) Formulation of nursing care plan — 100%

   b. Patient maintained on bed rest as ordered, and never left alone if on bed rest — 100%

   c. Ambulatory patient monitored for vomiting, abuse of laxatives and excessive exercise — 100%

   d. Patient weighed each morning upon awakening, after emptying bladder and before taking any food or fluids — 100%

   e. Weight chart maintained daily — 100%

   f. All intake and output charted daily — 100%

   g. Supportive attitude and behavior maintained — 100%

LENGTH OF STAY

10. Patient hospitalized until she has maintained a weight that is at least 90% of her ideal weight for a period of at least 2 weeks — 100%

DISCHARGE STATUS

11. Patient discharged under the following conditions:

   a. Weight has remained at a level of at least 90% of ideal weight for at least 2 weeks — 100%   **$7,728**
per 3 weeks

   b. Electrolytes stabilized — 100%   **10,304**
per 4 weeks

   c. Patient appearing free of guilt and depression concerning weight gain — 100%

   d. Patient able to meet developmental requirements in such areas as schooling, recreational activities and family and social interaction — 100%

   e. Documentation in the record of plans and initial schedule for continuing psychiatric monitoring and counseling for patient and family — 100%

   f. Patient and family instructed as to (1) diet, (2) activity level and (3) next appointment with psychiatrist — 100%

     Exception: Instructions on transfer form.

SUGGESTED SAMPLE

Patients whose primary discharge diagnosis and reason for admission was the occurrence of an acute episode of depressive or manic psychosis.

REVIEW

Criterion	Standard	Estimated Charge

DEPRESSIVE PSYCHOSIS

JUSTIFICATION FOR ADMISSION

1. The presence of an episode of severe depression associated with any of the following conditions: — 100%
   a. Suicidal tendency
   b. Psychomotor retardation such that the patient is unable to care for himself or to carry on his usual activities
   c. Protracted failure or refusal to take fluids or nourishment
   d. Extra-hospital family care inadequate to sustain the patient in the presence of psychosis

DIAGNOSTIC STUDY

2. In the chart within 24 hours after admission,
   a. History — 100%
   b. Physical examination report — 100%
   c. Initial note by psychiatrist — 100% — $ 60
   d. Initial written orders including medication orders — 100%
   e. CBC, urinalysis and admission panel test reports — 100% — 125
3. In the chart within 3 days after admission,
   a. Treatment history — 100%
   b. Psychiatric assessment — 100% — 60
   c. Treatment plan including specification of modalities to be employed — 100%

MANAGEMENT

4. At weekly or other intervals consistent with Psychiatric Service policies, rules and regulations, updating of
   a. Definition of primary problem — 100%
   b. Assessment by attending physician — 100% — 60
   c. Assessments by non-physician mental health personnel — 100%
   d. Psychiatric and medical diagnoses — 100%
   e. Treatment plan revised as indicated — 100%
5. Documented implementation of indicated modalities of care including as appropriate and as ordered
   a. Modified analytically oriented psychotherapy with interviews scheduled 1 or 2 times a week — 100% — 64 per week

b. In the presence of severe agitation, chlorpromazine therapy   100%

   Exception: Absence of severe agitation

c. Electroshock treatments 3 times per week during acute phase   100% $ 120
                                                                                        per week

   Exceptions: Presence of (1) decompensated cardiac disease;
   (2) active tuberculosis; (3) recent fracture.

d. High calorie diet   100%   35

e. Gavage   0%

   Exception (Indication):   Failure to eat voluntarily for a
   period of 24 hours or more.

f. Lithium therapy as indicated   100%

g. Milieu therapy with special attention to prevention of suicide   100%

h. Family counseling   100%   64
                                                                                        per week

i. Monitoring and treatment as reflected in physician's progress
    notes written at least 3 times a week   100%

LENGTH OF STAY

6. Length of stay dependent upon documented evidence of progress
    within time parameters established by Hospital or Psychiatric
    Service policy, applicable regulations or court-ordered retention.   100%   7,728
                                                                                      per 3 weeks

DISCHARGE STATUS

7. Patient discharged under the following conditions:

a. Improvement in condition with evidence of the patient's
    ability to face problems without decompensation   100%

   Exceptions: (1) Transfer of patient deemed not treatable
   within Hospital's program; (2) early departure against
   medical advice in the absence of court-ordered admission
   or retention.

b. Opinion of attending physician that the patient does not pose
    a hazard to his own welfare or that of others   100%

   Exception: Transfer of patient deemed not treatable
   within the Hospital's program.

c. Documented evidence of normal level of psychomotor activity   100%

   Exceptions: (1) Transfer of patient deemed not treatable
   within the Hospital's program; (2) early departure against
   medical advice in the absence of court-ordered admission or
   retention.

d. Patient and family or significant other instructed re
    (1) medication dosage, schedule and possible side effects as
    applicable and (2) schedule of outpatient appointments.
    Exception: Instructions on transfer form.

MANIC OR HYPOMANIC PSYCHOSIS

JUSTIFICATION FOR ADMISSION

1. The presence of a psychosis associated with extreme psychomotor
    activity and evidence of impairment of judgment such that effective
    outpatient therapy and control cannot be maintained   100%

DIAGNOSTIC STUDY

2. In the chart within 24 hours after admission,
   a. History 100%
   b. Physical examination report 100%
   c. Initial note by psychiatrist .... 100% $ 60
   d. Initial written orders including medication orders ... 100%
   e. CBC, urinalysis and admission panel test reports ... 100%   125
3. In the chart within 3 days after admission,
   a. Treatment history 100%
   b. Psychiatric assessment 100%   60
   c. Treatment plan including specification of modalities to be employed ... 100%

MANAGEMENT

4. At weekly or other intervals consistent with Psychiatric Service policies, rules and regulations, updating of
   a. Definition of primary problem 100%
   b. Assessment by attending physician 100%
   c. Assessments by non-physician mental health personnel ... 100%
   d. Psychiatric and medical diagnoses 100%
   e. Treatment plan revised as indicated 100%
5. Documented implementation of indicated modalities of care, including as appropriate and as ordered
   a. Psychotherapy directed toward the objective of converting manic or hypomanic symptoms into depressive type ... 100%   64
      per week
   b. Chlorpromazine therapy 100%
   c. Electroshock treatments twice a day for 3 or 4 days initially, then 3 times a week ... 100%   680

      Exceptions: Presence of (1) satisfactory response to psychotherapy and chlorpromazine; (2) decompensated cardiac disease; (3) active tuberculosis; or (4) recent fracture.
   d. Lithium carbonate orally 4 to 7 times per week ... 100%

      Exception: Satisfactory response to psychotherapy, chlorpromazine or electroshock therapy.

      Contraindication: Presence of impaired renal function.

      Record Analyst: Review BUN value as shown in admission panel or laboratory reports.
   e. Milieu therapy 100%
   f. Occupational therapy 100%
   g. Monitoring and treatment as reflected in physician's progress notes written at least 3 times per week ... 100%

LENGTH OF STAY

6. Length of stay dependent upon documented evidence of progress within time parameters established by Hospital or Psychiatric Service policy, applicable regulations or court-ordered retention ... 100%   7,728
   per 3 weeks

DISCHARGE STATUS

7. Patient discharged under the following conditions:

   a. Improvement in condition with evidence of the patient's ability to face problems without decompensation   100%

      Exceptions: (1) Transfer of patient deemed not treatable within Hospital's program; (2) Early departure against medical advice in absence of court-ordered admission or retention.

   b. Opinion of attending physician that the patient does not pose a hazard to his own welfare or that of others   100%

      Exception: Transfer of patient deemed not treatable within Hospital's program.

   c. Patient and family or significant other instructed re (1) medication dosage, schedule and possible side effects as applicable and (2) schedule of outpatient appointments   100%

      Exception: Instructions on transfer form.

SCHIZOPHRENIAS, ALL TYPES

SUGGESTED SAMPLE

Patients whose primary discharge diagnosis and reason for admission was the occurrence of an acute episode of schizophrenia of any type.

REVIEW

Criterion	Standard	Estimated Charge

JUSTIFICATION FOR DIAGNOSIS

1. The presence of an illness with some combination of the following signs and symptoms in the absence of a disorder of toxic or organic origin	100%	
a. Delusions		
b. Hallucinations		
c. Thinking disorder		
d. Inappropriate affect		
e. Bizarre motor signs and symptoms		

JUSTIFICATION FOR ADMISSION

2. The presence of suicidal or homicidal tendencies, of aggressive behavior or other manifestations of psychosis that cannot be controlled in an outpatient setting in a patient with the diagnosis of schizophrenia	100%	

DIAGNOSTIC STUDY

3. In the chart within 24 hours after admission,		
a. History	100%	
b. Physical examination report	100%	
c. Initial note by psychiatrist	100%	$ 60
d. Initial written orders including medication orders	100%	
e. Patient's self report	100%	
Exception: Not required in Hospital's program.		
4. In the chart within 3 days after admission,		
a. Treatment history	100%	
b. Psychiatric assessment	100%	60
c. Treatment plan including specification of modalities to be employed	100%	

MANAGEMENT

5. At weekly or other intervals consistent with Psychiatric Service policies, rules and regulations, updating of		
a. Definition of primary problem	100%	
b. Assessment by attending physician	100%	
c. Assessments by non-physician mental health personnel	100%	
d. Psychiatric and medical diagnoses	100%	
e. Treatment plan revised as indicated	100%	

6. Documented implementation of indicated modalities of care including as appropriate and as ordered

   a. Psychotherapy program including family counseling   100% $ 64 per week

   b. Efforts to help the patient resolve confusion as to his social and sexual identity   100%

   c. Adherence to medication regimen including phenothiazine therapy   100%

   d. Milieu therapy   100%

   e. Electroshock convulsive therapy as indicated   100%   240

      Contraindications: Presence of (1) decompensated cardiac disease; (2) active tuberculosis; (3) recent fracture.

   f. Monitoring and treatment as reflected in physician's progress notes written at least 3 times per week   100%

LENGTH OF STAY

7. Length of stay 30 days   100%   11,040

   Exceptions: (a) Earlier departure against medical advice in the absence of court-ordered admission or retention; (b) earlier transfer of patient deemed not treatable within Hospital's program; (c) documented presence of indications justifying longer stay; (d) other length of stay dictated by Hospital policy or applicable regulatory or court-ordered provisions.

DISCHARGE STATUS

8. Patient discharged under the following conditions:

   a. Improvement in or stabilization of condition   100%

      Exceptions: (1) Transfer of patient deemed not treatable within Hospital's program; (2) departure against medical advice in absence of court-ordered admission or retention.

   b. Opinion of attending physician that the patient does not pose a hazard to his own welfare or that of others   100%

      Exception: Transfer of patient deemed not treatable within hospital's program.

   c. Patient and family or significant other instructed re (1) medication dosage, schedule and possible side effects as applicable and (2) schedule of outpatient appointments   100%

      Exception: Instructions on transfer form.

INPATIENT DENTAL CARE

DENTAL EXTRACTION

REVIEW

Criterion	Standard	Estimated Charge

INDICATIONS FOR ADMISSION AND PROCEDURE

1. The presence of any of the following conditions: — 100%
   a. Infection
   b. Severe trauma precluding the possibility of salvage
   c. Severe malocclusion that has not responded to outpatient therapy
   d. Multiple extractions required as part of orthodontia plan
   e. Peridontal complications
   f. Impaction
   g. Planned pre-prosthetic extraction of several teeth, or full-mouth extraction
   h. Need for routine extraction in a patient who, as a result of the presence of physical or mental problems, is not a suitable candidate for outpatient extraction

PREOPERATIVE STUDY AND CARE

2. In the chart prior to surgery,
   a. History with specific reference to present complaint — 100%
   b. Physical examination report — 100%
3. Pre-admission laboratory and other studies including
   a. CBC, urinalysis and admission panel — 100% — $ 125
   b. Chest x-ray within past 3 months with report in record — 100% — 70
   c. Serology — 100% — 11
   d. Coagulation profile — 100% — 64
4. Preoperative nursing care including
   a. Patient assessment including vital signs, brief relevant history and present complaint — 100%
   b. Patient orientation to surroundings and planned procedures — 100%
   c. Formulation of care plan based on assessment and objectives — 100%
   d. Preoperative instruction consistent with anesthesia plan — 100%
5. Anesthesiologist's preoperative evaluation of patient — 100%

MANAGEMENT

6. Extraction as indicated — 100% — 38 per tooth
7. Report by operating practitioner covering (a) preoperative diagnosis, (b) procedures performed and (c) description of tissues and findings dictated or written immediately after surgery — 100% — 134 OR 53 anesthesia
8. Pathologist's report on any specimens submitted — 100%
   Exception: Teeth on exempt list.

9. Management of complications
   a. Postoperative infection
      (1) Culture and sensitivity before administration of anti-infective agent — 100% — $ 75
      (2) Anti-infective agent consistent with culture and sensitivity — 100%
      (3) In presence of cellulitis, incision and drainage — 100% — 55
   b. Postoperative hemorrhage
      (1) Early postoperative instruction of patient, warning against vigorous mouth rinsing, sucking and expectoration of blood following extraction — 100%
      (2) Cleansing and inspection of postextractive site — 100%
      (3) Control by pressure, with patient biting down on folded sterile gauze sponge for from 10-15 minutes — 100%
      (4) Where bleeding is controlled after 10-15 minutes, patient instructed to bite down on fresh folded sterile gauze sponge for 45 minutes — 100%
      (5) Where bleeding persists despite pressure, packing of socket with gauze saturated in hemostatic agent for 72 hours — 100%

      Exception: Bleeding controlled with pressure alone.

      (6) Suturing of any lacerations — 100%
      (7) Patient instructed to avoid rinsing and spitting for 24 hours after bleeding controlled — 100%
   c. Local osteitis ("Dry Socket")
      (1) Irrigation with warm saline solution — 100%
      (2) Socket packed lightly with gauze strips saturated in analgesic agent — 100%
      (3) Replacement of gauze packing every 2 days until subsidence of symptoms — 100%
10. Postoperative nursing care
    a. Pulse and respiration every 15 minutes until stable, then per postoperative care plan — 100%
    b. Oral hygiene maintained, consistent with orders — 100%
11. Dietetic services
    Soft diet provided — 100%

LENGTH OF STAY

12. Length of stay in absence of other diagnoses or complications, 2 days — 100% — 749

    Exceptions: (a) Earlier departure against medical advice; (b) presence of complications or other diagnoses justifying extension.

DISCHARGE STATUS

13. Patient discharged under the following conditions:
    a. Absence of complications — 100%
    b. Temperature below 99.6 F on day of discharge — 100%
    c. Patient and family instructed re (1) diet, (2) oral hygiene, (3) avoidance of vigorous rinsing, sucking and expectoration and (4) follow-up visit to dentist — 100%

    Exception: Instructions on transfer form.

MODALITIES OF CARE

ANTIBIOTIC USAGE
AMINOGLYCOSIDES

REVIEW

Criterion	Standard	Estimated Charge
INDICATIONS FOR THE USE OF AN AMINOGLYCOSIDE		
1. Documentation in progress notes of presence of an infection	100%	
Exception: Need for pre- or postoperative prophylaxis. and		
2. Presence of at least one of the following conditions:	100%	
a. An infection susceptible to Gentamicin, Tobramicin, Amikin or Kanamicin		
b. Hospital-acquired pneumonia or urinary tract infection not susceptible to cephalosporins or Ampicillin		
c. Debilitated patient with evidence of sepsis at initiation of therapy		
d. Need for pre- or postoperative prophylaxis		
LABORATORY INDICATOR FOR THE USE OF AN AMINOGLYCOSIDE		
3. Culture and sensitivity obtained before initiation of therapy and positive for an organism susceptible to an aminoglycoside	100%	$ 75
Exception: Need for pre- or postoperative prophylaxis.		
CONTRAINDICATION TO THE USE OF AMINOGLYCOSIDES		19 BUN
4. Presence of severely impaired renal function	0%	25 serum creatinine
Record Analyst: *Severe renal disease is reflected in BUN greater than 50, creatinine greater than 5 and creatinine clearance below 10.*		28 creatinine clearance
LABORATORY STUDIES		
5. Culture and sensitivity obtained before initiation of therapy	100%	75
Exception: Need for pre- or postoperative prophylaxis.		
6. CBC, urinalysis and admission panel	100%	125
DOSAGE AND ADMINISTRATION		
7. Dosage and administration as follows:		
In the following list, "kg" refers to kilograms of body weight		
a. Amikin		
(1) Adults: 15 mg/kg/day in 2 or 3 equally divided doses	100%	71 per day
(2) Route either intravenous or intramuscular	100%	
b. Gentamicin		
(1) Adults and children over the age of 1 week: 5 mg/kg/day in equally divided doses	100%	44 per day
(2) Route either intravenous or intramuscular	100%	

c. Kanamicin
   (1) Adults: Up to 15 mg/kg/day in equally divided doses 100%
   (2) Route either intravenous or intramuscular 100%
d. Tobramicin
   (1) Adults: 5 mg/kg/day in equally divided doses .... 100% $ 47 per day
   (2) Route either intravenous or intramuscular

MANAGEMENT

8. Monitoring carried on:
   a. Kidney function
      (1) Before start of therapy 100%   44
      (2) Every 3 days during therapy 100%   44
      (3) Upon termination of therapy 100%   44
   b. Peak and trough blood levels obtained during therapy:
      (1) On Day 1 .... 100%   37
      (2) On Day 5 .... 100%   37
      (3) More often than Days 1 and 5 .... 0%
      Exception (Indication): Presence of resistent infection.

9. Dosage regulated in accordance with kidney function 100%

10. Therapy maintained for from 7 to 10 days in presence of documented infection 100%
    Exception: To be discontinued in absence of documentation of infection with susceptible organism.

11. Patient's vital signs, intake and output and response to antibiotic therapy monitored and documented in progress notes and nursing notes 100%

12. Patient monitored for evidence of complications 100%

13. Management of complications
    a. Compromised kidney function
       Use of drug stopped 100%
    b. Ototoxicity
       Use of drug stopped 100%

DATA TO BE COLLECTED FOR INFORMATIONAL PURPOSES

Evidence in progress notes or nursing notes of any monitoring for ototoxic effects of drugs.

ANTIBIOTIC USAGE
AMPICILLIN

REVIEW

Criterion	Standard	Estimated Charge
INDICATION FOR THE USE OF AMPICILLIN		
1. Presence of an infection caused by any of the following organisms:	100%	
a. Susceptible Gram-positive bacteria including streptococci, pneumococci, penicillin G-sensitive staphylococci or enterococci		
b. Susceptible Gram-negative bacteria including H. influenzae, E. coli, Proteus mirabilis, N. gonorrhoeae, Shigella, Salmonella or N. meningitidis		
CLINICAL AND LABORATORY INDICATORS FOR THE USE OF AMPICILLIN		
2. One or more of the following elements:	100%	$ 75
a. Culture showing susceptible organism		
b. History of intractable dysentery accompanied by chills, fever above 102 F and nausea	100%	
CONTRAINDICATIONS TO THE USE OF AMPICILLIN		
3. Presence of an infection caused by enterobacter, pseudomonas or penicillinase-producing organism	0%	
4. Presence of severe renal or liver disease	0%	85
Record Analyst: Severe renal disease is reflected in BUN greater than 50, creatinine greater than 5 and creatinine clearance below 10. Severe liver disease is reflected in albumin less than 2, bilirubin greater than 10 and SGOT more than 3 times normal. Find data in laboratory reports.		
5. History of sensitivity to penicillin	0%	
LABORATORY STUDIES		
6. Culture and sensitivity obtained before initiation of therapy	100%	75
7. Admission studies including CBC, urinalysis and admission panel	100%	125
DOSAGE AND ADMINISTRATION		
8. Dosage		
a. Upper respiratory and soft tissue infections		
Weight *Dose*		
44 pounds + 250 mg/6 hours	100%	46 per day
Below 44 pounds (20 kg) 50 mg/kg/day in equally divided doses at 6 or 8 hour intervals	100%	

b. Gastrointestinal or genitourinary tract infections

Weight	Dose		
44 pounds +	500 mg/6 hours	100%	$ 46 per day
Below 44 pounds (20 kg)	100 mg/kg/day in equally divided doses at 6 or 8 hour intervals		

c. Uncomplicated gonorrhea

   Single oral dose of 3.5 grams administered simultaneously
   with 1.0 gram of probenecid 100%

9. Route oral, intramuscular or intravenous 100%

MANAGEMENT

10. Patient's vital signs, intake and output and response to antibiotic
    therapy monitored and documented in progress notes and nursing
    notes 100%

11. Patient monitored for evidence of complications 100%

12. Management of complications

    Rash attributed to drug

    (1) Use of Ampicillin stopped 100%

    (2) Antihistamine administered 100%

INDICATION FOR DISCONTINUATION OF AMPICILLIN

13. Presence of any of the following elements: 100%

    a. Temperature below 99.8 F for 48 hours 100%

    b. Failure of clinical response after 4 days 100%

    c. Culture report showing presence of an organism not
       susceptible to Ampicillin 100%

REVIEW

Criterion	Standard	Estimated Charge
INDICATIONS FOR THE USE OF CLINDAMYCIN		
1. Presence of a serious anaerobic infection susceptible to Clindamycin or of a serious infection caused by susceptible streptococci, pneumococci or staphylococci in a patient who cannot take penicillin	100%	
CLINICAL AND LABORATORY INDICATORS FOR THE USE OF CLINDAMYCIN		
2. Presence of one or more of the following elements:	100%	

   a. Culture showing susceptible organism

   b. Fever above 102 F

   c. Chest x-ray consistent with bacterial pneumonia, empyema or lung abscess

   d. Tender, hot, swollen, erythematous tissues on physical examination

   e. Peritonitis, perforation of a hollow viscus or intra-abdominal abscess

   f. Infection clinically present at surgery

   g. Contaminated wound

CONTRAINDICATIONS TO THE USE OF CLINDAMYCIN

Criterion	Standard	Estimated Charge
3. Presence of any of the following elements:	0%	

   a. Non-bacterial infection

   b. Allergy to Clindamycin or Lincomycin

   c. History of colitis

   Exception: No other appropriate antibiotic available

   d. Severe renal or liver disease

   Exception: No other appropriate antibiotic available. Dose to be reduced to 1.2 gm/day.

   Record Analyst: Severe renal disease is reflected in BUN greater than 50, creatinine greater than 5 and creatinine clearance below 10.

   Severe liver disease is reflected in albumin less than 2, bilirubin greater than 10 and SGOT more than 3 times normal.

   Find data in laboratory reports.

   e. Severe urinary tract infection

   f. Meningitis

g. Pregnancy

   Exception: Presence of life-threatening infection with no other appropriate antibiotic available.

h. Concomitant administration of Erythromycin

LABORATORY STUDIES

4. The following tests and findings:
   a. At least 1 appropriate culture (blood, sputum, vaginal or wound as applicable)   100% $ 75
   b. CBC, differential and urinalysis   100%   45
   c. Bilirubin less than 10 mg %   100%   25
   d. Albumin greater than 2 gm %   100%   24
   e. SGOT less than 3 times normal value   100%   25
   f. BUN equal to 50 mg/100 ml or less   100%   19

DOSAGE AND ADMINISTRATION

5. Dose 0.6-2.8 gms/24 hours   100%

   Exception: In presence of liver or renal disease, dose less than 1.2 gms/day

6. Route oral, intravenous or intramuscular   100%

MANAGEMENT

7. Vital signs, intake and output and response to Clindamycin monitored and documented   100%
8. Patient monitored for evidence of complications   100%
9. Management of complications
   a. Rash or other allergic reaction attributed to Clindamycin
      Use of Clindamycin stopped   100%
   b. Diarrhea or colitis
      (1) Clindamycin discontinued   100%
      (2) Where diarrhea persists for 48 hours, or patient passes blood, proctosigmoidoscopy performed for evaluation   100%   106-125

INDICATIONS FOR DISCONTINUATION OF CLINDAMYCIN

10. Presence of any of the following elements: 100%
    a. Temperature below 100 F for 48 hours
    b. Failure of clinical response after 4 days
    c. Culture report showing organism not susceptible to Clindamycin

ANTIBIOTIC USAGE
SODIUM CEPHALOTHIN (KEFLIN)

REVIEW

Criterion	Standard	Estimated Charge
INDICATION FOR THE USE OF SODIUM CEPHALOTHIN		
1. Presence of an infection susceptible to Keflin	100%	
CLINICAL AND LABORATORY INDICATIONS FOR THE USE OF SODIUM CEPHALOTHIN		
2. Presence of one or more of the following elements:	100%	
a. Culture showing susceptible organism		
b. Fever higher than 102 F		
c. Chest x-ray showing infiltrate consistent with presence of bacterial pneumonia		
d. Tender, hot, swollen erythematous tissues on physical examination		
e. Peritonitis or perforation of a hollow viscus		
f. Infection clinically present at surgery		
g. Contaminated wound		
h. Need for prophylaxis before surgery for vascular prosthesis		
CONTRAINDICATIONS TO USE OF SODIUM CEPHALOTHIN		
3. Presence of any of the following:	0%	
a. Meningitis		
b. Infections caused by enterobacter, P. vulgaris, P. rettgeri, P. morgani, P. inconstans, Pseudomonas aerruginosa, bacteroides or serratieae		
c. Allergy to Keflin or related drugs such as cephalozin sodium		
d. Allergy to penicillin		
e. Patient currently on low sodium diet		
f. Patient on digitalis		
g. Congestive heart failure		
h. Renal failure		
LABORATORY STUDIES		
4. The following tests and findings:		
a. At least one appropriate culture (blood, sputum, urine, stool, vaginal, wound or throat as applicable)	100%	$ 75
b. CBC, urinalysis and admission panel	100%	125
c. BUN 20 mg % or less	100%	
d. Fasting blood sugar (FBS) 140 mg % or less	100%	13

DOSAGE AND ADMINISTRATION

5. Maximum dose: 1 gm/2 hours   100%
   Exception: Dosage reduced in presence of renal failure.
6. Route intravenous   100%

MANAGEMENT

7. Vital signs, intake and output and response to antibiotic therapy
   monitored and documented   100%
8. Patient monitored for evidence of complications   100%
9. Management of complications
   a. Allergic reaction
      Keflin discontinued   100%
   b. Presence of suprainfection or emergence of resistant strain
      (1) Keflin discontinued   100%
      (2) Culture and sensitivity performed, followed by
          substitution of appropriate antibiotic   100% $ 75
   c. Thrombophlebitis
      (1) Intravenous site rotated   100%
      (2) Intravenous catheter replaced with needle   100%   20
   d. Presence of Coombs positive hemolytic anemia
      Dose reduced to less than 12 gms/day   100%
   e. Neutropenia
      Therapy limited to 10 days or less   100%

INDICATIONS FOR DISCONTINUATION OF SODIUM CEPHALOTHIN

10. Presence of any of the following elements: 100%
    a. Temperature below 99.8 F for at least 48 hours
    b. Failure of clinical response after 4 days
    c. Culture report showing presence of organism not susceptible
       to Keflin

BLOOD TRANSFUSIONS

REVIEW

Criterion	Standard	Estimated Charge

INDICATIONS FOR BLOOD REPLACEMENT

1. The presence of Condition a, b or c: **100%**
   a. Documented surgical or other blood loss exceeding 500 cc's
   b. A combination of at least two of the following conditions:
      (1) Any blood loss in an anemic patient
      (2) Pulse greater than 100 per minute
      (3) Systolic blood pressure drop of 30% or more
      (4) Hemoglobin (Hgb) decrease of more than 3 grams
      (5) Hematocrit (Hct) decrease of more than 10%
      (6) Hgb level below 8 gms %
   c. Need for exchange transfusion in a newborn

PROCEDURES TO BE REVIEWED

2. Documentation of type and cross match of patient's blood — 100% — $ 50
3. Packed red cells given — 100% — 45-88 per unit / 45 infusion fee
   Exception: Presence of need for protein replacement.

4. Whole blood given — 0%
   Exceptions (Indications):
   a. Unavailability of packed cells
   b. Other components not available
   c. Continued severe bleeding
   d. Need for exchange transfusion

5. Blood platelets given — 0%
   Exceptions (Indications):
   a. Presence of active bleeding with platelet count below 50,000
   b. Use of heart-lung machine
   c. Pre- or postoperative transfusion for patient undergoing splenectomy for thrombocytopenia or portacaval shunt
   d. Continued bleeding with prolonged bleeding time caused by platelet abnormality
   e. Presence of thrombocytopenia with active bleeding

6. Use of anti-hemophilic factor — 0%
   Exception (Indication): Presence of known hemophilia, von Willebrand's disease or hypofibrinogenemia.

7. Plasma protein fraction given — 0%
   Exception (Indication): Given as an adjunct to packed cells to reconstitute whole blood.

8. Factor IX Complex given — 0%

194

Exception (Indication): Presence of Factor IX Complex
deficiency or Christmas disease.

9. Fresh frozen plasma given 0%

Exception (Indication): Presence of coagulopathy.

10. Single unit transfusion 0%

Exception (Indication): Presence of hypovolemia corrected by
1 unit.

11. Administration of more than 6 units in 24 hours 0%

12. Blood unit released if not administered within 48 hours of date
and time of type and cross match 100%

13. For each transfusion, documentation of the following:
   a. Time transfusion started 100%
   b. Time transfusion completed 100%
   c. Date of transfusion 100%
   d. Transfusion number 100%
   e. Number of units transfused in each transfusion episode ... 100%
   f. Any transfusion reactions or complications 100%

MANAGEMENT OF COMPLICATIONS

14. Allergic reaction
   a. Blood transfusion stopped 100%
   b. Unused blood returned to blood bank for re-typing 100%
   c. Antihistamine administered in presence of hives 100%

15. Circulatory overload in presence of cardiopulmonary disease
   a. Monitoring of central venous pressure for evaluation 100%
   b. Administration of packed red cells in place of whole blood . 100%

16. Hemolytic reaction
   a. Blood transfusion stopped 100%
   b. Unused blood, blood sample in pilot tube and sample of
      recipient's blood re-cross matched 100%
   c. Patient's serum and urine tested for hemoglobin .... 100% $ 9
   d. Serum creatinine, bilirubin and electrolyte levels determined 100%   75
   e. Mannitol infusion administered in presence of incipient renal
      failure 100%   30

17. Contamination reaction
   a. Blood transfusion stopped 100%
   b. Cultures of transfused blood and of recipient's blood obtained 100%   150
   c. Volume repletion to correct hypotension 100%
   d. Evaluation of infection and administration of appropriate
      anti-bacterial agent 100%

SHORT TERM OUTCOMES

18. Restoration to the following levels:
   a. Hgb approaching 10 gms % as reflected in serial counts .... 100% ⎫
   b. Hct approaching 30% as reflected in serial counts .... 100% ⎬   38
   c. Systolic blood pressure approaching 100 or higher as reflected
      in serial readings .... 100% ⎭
   d. Pulse slower than 100 per minute 100%

TRANSFUSION DATA TO BE RETRIEVED FOR EVALUATION

19. The following information reported as applicable:
    a. Documentation of major cross match performed before transfusion   100%

       Exception: Need for emergency surgery.
    b. Documentation of minor cross match performed   100%

       Exception: Donor sera screened for irregular antibodies.
    c. Documentation of definitions of
       (1) Unit of whole blood in terms of cc's
       (2) Unit of packed cells in terms of cc's
       (3) Pediatric unit of whole blood in terms of cc's
       (4) Pediatric unit of packed cells in terms of cc's

DATA TO BE RETRIEVED FOR INFORMATIONAL PURPOSES

20. The following data for use in studies of blood transfusion services:
    a. Total number of units of packed cells ordered typed and cross matched
    b. Total number of units of blood or blood components ordered to be administered
    c. Total number of units of blood or blood components actually administered
    d. Number of instances in which more than 2 units were ordered for surgical standby
    e. Number of units discarded during the time frame of the study because the blood became outdated
    f. Number of units reassigned
    g. Number of units cross matched, later cancelled and eventually discarded

SAMPLE

Patients who have received, or who are receiving, parenteral nutrition.

REVIEW

Criterion	Standard	Estimated Charge
NUTRITIONAL ASSESSMENT PRIOR TO INITIATION OF PARENTERAL NUTRITION		
1. Construction of anergic-metabolic profile based on:	100%	
a. Serum transferrin estimated from total iron-binding capacity		$ 48
b. Total lymphocyte count		35
c. Measurement of any weight loss during past 6 months and of actual weight as percentage of ideal weight		
d. Estimate of fat reserves on basis of triceps skin fold measurement		
e. Estimates of degree of somatic protein depletion on basis of mid-arm circumference and arm muscle circumference		
f. Estimate of muscle stores on basis of creatinine height index		25
g. Skin test measure of immune competence		30
h. Estimated nitrogen balance		9
i. Estimate of degree of hypermetabolism on basis of 24 hour urea nitrogen excretion		24
		37 assessment
MANAGEMENT		
2. Protein-sparing or peripheral total parenteral nutrition		96 per day
a. Indicated in the presence of the following conditions:	100%	30 per dressing change
(1) Slight or absent protein nutritional deficit with adequate adipose tissue stores		
(2) Absence of hypermetabolic status		
(3) Medical condition such that a deficit will develop in the absence of nutritional support		
(4) Inability to provide adequate oral or enteral feeding		
b. Composition of protein-sparing formula:		
400-600 kcal/day of amino acids with vitamins, minerals and electrolyte additives	100%	
c. Treatment objective: 0 nitrogen balance, or imbalance no greater than −2	100%	
3. Peripheral total parenteral nutrition		96 per day
a. Indicated in the presence of the following conditions:	100%	30 per dressing change
(1) Minor nutritional deficit		
(2) Slightly hypermetabolic status		
(3) Inability to provide adequate oral or enteral feeding		

b. Composition

    1,400-2,000 kcal/day of amino acids, fat, dextrose
5%-7.5% with vitamins, minerals and electrolyte additives — 100%

c. Treatment objective: 0 nitrogen balance, or imbalance no
greater than —2 — 100%

4. Intravenous hyperalimentation or central total parenteral nutrition — $ 96 per day
   30 per dressing change

  a. Indicated in presence of either Condition 1 or Condition 2,
below — 100%

    (1) Severe protein-calorie malnutrition or

    (2) Nutritionally sound, hypermetabolic patient in whom a
major burn or other trauma has increased nutritional
needs to a level that cannot be met via oral intake
and

    (3) Inability to provide adequate oral or enteral feeding — 100%

  b. Composition

    (1) In intravenous hyperalimentation, 2,400-3,000 kcal/day
of amino acids and 25% dextrose with vitamins, minerals
and electrolyte additives — 100%

    (2) In central total parenteral nutrition, 2,400-3,000 kcal/day
of amino acids, fat and dextrose with vitamins, minerals
and electrolyte additives — 100%

  c. Treatment objectives

    (1) In presence of severe protein-calorie malnutrition,

      (a) Repair of deficits — 100%

      (b) Positive nitrogen balance of +4 to +6 g/day — 100%

    (2) In presence of a nutritionally sound, hypermetabolic
patient with increased nutritional needs due to trauma,

      (a) Current nutritional level maintained — 100%

      (b) 0 nitrogen balance — 100%

EVALUATION OF EFFECTIVENESS OF THERAPY

5. Patient monitoring including

  a. Daily weight measurement — 100%

  b. Intake and output measured — 100%

  c. Repeated measurement of nitrogen balance — 100%

  d. Weekly test of immune competence — 100%

MANAGEMENT OF COMPLICATIONS

6. Phlebitis at site of intravenous catheter

  a. Catheter removed — 100%

  b. New catheter inserted at alternate site by physician under
strict aseptic precautions — 100%   30

INTRAVENOUS THERAPY

REVIEW

Criterion	Standard	Estimated Charge
SITE AND PROCEDURES		
1. Vein of forearm or dorsum of hand	100%	$ 20
2. Veins of foot or leg	0%	
Exception (Indication): Absence of another usable site.		
3. Vein cut-down and insertion of cannula	0%	25
Exception (Indication): Usually accessible veins collapsed.		
4. Rate of flow 120 drops per minute or less	100%	
5. Needle strapped in place	100%	
6. Presence of filter recorded	100%	
7. Needle site rotated every 3 days	100%	20
Exceptions: (a) Appearance of redness at site necessitating earlier rotation; (b) catheter in subclavian vein for hyperalimentation.		
MANAGEMENT OF COMPLICATIONS		
8. Presence of edema, redness or phlebitis at site		
Site changed	100%	20
9. Extravasation of fluid into skin		
a. Needle removed	100%	
b. Area massaged gently to disperse fluid	100%	
OUTCOME OF PROCEDURE		
10. Absence of inflammation or phlebitis at site	100%	

UTILIZATION

SAMPLE

Patients admitted on Friday and Saturday, excluding the following types of admission:

- Patients who underwent UHDDS Class I procedures after admission
- Patients who underwent any of the following procedures either on the day of admission or on the first day after admission
    - Colonoscopy
    - Percutaneous angiography
    - Peritoneal dialysis
- Direct admission to the Coronary Care Unit or Intensive Care Unit
- Emergency admissions in the presence of life- or limb-threatening emergencies requiring immediate intervention
- Newborns
- Obstetrical patients delivered
- Patients who expired within 3 days following admission
- Transfers from other acute care hospitals

REVIEW

Criterion	Standard	Estimated Charge

JUSTIFICATION FOR ADMISSION ON FRIDAY OR SATURDAY

The ordering of and provision of at least one of the following services within 2 hours after admission: **100%**

1. Initiation of indwelling urinary or nasogastric catheter drainage
2. Order for immediate "nothing by mouth" (NPO) other than in preparation for procedures and tests
3. Order for complete bed rest without bathroom privileges
4. Continuous immobilizing traction
5. Continous telemetry
6. Vital signs monitored at a frequency of at least every 2 hours
7. Continuous intravenous fluid administration
8. Documented actual parenteral administration of analgesic PRN medication at a frequency of more than two times in one day
9. Repeated respiratory therapy services
10. Continuous administration of oxygen
11. Admission of patient with admitting diagnosis or impression of labor or ruptured membranes
12. Admission of patient with admission diagnosis of suspected or established child abuse
13. Restraints and intensive psychiatric observation for a patient admitted because of the sudden onset of signs and symptoms of psychiatric illness

Exclusions: Patients with diagnosed or apparent chronic brain syndrome whose symptoms have existed for more than 3 days.

DEPARTMENTAL STUDIES

PROBLEM

Excessive in-house transfers, resulting in delays in and the misdirecting of food trays, inability of diagnostic service units to return test results to the appropriate nursing station promptly and in the need for repeated preparation of rooms.

SUGGESTED SAMPLE

The last 100 discharges of patients over the age of 18 years who had been admitted under non-emergency, non-urgent conditions.

REVIEW

Criterion	Standard	Estimated Charge
For each admission,		
1. The patient had been admitted no later than the Hospital's admission deadline time	100%	
2. The patient had been accurately coded as either a smoker or a a non-smoker at the time of admission	100%	
3. The patient's sex was accurately recorded on the face sheet at the time of admission	100%	
4. The patient's attending physician had notified the Hospital's admitting office of the planned and scheduled admission at least 24 hours before the patient's arrival	100%	
5. Upon discharge from the Hospital, the patient had vacated his room no later than the Hospital's discharge deadline time	100%	
6. If the patient was transferred within the Hospital during his stay, the transfer was medically indicated	100%	

Record Analyst: The following are examples of medically indicated transfers:

- *To or from a special care unit, such as an ICU or CCU*
- *To or from a room equipped for telemetry*
- *From an acute care section to a step-down or self care section*
- *Following surgery, from the patient's original room to a room in a special surgical section*

Exception: Absence of transfer.

PROBLEM

Lack of timeliness in patient accounts billing operations.

SAMPLE

It is recommended that the criteria shown below be used in concurrent monitoring.

REVIEW

Criterion	Standard	Estimated Charge
1. The Medical Record Department obtains the records of all discharged patients or patients transferred out of the hospital by 12:00 noon on the day following the patient's departure	100%	
2. The backlog of uncoded and incomplete records is no greater than 1 month's discharges	100%	
3. The number of surgical operations for which, at the end of any day, no operative notes have been dictated is no greater than the average number of operations performed per day	100%	
4. Within 3 calendar days following his discharge or transfer to another facility, the final diagnosis has been entered on the face sheet of the medical record of each discharged or transferred patient	100%	
Record Analyst: *No allowance is made for Saturdays, Sundays or holidays.*		

PROBLEM

Failure to handle correspondence in an expeditious manner, resulting in a backlog.

SAMPLE

All requests for information received during the most recent calendar month.

REVIEW

Criterion	Standard	Estimated Charge
For each sample month, the number of second requests for patient information received from insurance companies, other health care facilities, outside physicians and attorneys is less than 1% of the average number of patient information requests received per month	100%	

PROBLEM

An unsatisfactory cash flow, associated with late charges, the denial of third party claims, the need for production of corrected statements, the write-off of late Medicare charges, the re-filing of claims and the presence of an unacceptably high number of accounts receivable that are more than 60 days old.

SUGGESTED SAMPLE

Two samples are to be used in a comparison of performance.

Sample 1

All claims submitted to Medicare and Medicaid fiscal intermediaries as well as to other third party payers during the calendar quarter most recently ended.

Sample 2

All claims submitted to Medicare and Medicaid fiscal intermediaries as well as to other third party payers during the calendar quarter that ended six months prior to the close of the most recent calendar quarter.

REVIEW

	Criterion	Standard	Estimated Charge
1.	The sampling time frames and numbers of claims used for this review are defined and documented in the report	100%	
2.	A reduction of at least 10% has occurred in the number of claims denied by private insurers such as Blue Cross or the local equivalent	100%	
3.	A reduction of at least 10% has occurred in the number of claims denied by the Medicare intermediary	100%	
4.	A reduction of at least 10% has occurred in the number of claims denied by the Medicaid intermediary	100%	
5.	A reduction of at least 10% has occurred in the number of third party accounts receivable that are more than 60 days old	100%	
6.	Productivity as measured by the account processing rate (APR) has increased by at least 3% since the earlier sample quarter	100%	

Record Analyst: The account processing rate is calculated in the following manner:

   a. *Determine the number of Full Time Equivalent personnel in the department for each of the 2 calendar quarters used as samples*

   b. *For each calendar quarter, determine the total number of patient accounts that were paid*

   c. *For each quarter, divide the number of paid patient accounts by the number of Full Time Equivalent personnel in the department that calendar quarter*

7.	In the second calendar quarter studied, there were no late charges	100%	

SUGGESTED SAMPLE

Patients discharged or transferred from the hospital following treatment of alcoholism as the primary problem and reason for admission.

REVIEW

Criterion	Standard	Estimated Charge
JUSTIFICATION FOR ADMISSION		
1. The presence of either of the following conditions in the absence of dementia or other mental illness:	100%	
a. The patient's request for inpatient treatment in the presence of a history of excessive drinking interfering with his occupational functioning and interpersonal relations		
b. An acute episode of any of the following conditions:		
(1) Pathological alcoholic intoxication		
(2) Delirium tremens		
(3) Alcoholic hallucinosis		
(4) Impending hepatic coma in established or suspected alcoholism		
DIAGNOSTIC STUDY		
2. In the chart within 24 hours after admission,		
a. History including history of present complaint	100%	
b. Physical examination report	100%	
c. Pulse, respiration and blood pressure on admission and on each shift	100%	
d. Physician's admission note	100%	
e. Initial written orders	100%	
f. Laboratory test reports including		
(1) CBC, urinalysis and admission test panel	100%	$ 125
(2) Electrolytes	100%	25
(3) Direct bilirubin	100%	29
(4) Creatinine clearance	100%	28
(5) Prothrombin time	100%	15
(6) Blood ammonia level	100%	50
Exception: Absence of hepatic coma or pre-coma.		
3. In the chart within 3 days after admission,		
a. Treatment history	100%	
b. Psychiatric assessment and assessment of rehabilitation potential	100%	60
c. Psychosocial history and evaluation	100%	
d. Treatment plan	100%	

MANAGEMENT

4. Milieu therapy and structured control including the following provisions:

    a. Patient confined to unit during detoxification and evaluation phase of treatment · · · 100%

    b. Hospital pajamas to be worn during detoxification and evaluation phases of treatment · · · 100%

    c. No incoming or outgoing telephone calls until authorized in physician's written orders · · · 100%

    d. Any packages received to be inspected by unit personnel · · · 100%

5. Detoxification measures

    Exception: Patient not in a state of intoxication at admission.

    a. Intravenous saline solution with 5% dextrose, vitamin B complex and ascorbic acid as indicated to combat dehydration · · · 100% · · · $ 20

    b. In presence of hepatic pre-coma, measures to reduce blood ammonia level · · · 100% · · · 5

    Exception: Absence of hepatic pre-coma.

    c. In presence of hepatic pre-coma, protein-free diet with ample fruit juices · · · 100% · · · 35

    Exception: Absence of hepatic pre-coma.

    d. In presence of delirium tremens, gastric lavage as indicated · · · 100% · · · 22

    Exceptions: (1) Presence of abnormalities in fluid and electrolyte balance; (2) absence of delirium tremens.

    e. In presence of delirium tremens, administration of 3,000-4,000 ml of fluids per day · · · 100% · · · 20 per day

    Exception: Absence of delirium tremens.

    f. In presence of delirium tremens, administration of 3,000-4,000 calorie per day high carbohydrate soft diet · · · 100% · · · 35

    Exception: Absence of delirium tremens.

    g. Administration of chlorpromazine as indicated · · · 100%

    Exceptions: (1) Presence of pre-coma or somnolence; (2) recent administration of other drugs.

6. Therapeutic program

    When the patient is medically stable,

    a. Re-evaluation of rehabilitation potential · · · 100%

    b. Daily psychotherapeutic counseling · · · 100% · · · 150 per week

    Contraindicated: Psychoanalytically oriented intervention.

    c. Documented participation in structured rehabilitation program 6-7 hours per day, including

    (1) Patient's acknowledgement of existence of problem · · · 100%

    (2) Efforts directed toward resolution of identity problem · · · 100%

    (3) Development of more effective behavioral and attitudinal patterns · · · 100%

    (4) Efforts to establish personal priorities and objectives · · · 100%

    (5) Learning techniques for maintaining continuing sobriety · · · 100%

    (6) Development of new patterns of problem solving · · · 100%

    d. Documented participation of patient with his family or significant others in weekly group therapy sessions · · · 100% · · · 90 per week

e. Documented participation of patient's family with families of other patients in weekly group sessions	100%	$ 60 per week
f. After first week of treatment, weekly participation in meetings of Alcoholics Anonymous or similar group	100%	
g. Documented participation in group therapy	100%	100 per week
h. Documented participation in occupational and recreational therapy programs	100%	

7. Provision of diet meeting any special nutritional needs of patient — 100%

8. Continuing medical surveillance as reflected in physician's progress notes — 100%

9. Continuing nursing surveillance as reflected in nursing notes — 100%

10. Weekly updating of evaluation — 100%

11. Weekly updating of therapy plan — 100%

LENGTH OF STAY

12. Length of stay
    a. Inpatient LOS 3-4 weeks — 100% — 4,200-5,600
       Exceptions: (1) Early departure against medical advice; (2) transfer of patient deemed not treatable within this program.
    b. Participation in post-hospital outpatient program minimum of 10 weeks — 100% — 1,200
       Exceptions: (1) Early termination against medical advice; (2) Transfer of patient deemed not treatable within this program.

DISCHARGE STATUS

13. Patient discharged under the following conditions:
    a. Free of alcohol since admission to program — 100%
    b. Has verbalized intention to maintain abstinence from alcohol — 100%
    c. Psychological symptoms present on admission alleviated — 100%
    d. Post-hospital outpatient treatment plan accepted by patient and family or significant others — 100%

POST-HOSPITAL OUTPATIENT PROGRAM

14. Outpatient record documentation showing that patient and his family or significant others are participating in, or have participated in, the follow-up program including
    a. Weekly counseling sessions for the patient — 100%
    b. Weekly family group therapy sessions — 100%

15. Evidence in record indicating or suggesting that patient has remained abstinent since discharge — 100%

16. Documentation in record showing participation in outpatient program for at least 10 weeks — 100% — 1,200

Exception to Criteria Numbers 14, 15 and 16: Not applicable as a result of early departure from program or transfer to another facility.

SUGGESTED SAMPLE

Patients presenting dyspnea, tachypnea, breathing difficulties, asthma or chronic cough in the absence of congestive heart failure or other evidence of cardiac disease.

REVIEW

Criterion	Standard	Estimated Charge
EVALUATION AND STUDY		
1. History with specific inquiries concerning each of the following:	100%	
a. Upper respiratory infection		
b. Allergies		
c. Tuberculosis exposure or history		
d. Cardiac problems		
e. Smoking		
f. Environmental and occupational exposure, going back to earliest employment		
g. Medication and drug history		
h. Childhood illnesses		
2. Medical problems of parents and siblings reported	100%	
3. Physical examination	100%	
4. Laboratory and other studies including		
a. CBC	100%	$ 19
b. Urinalysis	100%	10
c. Sputum culture	100%	40
d. Chest x-ray	100%	70
e. Pulmonary function study	100%	10
f. Arterial blood gas analysis	100%	70
g. Blood urea nitrogen (BUN)	100%	19
h. Skin tests	100%	50
Exception: Absence of history of allergy and of evidence suggesting allergic etiology.		
i. Sweat test	0%	37
Exception (Indication): Needed to rule out cystic fibrosis in presence of asthma.		
5. Pulse, respiration and temperature recorded on each visit	100%	
6. Blood pressure recorded on each visit	100%	

MANAGEMENT

7.	Diagnosis established and documented	100%
8.	Discussion with patient and relative for purpose of explaining his respiratory problem and the management plan	100%
9.	Plan of management documented, including	
	a. Any respiratory treatments to be provided at home	100%
	b. Medication schedule and dosage as indicated	100%
	c. Any applicable restrictions on diet or activity explained	100%
	d. In presence of a food allergy, dietary counseling session or scheduling of an appointment with dietician for counseling	100%
	e. Scheduling of periodic return visits	100%

SUGGESTED SAMPLE

Patients in whom routine or special urinalysis has revealed glycosuria in the absence of documented diabetes.

REVIEW

Criterion	Standard	Estimated Charge
EVALUATION AND STUDY		
1. History with specific inquiries concerning each of the following:	100%	
a. Any previous episode of glycosuria or high blood sugar levels	100%	
b. Polyuria	100%	
c. Excessive thirst	100%	
d. Excessive hunger	100%	
e. Weakness	100%	
f. Weight loss	100%	
g. Itching	100%	
h. Childhood diseases	100%	
2. Medical problems of parents and siblings reported	100%	
3. Physical examination	100%	
Exception: Diabetes screening being performed following recent documented complete physical examination.		
4. Blood pressure in both arms, with patient lying down and sitting up, on each visit	100%	
5. Pulse, respiration and temperature recorded on each visit	100%	
6. Laboratory and other studies including		
a. Urinalysis	100%	$ 10
b. Oral glucose tolerance test	100%	68
c. Funduscopy on each visit	100%	
d. Arterial blood gas analysis	100%	70
e. Arterial blood pH level	100%	18
f. Blood acetone	100%	377
CATEGORIZATION OF PATIENT		
7. Establishment of diagnosis in presence of diabetes and categorization of patient in terms of severity of problem, such as	100%	
a. Obese mild diabetic		
b. Nonobese mild diabetic		
c. Severe diabetic		
d. Brittle diabetic		
e. Juvenile diabetic		

MANAGEMENT

In the presence of established diabetes,

8. Discussion with patient and relative for purpose of explaining nature of problem and plan of management, documented in the record   100%

9. Management plan formulated, including

    a. Medication regimen, whether insulin or oral hypoglycemic agents   100%

        Exception: Diabetes controlled by diet alone.

    b. Designing of appropriate diet in consultation with dietician   100% $ 35

    c. Training of patient and relative with documentation of the following:

        (1) Patient/relative showing ability to test urine for sugar and acetone   100%

            (a) Urine analyzed 4 times daily until stabilized

            (b) After stabilization and visit to physician, analyzed once daily upon awakening

        (2) Patient/relative showing ability to administer insulin   100%

        Exception: Not insulin dependent.

        (3) Patient/relative showing ability to administer medications and to identify early signs of adverse reactions   100%

        Exception: Medication not to be used.

        (4) Patient/relative showing ability to provide foot care   100%

        (5) Patient/relative instructed in diet restrictions and given copies of appropriate diet   100%

        (6) Patient/relative instructed as to weight controls or goals   100%

        (7) Patient/relative instructed as to exercise restrictions   100%

        Exception: No restrictions indicated.

    d. Patient and relative instructed as to symptoms and treatment of hypoglycemia   100%

        Patient instructed to carry diabetic identification card and small supply of sugar or candy   100%   15

    e. Scheduling of periodic return visits explained to patient and relative and documented   100%

10. Patient admitted to hospital in presence of any of the following: 100%

    a. Diabetic ketoacidosis

    b. Hypokalemia

    c. Evidence suggestive of peripheral vascular occlusion

Note: For a diet review model, you are referred to the model on dietetic study of patients with uncontrolled diabetes in the section on Dietetic Service.

SUGGESTED SAMPLE

Patients complaining of chronic or recurrent headache.

REVIEW

Criterion	Standard	Estimated Charge
PRELIMINARY EVALUATION		
1. History with specific inquiries concerning each of the following:	100%	
a. With reference to the headaches,		
(1) Frequency		
(2) Severity		
(3) Duration		
(4) Location with identification of unilateral site if present		
(5) Character with identification of throbbing character if present		
b. Any recent or remote head injury		
c. Alcohol consumption pattern		
d. Medications recently or presently taken		
e. Any visual problems		
f. Allergies		
g. Frequency of upper respiratory infections		
h. Any hearing problems		
i. Sinusitis		
j. Hypertension		
k. Any neurological symptoms such as weakness, numbness or tingling		
l. Occupation		
m. Childhood illnesses		
2. Report of medical problems of parents and siblings	100%	
3. Physical examination including neurological survey	100%	
Exception: Recent complete physical examination with neurological survey documented in record.		
4. Pulse, respiration and temperature on each visit	100%	
5. Blood pressure in both arms, taken with patient lying down and sitting up, on each visit	100%	
6. Laboratory and other studies including		
a. CBC	100%	$ 19
b. Urinalysis	100%	10
c. Blood serology	100%	11
d. Blood urea nitrogen (BUN)	100%	19
e. Visual acuity and visual fields	100%	50
Exception: Documentation of recent ophthalmological study.		

f. Funduscopy on each visit	100%	
g. Chest x-ray	100%	$ 70

INDICATIONS FOR SPECIAL STUDIES

7. Suspected brain tumor, brain abscess or subdural hematoma
   a. Studies

   Skull x-ray, lumbar puncture, EEG and either encephalography, brain scan or arteriogram — 450-1,017

   b. Indications

   Any of the following listed physical findings in conjunction with a history of progressively increasing weakness on one side, neurological signs and symptoms, vomiting, ear disease, sinusitis, bronchieactasis, lung abscess, rheumatic or congenital heart disease, or trauma with loss of consciousness: — 100%

   (1) Papilledema
   (2) Visual field changes
   (3) Aphasia
   (4) Paralysis
   (5) Mental changes
   (6) Infective focus
   (7) Signs of recent head injury

8. Suspected meningeal irritation
   a. Studies

   Blood culture and lumbar puncture with smear and culture of cerebrospinal fluid — 187

   b. Indications

   In an acutely ill patient, severe, generalized, constant headache radiating down neck, accompanied by malaise, fever and vomiting, following sore throat or respiratory infection — 100%

9. Suspected chronic meningitis
   a. Studies

   Lumbar puncture with smear and culture of cerebrospinal fluid, cerebrospinal fluid protein and sugar, and blood and spinal fluid serologies — 178

   b. Indications

   (1) History of syphilis or tuberculosis with
   (2) Signs of meningeal irritation and/or
   (3) Cranial nerve palsies — 100%

10. Suspected subarachnoid hemorrhage
    a. Studies

    Lumbar puncture and arteriogram — 791

    b. Indications

    Following sudden onset of severe and constant headache, the presence of any of the following: — 100%

    (1) Drowsy or comatose patient
    (2) Stiff neck
    (3) Positive Kernig's sign
    (4) Bilateral Babinski reflexes

215

(5) Third nerve paralysis

(6) Elevated blood pressure

11. Suspected Paget's disease
    a. Studies
       Skull x-ray and serum alkaline phosphatase $ 154
    b. Indications
       In the presence of a history of increasing skull size, either
       of the following: 100%
       (1) Tenderness of skull
       (2) Evidence of compression of brain and cranial nerves

12. Suspected metastatic neoplasm
    a. Study
       X-ray and scan of skull 430
    b. Indication
       Evidence of a primary neoplasm or metastases at other
       sites 100%

13. Suspected migraine
    a. Studies
       Studies to rule out organic disease and a trial course with
       a vasoconstrictor 309
    b. Indications
       A combination of the following: 100%
       (1) History of recurrent episodes of severe, throbbing pain
           accompanied by anorexia, nausea and vomiting
       (2) Negative findings on physical examination

14. Suspected or established hypertension
    a. Studies
       Blood glucose studies and urinalysis 19
    b. Indications
       Any of the following: 100%
       (1) Elevated blood pressure
       (2) Retinal changes
       (3) Edema
       (4) Cardiac findings suggestive of hypertension

15. Suspected histamine headache
    a. Studies
       Trial of vasoconstrictor drugs
    b. Indications
       Presence of a combination of the following: 100%
       (1) History of unilateral pain involving eye, temple, face and
           neck with symptoms of vasodilatation on same side as
           pain
       (2) Swelling of temporal vessels
       (3) Injection of conjunctiva
       (4) Flushing of side of face and other evidence of vasodilatation

16. Suspected toxic state
    a. Studies
       Lumbar puncture, blood and urine studies to identify agent 212

b. Indications

Severe, generalized, constant pain following exposure to toxins or associated with other symptoms caused by toxic agent | 100%

17. Suspected eyestrain, iritis or glaucoma
   a. Study

   Ophthalmological examination | $ 50

   b. Indications

   History of frontal or supraorbital pain with any of the following: | 100%
   (1) Increased intraocular pressure
   (2) Errors of refraction
   (3) Change in appearance of iris

18. Suspected otitis media or mastoiditis
   a. Studies

   Otoscopic examination and mastoid x-ray | 147

   b. Indications

   Presence of a combination of the following: | 100%
   (1) In an acutely ill patient with fever, a temporal, unilateral, stabbing pain accompanied by sensations of fullness in the ear with increasing tinnitus and deafness
   (2) Tenderness over the mastoid with a red, congested or retracted drum on the affected side

19. Suspected lesions of nasal sinuses
   a. Studies

   Transillumination and x-ray of sinuses | 126

   b. Indications

   Presence of a combination of the following: | 100%
   (1) History of frontal pain following upper respiratory infection
   (2) Nasal obstruction with swollen mucous membranes, purulent discharge and tenderness over affected sinus

20. Suspected anxiety state
   a. Studies

   Studies for purpose of ruling out organic disease, followed by evaluation of personality | 315

   b. Indications

   Presence of a combination of the following: | 100%
   (1) History of headache following or associated with stress
   (2) Normal physical and neurological examination

MANAGEMENT

21. Diagnosis established and documented | 100%
22. Discussion with patient and relative to explain nature of problem and management plan | 100%
23. Management plan documented in record | 100%
24. Instructions given relevant to management plan documented in record | 100%
25. Follow-up appointment scheduled | 100%

REVIEW

Criterion	Standard	Estimated Charge

INDICATIONS FOR HEMODIALYSIS

1. The presence of either of the following conditions: — 100%
   a. Acute intrinsic renal failure associated with any of the following conditions:
      (1) Protein catabolism, reflected by
         (a) Non-protein nitrogen level from 100-120 mg %
         (b) Urea nitrogen level from 120-150 mg %
         (c) Hyperuricemia
      (2) Electrolyte disorders, reflected by
         (a) Hyperkalemia (6.2 mEq per liter) or
         (b) Hypernatremia (more than 160 mEq per liter)
      (3) Acid-base disorder, reflected by
         (a) Acidosis with arterial blood pH below 7.25 or
         (b) Alkalosis, either respiratory or metabolic
      (4) Overhydration, reflected by persistent elevation of central venous pressure or of pulmonary artery wedge pressure, S_3 or S_4 gallop, moist rales or pleural effusion
      (5) Platelet defect coagulopathy
   b. Chronic renal failure associated with at least 3 of the following:
      (1) Glomerular filtration rate of 5 ml per minute or less
      (2) Blood urea nitrogran greater than 130 mg per 100 ml
      (3) Blood creatinine above 10 mg per 100 ml
      (4) Elevated serum uric acid, above 12-15 mg per 100 ml
      (5) Hyperphosphatemia above 8-10 mg per 100 ml
      (6) Clinical signs including
         (a) Pericarditis
         (b) Deterioration of motor nerve conduction velocity
         (c) Anemia
         (d) Anorexia and vomiting with inability to maintain adequate calorie intake and nitrogen balance
         (e) Cachexia, malaise and weakness
         (f) Chronic congestive heart failure
         (g) Presence of a severe infection
   c. Exogenous intoxication following the ingestion of a dialyzable poison, associated with prolonged apnea, hypotension, underlying pulmonary, renal or hepatic disease or diabetes mellitus, pneumonia or other infections, or followed by a deterioration of the patient's condition despite therapy

EVALUATION OF THE PATIENT'S CONDITION

2. Documented in the record prior to dialysis,
   a. Complete blood count — 100% — $ 19
   b. Chest x-ray — 100% — 70
   c. Renal ultrasound examination — 100% — 278
   d. Renal scan — 100% — 409
   e. EKG — 100% — 48
   f. SMAC 24 or equivalent battery or admission panel — 100% — 85
   g. Serum electrolytes — 100% — 25
   h. Blood gas analysis — 100% — 70

TREATMENT PROGRAM

3. Vascular access established by means of external shunt or arteriovenous fistula — 100%
4. Maturation of arteriovenous fistula (AVF) — 100%
   Exception: Presence of external shunt.
5. Hemodialysis schedule established — 100%
   a. 3-5 hours per treatment 3 times a week, or — 741 per week
   b. Total of 9-15 hours per week in 3 or 4 sessions — 100% — 741-988 per week
6. Establishment of therapeutic nutritional program providing for:
   a. Protein — 1-1.2 g/kg of body weight per day, with 60% being of high biological value — 100% — 35
   b. Calories — 25-30 cal/kg of body weight per day — 100%
   c. Sodium — No more than 50 mEq per day — 100%
   d. Potassium — 44 mEq per day — 100%
   e. Fluid intake — In the anuric patient on dialysis 3 times a week, 700 to 800 ml of fluids per day — 100%

MANAGEMENT OF COMPLICATIONS OF HEMODIALYSIS AND OF VASCULAR ACCESS

7. Dialysis disequilibrium syndrome (DDS)
   In the presence of any combination of headache, nausea, blurring of vision, muscular twitching, disorientation, hypertension with or without tremor and seizure,
   a. Prevention of rapid fall in plasma osmolality during hemodialysis with use of osmotically active solutes — 100%
   b. Prevention of rapid removal of solutes during hemodialysis — 100%
8. Bleeding
   a. Pressure dressing and surgical revision — 100% — 267
   b. Complete clotting profile — 100% — 65
   c. Protamine sulfate intravenous — 100% — 20
   d. Transfusion of fresh whole blood or plasma — 100% — 183
9. Cannula infection
   a. Culture and sensitivity — 100% — 75
   b. Antibiotic therapy consistent with culture and sensitivity — 100%
   c. Removal of cannula — 100%

10. Poor flow
    a. Declotting — 100%
    b. Heparinization and surgical revision as indicated — 100%
    c. Angiography — 100% $ 140
11. Clotting
    a. Declotting, heparinization, use of Fogarty catheter as indicated — 100%
    b. Angiography — 100%   140
12. Skin erosion
    a. Secure cannula with tape — 100%
    b. Rigorous skin care maintained — 100%
13. False aneurysm
    Removal of cannula — 100%
14. Septicemia
    a. Removal of cannula — 100%
    b. Culture and sensitivity of blood — 100%   75
    c. Antibiotic consistent with culture and sensitivity — 100%

ONGOING MONITORING

15. Before initiation of dialysis, and every 2 to 4 weeks thereafter: 114
    Blood levels of
    a. Urea — 100%
    b. Creatinine — 100%
    c. Uric acid — 100%
    d. Total proteins — 100%
    e. Hematocrit and hemoglobin — 100%
    f. Sodium — 100%
    g. Potassium — 100%
    h. Chloride — 100%
    i. Bicarbonate — 100%
    j. Calcium — 100%
    k. Phosphate — 100%
16. Every 3 months while the patient is on dialysis: 104
    a. Serum protein — 100%
    b. HBs antigen and anti-HBs antibody — 100%
    c. Serum lipids, cholesterol and triglycerides — 100%
    d. Serum transaminase — 100%
17. Every 6 months while the patient is on dialysis: 872
    a. Alkaline phosphatase — 100%
    b. Bilirubin — 100%
    c. Where chronic hepatitis is suspected, further liver function studies — 100%
    d. CBC, platelets and reticulocytes — 100%
    e. Serum transferrin — 100%
    f. Urine culture if patient is not anuric — 100%
    g. EKG — 100%
    h. Funduscopy — 100%

i.	EMG and motor nerve conduction velocity	100%
j.	Bone survey	100%

OUTCOMES IN TERMS OF PATIENT'S STATUS

18. Documentation of the following:

a.	Good personal, social and occupational rehabilitation	100%
b.	Good general and nutritional status	100%
c.	Normal blood pressure, with or without medication	100%
d.	Well tolerated anemia	100%
e.	Absence of major disorders of phosphorus and calcium metabolism	100%
f.	Absence of uremic polyneuritis	100%
g.	Before each dialysis, plasma urea and creatinine concentration in optimal range	100%
h.	Electrolyte and plasma balance near normal	100%

SUGGESTED SAMPLE

Patients found in the course of examination to have elevated blood pressure with the diastolic pressure above 95.

REVIEW

Criterion	Standard	Estimated Charge
EVALUATION AND STUDY		
1. History with specific inquiries concerning each of the following:	100%	
a. Cardiac problems		
b. Diabetes		
c. Changes in weight		
d. Headaches		
e. Episodes of dizziness or fainting		
f. Renal problems		
2. Medical problems of parents and siblings reported	100%	
3. Physical examination	100%	
Exception: Hypertension screening following recent complete documented physical examination.		
4. Blood pressure in both arms, taken with patient lying down and sitting up	100%	
5. Pulse, respiration and temperature recorded	100%	
6. Laboratory and other studies including		
a. Urine analysis		$ 11
(1) Specific gravity	100%	
(2) Albumin	100%	
(3) Microanalysis	100%	
b. Serum potassium prior to any therapy with diuretics	100%	18
c. Hemogram with differential analysis	100%	35
d. Chest x-ray	100%	70
e. EKG	100%	48
f. Creatinine level	100%	10
g. Creatinine clearance	0%	11
Exception (Indication): Presence of elevated creatinine.		
h. Intravenous pyelogram (IVP)	0%	125
Exceptions (Indications): (1) Elevated creatinine; (2) diagnosis of hypertension in a patient under 30 with history of previous trauma.		

i. Catecholamines		0%	$ 66
Exception (Indication): Diastolic pressure over 110 mm Hg in a patient under 30.			
j. Funduscopy		100%	

CATEGORIZATION OF PATIENT

7. Categorization either   100%
   a. Group A, borderline hypertension
      Diastolic pressure 96-100 mm Hg, or
   b. Group B, definite hypertension
      (1) Diastolic pressure 100 mg Hg or higher, or
      (2) Presence of retinal abnormalities on funduscopy

MANAGEMENT PLAN

8. Discussion with patient including explanation of etiology of hypertension, documented in record   100%
9. Management plan documented, including
   a. Medication schedule and dosage as indicated   100%
   b. Explanation of any side effects of medication   100%
   c. Statement of any dietary restrictions including low sodium diet as indicated   100%
   d. Dietary counseling session or scheduling of appointment with dietician for counseling   100%
   e. Weight reduction program outlined as indicated   100%
   f. Scheduling of periodic return visits   100%

PERIODIC RETURN VISIT

SUGGESTED SAMPLE

Previously screened patients with known hypertension of either Group A or Group B.

REVIEW

Criterion	Standard	Estimated Charge

EVALUATION

1. History covering period since previous visit, with reference to:
   a. Adherence to medication schedule   100%
      Exception: Patient not receiving medication for hypertension.
   b. Headaches   100%
   c. Episodes of dizziness or fainting   100%
   d. Intercurrent illnesses   100%
   e. Adherence to low sodium diet as indicated   100%
   f. Any stressful situations   100%
2. Pulse, respiration and temperature recorded   100%
3. Blood pressure in each arm, lying down and sitting up   100%
4. Urinalysis   100% $ 11
5. Funduscopy   100%

6. Diastolic blood pressure either lower than on previous visit by 10 mm Hg, or no higher than 95 mm Hg   100%
7. Absence of eyeground abnormalities   100%
8. Absence of proteinuria   100%
9. Absence of edema   100%

SUGGESTED SAMPLE

Patients with complaints of coryza, pharyngitis and cough.

REVIEW

Criterion	Standard	Estimated Charge
EVALUATION		
1. History with specific inquiries concerning each of the following:	100%	
a. Duration of symptoms		
b. Presence of sore throat, chest pain or thoracic pain		
c. Chills		
d. Fever		
e. Character of cough, whether dry or productive		
f. Presence of headache		
g. Any medications taken for this illness prior to visit to physician		
2. Physical examination including evaluation of breath sounds	100%	
3. Pulse, respiration and temperature documented	100%	
4. Laboratory and other studies including		
a. Chest x-rays, anterior-posterior and lateral	100%	$ 70
Exception: Lungs normal to auscultation and percussion.		
b. CBC	100%	11
c. Urinalysis	100%	11
d. Nasopharyngeal culture and sensitivity	0%	40
Exception (Indication): Presence of fever and sore throat.		
e. Sputum culture and sensitivity	0%	40
Exception (Indication): Presence of fever and thoracic pain.		
f. Blood culture	0%	40
Exception (Indication): History of persistent high fever longer than 4 days with inability to raise sputum.		
MANAGEMENT		
5. Bed rest at home until temperature has been no higher than 99 F for at least 24 hours	100%	
Exception: Provisional diagnosis of pneumonia justifying admission to hospital.		
6. Patient instructed to drink large amounts of fluids	100%	
7. Antipyretic analgesic ordered	100%	
8. Cough mixture ordered	100%	
9. Antibiotic	0%	
Exception (Indication): (a) X-ray evidence of pneumonia, (b) persistent high fever in bronchitis or (c) positive culture.		
10. Admission to hospital	0%	
Exception (Indication): Provisional diagnosis of pneumonia.		

SAMPLE

Patients who have undergone augmentation mammoplasty on an outpatient basis.

REVIEW

Criterion	Standard	Estimated Charge
INDICATION FOR AUGMENTATION MAMMOPLASTY		
1. The presence of small breasts, usually representing collapse following pregnancy with decrease in breast mass	100%	
PREOPERATIVE STUDY AND CARE		
2. Patient instructed to abstain from taking aspirin for 2 weeks preoperative	100%	
3. In the chart prior to surgery,		
a. History including present complaint	100%	
b. Physical examination report with specific reference to		
(1) Breast size and shape	100%	
(2) Absence of contraindications to elective surgery	100%	
4. Documentation of the patient's desire for the surgery and of her understanding of the consequences of the surgery	100%	
5. Laboratory and other studies performed prior to the day of surgery		
a. CBC, urinalysis and admission panel	100%	$ 77
b. Chest x-ray	100%	70
6. Preoperative nursing care		
a. Patient assessment including vital signs, brief relevant history and patient's reason for surgery	100%	
b. History of allergies and drug sensitivities	100%	
c. Patient orientation to planned nursing care and procedures	100%	
d. Preoperative instruction, preparation and medication	100%	
SURGICAL MANAGEMENT		695 OR
7. Under local anesthesia, augmentation mammoplasty with implants	100%	50 anesthesia
8. Report by operating surgeon of (a) preoperative diagnosis, (b) procedures performed and (c) description of tissues and findings, dictated or written immediately after surgery	100%	160 RR
9. Management of complications		
a. Hemorrhage		350 per day
(1) Patient readmitted to hospital	100%	
(2) Hemorrhage controlled	100%	
b. Infection occurring 4 or 5 days postoperative		75
(1) Culture and sensitivity	100%	
(2) Antibiotic consistent with culture and sensitivity	100%	

    c. Scar contracture of the capsule around an implant resulting
        in excessive firmness of the breast $ 350

per day

Where the result is completely unsatisfactory to the
patient, removal of the implant   100%

POSTOPERATIVE CARE

10. Patient kept under observation for 6 hours   100%

11. Patient instructed to avoid arm movements and strenuous activity   100%

12. Postoperative nursing care
    a. Vital signs recorded per outpatient postoperative plan   100%
    b. Patient monitored for evidence of complications   100%

LENGTH OF STAY

13. Length of stay 6 hours postoperative   100%
    Exceptions: (a) Earlier departure against medical advice;
    (b) complicating condition justifying longer stay or admission.

DISCHARGE STATUS

14. Patient discharged under the following conditions:
    a. Patient's temperature below 99.6 F   100%
    b. Patient not showing evidence of severe discomfort   100%
    c. Patient instructed to
       (1) Follow her normal routine with restriction of activities
            and avoidance of strenuous arm motion   100%
       (2) Schedule an office appointment for follow-up visit within
            several days   100%

SAMPLE

Patients who have undergone surgical removal of facial cysts on an outpatient basis.

REVIEW

Criterion	Standard	Estimated Charge
PREOPERATIVE STUDY AND CARE		
1. In the chart prior to surgery,		
a. Documentation of the presence of an epidermal or sebacious cyst on the face, associated with any of the following:	100%	
(1) Disfigurement		
(2) Site and size such that the lesion is repeatedly traumatized in shaving or washing		
(3) Infection, discharge or local swelling		
(4) Presence of potential for infection		
b. History with reference to etiology and duration	100%	
c. Physical examination report	100%	
2. Laboratory tests performed within 1 week before scheduled surgery, including		
a. CBC	100%	$ 11
b. Urinalysis	100%	11
3. History of any allergies and drug sensitivities documented	100%	
4. Documentation of any preoperative medication	100%	
SURGICAL MANAGEMENT		133 OR 50 anesthesia
5. Under local anesthetic, excision of lesion in operating room	100%	
6. Report by operating surgeon of (a) preoperative diagnosis, (b) procedures performed and (c) description of tissues and findings, dictated or written immediately after surgery	100%	
7. Pathologist's report on tissue specimen submitted, consistent with preoperative diagnosis	100%	
LENGTH OF STAY		
8. Length of postoperative stay from ½ hour to 2 hours, depending upon extent of surgery	100%	
Exceptions: (a) Earlier departure against medical advice; (b) complicating condition justifying longer observation.		
POSTOPERATIVE CARE		
9. Patient observed until condition stable	100%	
10. Patient's condition and condition of wound documented before discharge	100%	

DISCHARGE STATUS

11. Patient instructed re (a) wound care, (b) activity level, (c) any
medication prescribed and (d) follow-up visit to physician   100%
Exception: Instructions on transfer form.

*Record Analyst: The presence in the record of a copy of the
surgeon's standard instruction sheet covering at least these elements,
with an indication that a copy was given to the patient, satisfies
this requirement.*

AMBULATORY CARE SERVICES □ SURGERY
VASECTOMY

SAMPLE

Patients presenting themselves for vasectomy.

REVIEW

Criterion	Standard	Estimated Charge
INDICATIONS FOR PROCEDURE		
1. The presence of either of the following objectives:	100%	
a. Elective sterilization		
b. Prevention of retrograde epididymitis		
PREOPERATIVE STUDY AND CARE		
2. In the chart prior to surgery,		
a. History showing absence of contraindications to elective surgery	100%	
b. Physical examination report showing absence of contra-indications to elective surgery	100%	
c. Documentation of informed consent	100%	
d. CBC, urinalysis and admission panel	100%	$ 77
e. Serology	100%	11
MANAGEMENT		
3. Under local anesthesia, vasectomy with removal of a section of the vas and closure of the cut ends or electrocoagulation of the distal centimeter of vas	100%	133 OR 50 anesthesia
4. Report by operating surgeon of (a) procedures performed and (b) description of tissues and findings, dictated or written immediately after surgery	100%	
5. Pathologist's report on specimen submitted	100%	22
6. Management of complications		
Capillary bleeding or hematoma		
Conservative care and analgesics for discomfort	100%	
LENGTH OF STAY		
7. Length of postoperative stay from 1 to 2 hours	100%	
POSTOPERATIVE CARE AND INSTRUCTIONS		
8. The following measures prescribed	100%	
a. Scrotal support to be worn		17
b. Ice pack to be used at home for 24 hours after surgery		
c. Warm baths for relief of discomfort after first 24 hours		
d. Avoidance of vigorous activity for 3 days		
e. Analgesic given for pain		
9. Patient instructed to use contraceptive precautions after surgery until from 10 to 12 ejaculations have occurred	100%	
10. Follow-up visit to physician scheduled and documented	100%	

SAMPLE

Patients presenting themselves for amniocentesis.

REVIEW

Criterion	Standard	Estimated Charge
INDICATIONS FOR AMNIOCENTESIS		
1. The presence of either of the following conditions:	100%	
a. History of high exposure to genetic risk factors, such as:		
(1) Pregnancy in a woman 35 years of age or older		
(2) Previous birth of a child with Down's syndrome		
(3) Previous birth of a child with myelomeningocele		
(4) Previous birth of a child with amencephaly		
(5) Previous birth of a child with a metabolic disorder		
b. Need to assess fetal status, including any of these concerns:		
(1) Need to determine fetal maturity		
(2) Monitoring the severity of hemolytic disease		
(3) Monitoring surfactant activity as a predictor of possible respiratory distress syndrome		
(4) Presence of suspected chronic fetal distress		
PREOPERATIVE STUDY AND CARE		
2. Preoperative genetic counseling, covering the family's medical history, documented	100%	$ 112
Exception: Absence of genetic risk factors.		
3. Ultrasound examination for fetal age and status, as well as placental localization	100%	113
4. Determination of mother's blood group	100%	20
5. Interview with parents to explain the procedure and risks entailed	100%	
MANAGEMENT		
6. Ultrasound examination	100%	
7. Amniocentesis with		
a. Local anesthetic in skin	100%	60
b. Cleaning of area	100%	36
c. Insertion of needle and withdrawal of fluid specimen	100%	supplies
8. Surgeon's operative report describing procedure, dictated or written immediately following procedure	100%	
9. Genetic studies performed on specimen		
a. Chromosomal studies	100% ⎫	
b. Assay for Alpha fetoprotein	100% ⎬	214
c. Analysis to evaluate risk relevant to specific disease reported in history	100%	
Exception: Absence of genetic risk factors.		

231

10. Analysis of fetal well-being, age and status
    a. Fetal maturity based on study of bilirubin, creatinine, lipid-staining cells and surfactant — 100%
    b. Evaluation for presence of hemolytic disease — 100%
    c. Evaluation of lecithin/sphingomyelin ratio and risk of later respiratory distress syndrome — 100%
    d. Determination of presence or absence of chronic fetal distress — 100%

LENGTH OF STAY

11. Length of stay less than 2 hours — 100%
    Exception: Presence of complicating factors justifying longer stay.

STATUS FOLLOWING AMNIOCENTESIS

12. Patient discharged under the following conditions:
    a. Ambulatory — 100%
    b. Absence of any bleeding or leaking of amniotic fluid — 100%
    c. Patient instructed to engage in her normal activities — 100%
    Exception: Presence of bleeding or of leaking of amniotic fluid.

SAMPLE

Patients presenting themselves for pre-natal evaluation and care.

REVIEW

Criterion	Standard	Estimated Charge

FIRST PRE-NATAL VISIT

EVALUATION

1. History including the following: — 100%
   a. Previous pregnancies
   b. Previous deliveries and any problems encountered
   c. Abortions, miscarriages and perinatal deaths
   d. Number and health status of living children
   e. Any history of hypertension or pre-eclampsia
   f. Any history of diabetes
   g. Childhood illnesses
2. Medical problems of parents and siblings reported — 100%
3. Physical examination including pelvic examination and measurements — 100%
4. Weight recorded — 100%
5. Pulse, respiration and temperature recorded — 100%
6. Blood pressure in both arms, taken with patient lying down and sitting up — 100%
7. Chest x-ray — 100% — $ 70
   Exception: First visit before 5th month of pregnancy.
8. Pap smear test — 100%
9. Laboratory studies including — 100%
   a. CBC — 11
   b. Urinalysis — 11
   c. VDRL — 11
   d. Gc culture — 42
   e. Sickle cell test — 14
      Exception: Patient not black.
   f. Rubella titer — 30
      Exceptions: (1) First visit after 1st trimester; (2) record of rubella history or of rubella titer is documented
   g. Pregnancy test — 37
      Exception: Existence of pregnancy already confirmed.

MANAGEMENT AND INSTRUCTIONS

10. Patient given instructions on appropriate diet — 100%
11. Patient given instructions on weight control as indicated — 100%
12. Any anticipated obstetrical problems discussed with patient — 100%
13. Expected date of confinement specified in record — 100%
14. Return visit schedule specified in record and explained to patient — 100%

SUBSEQUENT PRE-NATAL VISITS

EVALUATION

1. The following data collected and recorded:
   a. Weight — 100%
   b. Blood pressure in both arms, with patient lying down and sitting up — 100%
   c. Urinalysis — 100% $ 11
   d. Height of uterus — 100%
   e. Fetal heart tones — 100%
2. Signs and symptoms reported, including headache, nausea, vomiting, blurring of vision or edema if present — 100%

MANAGEMENT AND OUTCOMES

3. Blood pressure below 140 systolic and 90 diastolic — 100%
4. Absence of proteinuria — 100%
5. Absence of edema — 100%
6. Absence of glycosuria — 100%
7. On admission for delivery, fetal heart rate from 120 to 160 — 100%

MANAGEMENT OF COMPLICATIONS OF PREGNANCY

8. Mild pre-eclampsia
   a. Bed rest — 100%
   b. Low sodium diet — 100%
   c. Diuretics — 100%
   d. Sedation as indicated — 100%
   e. Monitoring of blood pressure and of urine albumin — 100%   11
9. Threatened abortion
   a. Bed rest and observation until bleeding subsides — 100%
   b. Urinary chorionic gonadotropin (UCG) test — 100%   32
   c. Mild sedation — 100%

SUGGESTED SAMPLE

Patients who have experienced such post-anesthesis complications as headache, cardiovascular or respiratory problems.

REVIEW

Criterion	Standard	Estimated Charge
PRE-ANESTHESIA STUDY		
1. History including specific reference to	100%	
a. Any cardiac or pulmonary disease		
b. Use of any medications that pose an anesthetic risk, such as tricyclic antidepressants or monoamine oxydase inhibitors		
c. Smoking habits		
d. Alcohol intake		
e. Documentation of time of last food intake before surgery		
Exception: Non-emergency surgery with patient's food intake under hospital control before surgery and documented in record.		
2. Report of physical examination with specific reference to	100%	
a. Evaluation of respiratory function		
b. Cough test		
c. Any respiratory signs including hoarseness, stridor or vocal abnormalities		
3. Documentation in the record of		
a. CBC, urinalysis and admission panel	100%	$ 125
b. Hemoglobin greater than 10 gms %	100%	
c. Clotting and prothrombin times within normal limits	100%	85
d. Plasma protein level higher than 5.0 gms	100%	24
e. Blood sodium and potassium levels	100%	37
Exception: Need for emergency surgery before test results are obtainable.		
4. Chest x-ray within past 3 months with report in record	100%	70
5. EKG	100%	48
Exception: Patient under 40 years of age.		
SPECIAL PRE-ANESTHESIA PROCEDURES		
6. Documentation of anesthesiologist's preoperative evaluation of patient including		
a. Review of chart	100%	
b. Interview with patient to discuss his medical, anesthetic and drug history	100%	
Exception: Need for emergency surgery in a patient unable to cooperate in interview.		

c. "Match Test," breath holding and pulmonary function tests	100%
Exception: Absence of history of impaired pulmonary function.	
d. Presence of dentures, contact lenses or other prostheses noted	100%
e. Classification of patient with reference to criteria of American Society of Anesthesiologists	100%
f. Cardiac Risk Index	100%
Exception: Patient scheduled for cardiac surgery.	
g. Assessed anesthetic risk level	100%
h. General plan of anesthetic management outlined	100%

NURSING CARE, PRE-ANESTHETIC

7. Preoperative instructions by nursing personnel appropriate to anesthesia plan and nature of surgery   100%

Record Analyst: For patients scheduled for general anesthesia, such instructions usually include reference to coughing, deep breathing and reminders to turn in bed periodically following surgery.

Frequent turning in bed may be unnecessary or contraindicated in certain types of short-stay surgery, use of local anesthetic or certain operations on the head, eyes, face or neck. Review this matter with your Review Committee.

8. Restrictions on oral intake as ordered   100%
9. Nursing note on disposition of dentures, contact lenses, hearing aids or prostheses   100%
10. Preoperative medication documented   100%

MONITORING DURING SURGERY

11. Documentation of the following data:

a. Blood pressure, pulse and ventilation including volume and rate	100%
b. Agent used and method of induction	100%
c. All drugs used with dosage and time of administration	100%
d. Blood and urine loss during procedure	100%
e. All anesthesia procedures performed with time of performance	100%
f. All fluid replacement during anesthesia including	
(1) Blood or blood components and	100%
(2) Other fluids	100%

POST-ANESTHESIA CARE

12. Documentation of patient's status on admission to Recovery Room   100%
13. Monitoring and documentation of vital signs per routine plan in Recovery Room   100%
14. Evaluation of level of pain and of any need for pain medication   100%
15. Documentation of any medication or treatment administered, including

a. Indications	100%
b. Time of administration	100%
c. Dosage	100%

16. Documentation of discharge order from Recovery Room signed by physician   100%

17. Anesthetist's post-anesthesia evaluation note following transfer from Recovery Room   100%

PREVENTION AND MANAGEMENT OF COMPLICATIONS

18. Headache following spinal anesthesia
    a. Evaluation by physician   100%
    b. Bed rest maintained   100%
    c. Forced fluids administered orally or by intravenous route   100%
    d. Re-evaluation by physician within 12 hours of onset, documented in progress notes   100%

19. Cardiovascular complications
    a. Surveillance adequate to facilitate early identification of the presence of shock, the development of cardiac arrhythmias or of chest pain   100%
    b. Blood pressure, pulse and respiration checked every 5 minutes   100%
    c. EKG monitored   100%
    d. Oxygen administered to all patients with histories of cardio-respiratory diseases, following major abdominal surgery, and to patients in whom controlled ventilation was used during surgery   100% $ 26

20. Respiratory complications
    a. Patent airway established and maintained   100%
    b. Adequate ventilation maintained   100%
    c. Medical review of anesthetic agent employed, dosage and duration of anesthesia   100%
    d. As part of the anesthetic procedures, intubation of the trachea in the presence of any of the following: 100%   51
        (1) Any condition that might compromise patency of the airway
        (2) Need to prevent aspiration
        (3) Need to facilitate ventilation
        (4) Administration of a general anesthetic to a patient with a full stomach
        (5) Position of patient other than supine
        (6) Use of muscle relaxants
        (7) Specific operative procedures including
            (a) Head and neck surgery under general anesthesia
                Exception: Use of Ketamine.
            (b) Intrathoracic procedures including cardiac and vascular
            (c) Intraabdominal procedures under general anesthesia
    e. In patients who present technical difficulties in the establishment and maintenance of a patent airway, an indication in the record that special precautions such as the availability of a tracheotomy set or of a fiberoptic bronchoscope have been taken   100%   64

It is recommended that Central Services conduct a periodic concurrent review. The needed data can be gathered by means of direct observation of the manner in which each procedure in the preparation of materials for hospital distribution is performed. The purpose of this type of review is to compare actual behavior with the guidelines that are set forth in the Central Services Policy and Procedure Manual. For use in data collection, a checklist reflecting the criteria to be applied should be prepared and filled in as the observation and data gathering take place. In our experience, this approach has proven to be very practical, and it facilitates documentation of the review findings.

REVIEW

Criterion	Standard	Estimated Charge

PROCEDURES

PREPARATION OF MATERIALS FOR STERILIZATION

1. All caps, plugs, valves, stylettes and similar removable parts removed from devices — 100%
2. Syringes disassembled, with plungers outside barrels — 100%
3. Hollow bore needles and plastic or rubber tubing open at both ends and free of plugs — 100%
4. Jointed instruments in unlocked position — 100%
5. Instruments pre-cleaned with ultrasonic device until free of oil, grease, blood and organic debris — 100%
6. Catheters pre-cleaned in an alkaline detergent and rinsed with water just before packing — 100%
   Exception: Not applicable because reusable catheters not used.

Special Procedures for Gas (Ethylene Oxide) Sterilization

7. Materials towel-dry and free of water drops — 100%
8. Prepared materials kept in an area with relative humidity at 30% or higher — 100%
9. Use of hot oven to force dry materials — 0%
   Exception: Such procedure specifically approved by manufacturer of gas sterilizer.

WRAPPING AND PACKING MATERIALS FOR STERILIZATION

10. Articles in pack arranged in alternate layers to permit circulation of sterilizing agent — 100%
11. Lightest materials placed near center of pack — 100%
12. Gloves placed in billfold-style muslin wrapper — 100%
13. Packs not to exceed 12 inches by 20 inches in size — 100%
    Exception: If processed in steam sterilizer, sterilizing time increased to 40-60 minutes.

14. Materials wrapped in any of the following, according to process used: 100%

Steam Sterilization	Ethylene Oxide Sterilization
Double-thickness muslin	Double-thickness muslin
	Heat-sealed plastic or paper pouches if designed for use with gas sterilizer

15. Materials wrapped in aluminum foil, nylon film, canvas, Saran, Mylar, cellophane or polyamide, polyester and polyvinylidene films   0%

16. Labeling of any packs requiring aeration following ethylene oxide sterilization   100%

PRECAUTIONS TO ENSURE STERILIZATION

17. Live spore strip test performed daily on each sterilizer   100%

18. Live spore strip test on each gas sterilizer load containing implantable or intravascular material   100%

19. Packs containing biological control monitors placed as follows: 100%

Steam Sterilizer	Ethylene Oxide Sterilizer
In coolest part of chamber, usually near the front	At geometric center of load

20. An external chemical indicator placed on each pack   100%

21. Recording thermometer on each steam sterilizer   100%

LOADING THE STERILIZER

22. Packs placed on edges   100%

23. Each pack labeled to show load control number   100%

24. Load record filled in, showing for each load   100%

Steam Sterilizer	Ethylene Oxide Sterilizer
Date	Date
Load control number	Load control number
Sterilizer identification	Sterilizer identification
Temperature	Temperature
Cycle	Gas concentration
	Cycle

AERATION FOLLOWING ETHYLENE OXIDE STERILIZATION

25. All items composed of materials other than metal or glass segregated for aeration   100%
    a. At temperature 50C (122F)   12 hours
    b. At temperature 60C (140F)   8 hours
    c. At room temperature   7 days
    Exception: Not subjected to ethylene oxide sterilization.

STORAGE OF STERILIZED MATERIALS

26. All packages marked with date sterilized and expiration date   100%
    Exception: Commercially prepared packs not showing this information.

27. In the absence of an expiration date on a commercially prepared package, presence of a label statement to the effect that unless the package cover is compromised the material may be considered sterile 100%

28. All sterilized materials used within 4 weeks following sterilization 100%
  Exception: Outdated packs recalled and reprocessed.

29. Storage areas and storage shelves and bins free of evidence of insects and rodents 100%

30. Central Services area cleaned daily with same disinfectant-detergent as is used on nursing units 100%

DIETETIC SERVICE
FOR PATIENTS ON MODIFIED DIETS

SUGGESTED SAMPLE

Patients with any of the following diagnoses who have received modified diets as inpatients: Acute myocardial infarction, cirrhosis, congestive heart failure, diabetes mellitus, duodenal ulcer, fractured hip, gastric ulcer, hepatitis, hypertension, lower gastrointestinal disorders, malnutrition, obesity, renal disorders or other conditions requiring therapeutic diets.

REVIEW

Criterion	Standard	Estimated Charge
NUTRITIONAL AND OTHER STUDIES OF THE PATIENT		
1. Documentation of the patient's nutrition history and status including	100%	
a. Diagnosis		
b. Diet order		
c. Allergies and sensitivities if any		
d. Usual food intake for		
(1) Breakfast		
(2) Midday meal		
(3) Evening meal		
e. Usual place of		
(1) Breakfast		
(2) Midday meal		
(3) Evening meal		
f. Snacks usually eaten		
g. Patient's food preferences and aversions		
2. Review and documentation of social and environmental factors influencing nutrition, including	100%	
a. Patient's occupation		
b. Number of members in his household		
c. Patient's usual recreation and physical activity		
d. Estimate of his or his household's monthly food budget		
e. Number of meals per month usually eaten away from home		
3. Report of clinical data including	100%	
a. Height and actual weight		
b. Ideal weight		
c. Any recent change in weight, whether or not voluntary		
d. Any medications currently being taken that might affect nutritional status, needs or appetite		
MANAGEMENT		
4. Development of diet plan		
a. Diet patterns for calculated diets showing comparison of diet composition with patient's known nutritional needs	100%	$ 37

b. Composition of tube feeding as applicable 100%

    Exception: Tube feeding not required.

5. Dietician's consulting reports in record, covering quality of appetite, adequacy of intake and any recommended or ordered changes in diet 100%

    Exception: Length of stay less than 2 days.

6. Patient's nutrition intake and response to diet plan monitored, with changes made in diet as indicated 100%

7. Patient/significant other instructed in patient's nutrition requirements and appropriate food choices 100%

    Exception: Length of stay less than 2 days.

DISCHARGE STATUS

8. Patient/significant other able to verbalize instructions as to: 100%
   a. Patient's nutrition requirements
   b. Reasons for any dietary modifications or limitations
   c. Appropriate food choices

    Exception: Instructions on transfer form.

PATIENTS WITH UNCONTROLLED DIABETES

SAMPLE

Patients with newly diagnosed uncontrolled diabetes.

REVIEW

Criterion	Standard	Estimated Charge

NUTRITIONAL AND OTHER STUDIES OF THE PATIENT

1. Documentation of the patient's nutritional history and status including 100%
   a. Diagnosis
   b. Diet order
   c. Allergies and sensitivities if any
   d. Usual food intake for
     (1) Breakfast
     (2) Midday meal
     (3) Evening meal
   e. Usual place of
     (1) Breakfast
     (2) Midday meal
     (3) Evening meal
   f. Snacks usually eaten with particular attention to carbohydrate intake
   g. Patient's food preferences and aversions

2. Review and documentation of social and environmental factors influencing nutrition including 100%
   a. Patient's occupation
   b. Number of members in his household

    c. Patient's usual recreations and level of physical activity

    d. Estimate of his or his household's monthly food budget

    e. Number of meals per month usually eaten away from home

3. Report of clinical data including   100%

    a. Height and actual weight

    b. Ideal weight

    c. Any medications currently being taken that might affect nutritional status, needs or appetite

    d. Plasma glucose level

    e. Hemoglobin and hematocrit levels

    f. Cholesterol and triglyceride levels

    g. Urine glucose, acetone and 24 hour protein levels

    h. Blood urea nitrogen, creatinine and creatinine clearance levels

MANAGEMENT

4. Development of diet plan based on diet prescription, type and times of insulin injections as applicable and patient's food preferences and life style   100% $ 37

5. Patient's nutrition intake and responses to diet plan monitored, with changes made in diet as indicated, to ensure   100%

    a. Patient's acceptance of diet

    b. Absence of hypoglycemic or hyperglycemic reactions

6. Dietician's consulting reports in record, covering quality of appetite, adequacy of intake, degree of patient's understanding of diet plan and any recommended or ordered changes in diet   100%

    Exception: Length of stay less than 2 days.

7. Documentation of systematic instruction of patient/significant other with reference to reasons for modified diet and appropriate menu planning and food choices under various conditions   100%

    Exception: Length of stay less than 2 days.

DISCHARGE STATUS

8. Patient/significant other able to verbalize instructions and understanding as to: 100%

    a. Rationale for modified diet, menu planning and appropriate food choices

    b. Correct food choices from a food grouping system with reference to

        (1) Various settings such as home and restaurants

        (2) Portion measurements

        (3) Varying levels of activity

        (4) Insulin reaction

        (5) Appropriate substitutions for carbohydrates in individual meal plan as indicated

        (6) Selection of an appropriate concentrated source of carbohydrate to be carried on person at all times

    Exceptions: (a) Length of stay less than 2 days; (b) instructions on nursing home or other extended care facility transfer form.

DRUG ABUSE PROGRAM

For a model for the evaluation of Emergency Room treatment of patients suffering from drug overdose or an acute drug-related psychosis, please refer to the section on Emergency Services.

SUGGESTED SAMPLE

Patients discharged following inpatient treatment for opiate or barbiturate addiction as the primary problem and reason for admission.

REVIEW

Criterion	Standard	Estimated Charge
JUSTIFICATION FOR ADMISSION TO THE PROGRAM AS AN INPATIENT		
1. The presence of one of the following conditions:	100%	
a. The patient's request for inpatient treatment of his addiction to opiates or barbiturates		
b. Emergency Room referral of a patient suffering from an acute episode of opiate or barbiturate related psychosis		
c. Emergency Room referral of a patient diagnosed as suffering from an overdose of an opiate or a barbiturate		
DIAGNOSTIC STUDY		
2. In the chart within 24 hours after admission,		
a. History including obtainable history of present complaint	100%	
b. Physical examination report	100%	
c. Pulse, respiration and blood pressure on admission and on each shift since admission	100%	
d. Physician's admission note	100%	
e. Initial written orders	100%	
f. Laboratory test reports including		
(1) CBC, urinalysis and admission panel	100%	$ 125
(2) White blood count	100%	
3. In the chart within 3 days after admission,		
a. Treatment history	100%	
b. Psychiatric assessment and assessment of rehabilitation potential	100%	60
c. Psychosocial history and assessment	100%	
d. Treatment plan	100%	
MANAGEMENT		
4. Milieu therapy and structured control including the following provisions:		
a. Patient confined to unit during detoxification and evaluation phase of treatment	100%	
b. Hospital pajamas to be worn during detoxification and evaluation phase of treatment	100%	

244

c. No incoming or outgoing telephone calls until authorized in physician's written orders   100%

d. No mail or packages to be received   100%

e. No visitors   100%

5. Before commencement of drug withdrawal,

   a. Completion of general medical evaluation   100%   **$ 125** toxic screen

   b. Treatment and alleviation of any illnesses   100%

6. Detoxification measures

   a. Abrupt withdrawal   0%

   b. Rapid withdrawal staged over 7-10 days, including

     (1) Determination of appropriate stabilization dosage of drug   100%

     (2) In opiate addiction,

       (a) Methadone substitution course   100%

       (b) Gradual withdrawal of Methadone over 7-10 days, with reduction not to exceed 20% per day   100%

     (3) In barbiturate addiction,

       (a) Pentobarbitol substitution course   100%

       (b) Gradual withdrawal of pentobarbitol over 7-10 days   100%

   c. Chlorpromazine as needed for relief of tension during withdrawal   100%

   d. Mild bedtime sedation during withdrawal   100%

   Contraindicated: Heavy sedation.

   e. High calorie diet during withdrawal   100%

   f. Management of severe abstinence signs such as convulsions   **37** assay

     (1) Identification of any other drugs that the patient may have been taking in addition to known drug   100%

     (2) Adjustment of substitution agent and dosage to alleviate severe withdrawal symptoms   100%

   g. Continuing medical surveillance as reflected in physician's progress notes   100%

   h. Continuing nursing surveillance as reflected in nursing notes   100%

   i. Interim updating of evaluation and treatment plan   100%

LENGTH OF STAY

7. Length of stay

   a. Inpatient LOS 10-14 days   100%   3,680-5,152

   Exceptions: (1) Early departure against medical advice; (2) Transfer of patient deemed not treatable in this program.

   b. Participation in outpatient program, minimum of 6 months   100%

   Exceptions: (1) Early departure from inpatient program against medical advice; (2) transfer of patient deemed not treatable in this program

DISCHARGE STATUS

8. Patient discharged from inpatient unit under the following conditions:

   a. Patient abstinent from drugs other than those ordered since admission   100%

    b. Patient has verbalized intention to try to remain abstinent
        from addictive drugs   100%
    c. Any symptoms present on admission alleviated   100%
    d. Patient planning to participate in post-hospital outpatient
        program   100%

POST-HOSPITAL OUTPATIENT PROGRAM

9. Documentation present showing
    a. Patient participating in psychotherapy daily for at least
        6 months   100% $1,800[1]
    b. Patient on Methadone maintenance program as indicated   100%
        Exception: Addictive drug was other than an opiate.

Exception to Criterion Number 9:   Not applicable as a result of earlier departure from inpatient program against medical advice or to transfer of patient deemed not treatable in this program.

---

[1] 120 days at $15 per day.

SAMPLE

Emergency Room patients.

REVIEW

Criterion	Standard	Estimated Charge

EVALUATION

1. Documentation by the Emergency Room nurse of the following: — 100% — $ 70
   a. History with specific reference to
      (1) Circumstances of injury or present illness — 100%
      (2) Allergies and drug sensitivities — 100%
      (3) Tetanus immunization history — 100%
   b. Vital signs — 100%
2. Physical examination by physician with documentation of signs and symptoms — 100%

DIAGNOSTIC STUDY

3. Physician's orders for laboratory tests, x-ray or other studies as indicated by results of evaluation — 100%

   As review criteria, use the studies listed in the Emergency Room protocol for the specific clinical problem under study.

MANAGEMENT

4. If the patient is not to be admitted,

   Using the Emergency Room protocol for the specific clinical problem as a guide, set up review criteria including the appropriate

   Management plans and procedures including such measures as medications, gastric lavage, wound cleansing, suturing and dressing, splinting, observation in Emergency Room or other therapeutic procedures as may be indicated — 100%

5. If the patient is to be admitted,

   The review criteria would include such measures as

   Appropriate monitoring, management of any life-threatening problems and preparation for transport to inpatient area of hospital — 100%

   Exception: Patient not admitted.

DISPOSITION OF PATIENT NOT ADMITTED

6. Discharged patient is
   a. Referred to his own physician, to physician on call or to Outpatient Service as indicated — 100%
   b. Given written or printed instructions on follow-up care specific to the diagnosis, procedure or problem, with the patient's signature on the hospital's copy of the instructions — 100%

   Exception: Patient admitted.

SCHEDULE OF CARE

7. Documentation of the following information:
   a. Time of arrival at the Emergency Room   100%
   b. Time first seen by a nurse   100%
   c. Time first seen by a physician   100%
   d. Time of departure or transfer from Emergency Room   100%

EMERGENCY SERVICES
CHILD ABUSE, SUSPECTED

SUGGESTED SAMPLE

Children under the age of 16 whose presenting complaints are accidental injuries.

REVIEW

Criterion	Standard	Estimated Charge
EVALUATION		
1. Documentation by the Emergency Room nurse of the following:		
a. History with specific reference to		
(1) Circumstances of present injury	100%	$ 70
(2) Any previous injuries, including fractures, lacerations, burns and severe blows	100%	
(3) Any systemic disease	100%	
b. Vital signs	100%	
c. Observations with reference to		
(1) Evidence of recent trauma including bruises, lacerations, scald marks and other burn marks	100%	
(2) Evidence of old scars from lacerations, lash marks, scald and cigarette or other burns	100%	
(3) Differentiation between cigarette burns and evidence of impetigo, as applicable	100%	
(4) In a child under the age of 5, any evidence of failure to thrive	100%	
Exception: Child 5 years or over.		
2. Evaluation and physical examination by physician, including		
a. Physical examination with reference to present complaint	100%	
b. Orders for radiological and other studies as needed to establish diagnosis	100%	
c. Assessment of degree of correlation between history of injury and physical evidence	100%	
d. Diagnosis of accidental injury	100%	
Exception: Findings inconsistent with accidental basis of injury.		
e. Photographs taken of injury and surrounding area, for the Emergency Room record	100%	
Exception: Conclusion that the injury was of accidental origin.		

MANAGEMENT AND DISPOSITION

3. Treatment administered for present injury, as indicated — 100%

4. Patient discharged from Emergency Room and referred for follow-up visit to own physician or to Hospital's Outpatient Department, as appropriate — 100%

   Exception: Patient detained for further study on basis of suspicion of non-accidental origin of injury.

5. Discharged patient's parent given instructions for home care and follow-up visit to physician — 100%

   Exceptions: (a) Instructions on transfer form; (b) patient detained for further review of possibility of child abuse.

6. In presence of suspicion of child abuse, the following procedures followed and documented:

   a. Consultation obtained immediately with Social Service representative responsible for handling instances of suspected child abuse — 100%

   b. Detailed interview conducted by Social Service representative and physician with child and parent or significant other — 100%

   c. Evaluation of risk to child arrived at, and report on the situation and risk entered in chart — 100%

   d. In presence of confirmatory evidence developed on basis of physical findings and interview material, presumption of child abuse documented in record — 100%

7. Patient admitted as preventive measure — 100%

   Exception: Absence of presumption of child abuse.

8. After admission as an inpatient, further investigation of possibility of child abuse through bone surveys — 100% $ 214

9. After admission, parent(s) contacted for further discussion concerning Hospital's obligation to report the case to the relevant local government agency, such as a child protective service — 100%

10. Appropriate local government agency notified of instance of child abuse — 100%

11. Social Service follow-up documented in record, with report of return of child to family or foster home placement by agency — 100%

EMERGENCY SERVICES
DRUG ABUSE

SAMPLE

Patients treated in the Emergency Room for suspected or established drug abuse.

REVIEW

Criterion	Standard	Estimated Charge
PRELIMINARY EVALUATION		
1. Documentation by Emergency Room nurse of the following:		$ 70
a. History where obtainable with specific reference to type of drug involved and pattern of use	100%	
b. History of allergies and drug sensitivities if obtainable	100%	
c. Vital signs	100%	
2. Physician's examination with report on:		
a. Level of consciousness	100%	
b. Assessment of neurological, pulmonary and cardiovascular systems with report of any positive findings	100%	
DIAGNOSTIC STUDY		
3. Blood levels of the following:		
a. Salicylates	100%	20
b. Barbiturates	100%	57
c. Alcohol	100%	46
Exception: Agent is known and is not one of those listed.		
4. CBC	100%	11
5. Blood glucose	100%	9
Exception: Patient conscious.		
6. Urine sugar level	100%	4
Exception: Patient conscious.		
7. Portable x-ray of chest	0%	38
Exception (Indication): Presence of pulmonary or respiratory symptoms or complications.		
8. Portable skull x-ray in presence of persistent or progressive neurological deficit referable to possible head injury	100%	88
Exception: Patient not comatose.		
9. EKG	100%	44
Exception: Absence of cardiac irregularity.		
MANAGEMENT		
10. Gastric lavage	100%	20-29
Exception: Established use pattern was injection or sniffing.		
11. Intravenous administration of D5/W	100%	20

12. Narcan 1 ampule intravenous in rapid bolus   100%

    Exception: Patient conscious with dilated pupils.

13. Oxygen   100% $ 26

    Exception: Absence of respiratory distress.

14. In the presence of:

    a. Hyperexcitability or Phencyclidine (PCP) intoxication: Haldol 2-5 mg   100%

        Exception: Absence of hyperexcitability.

    b. Methadone intoxication: Narcan   100%

        Exception: Absence of Methadone intoxication.

    c. Convulsions: Valium 10 mg intravenous slowly   100%

15. Patient kept under observation for at least 3 hours in Emergency Room   100%

    Exceptions: (a) Early departure against medical advice or (b) patient admitted to hospital before expiration of 3 hours.

16. Patient monitored for evidence of complications   100%

DISPOSITION

17. Patient discharged and referred to own physician, to physician on call or to outpatient service   100%

18. Discharged patient referred to a psychiatrist, mental health center or a program for long range treatment   100%

Exception to Criteria Numbers 17 and 18: Patient's condition justifies admission.

SCHEDULE OF CARE

19. Documentation of the following information:

    a. Time of arrival at the Emergency Room   100%

    b. Time first seen by a nurse   100%

    c. Time first seen by a physician   100%

    d. Time of departure or transfer from Emergency Room   100%

SAMPLE

Patients treated in the Emergency Room for suspected or established frostbite.

REVIEW

Criterion	Standard	Estimated Charge
EVALUATION		
1. Documentation by the Emergency Room nurse of the following:		$ 70
a. History, if obtainable, with specific reference to		
(1) Exposure to cold or moisture, with estimate of temperature prevailing during exposure, and duration of exposure	100%	
(2) Effect of alcohol if applicable	100%	
(3) Any vascular or systemic disease	100%	
(4) Allergies and drug sensitivities	100%	
b. Vital signs	100%	
2. Physical examination with documentation of any of the following:	100%	
a. Flesh frozen hard and white or discolored		
b. Flesh frozen red and mottled		
c. Presence of edema		
d. Presence of anesthesia or paresthesia		
e. Presence of itching, burning dermatitis		
MANAGEMENT		
3. Rapid warming of the affected part in warm water between 100 F and 104 F, with constant monitoring of water temperature	100%	
4. Maintenance of maximal circulation by relief of vasospasm and prevention of thrombosis with vasodilating agents	100%	
5. Application of non-irritating bulky dressing	100%	7
6. Administration of analgesics for pain	100%	
7. Administration of tetanus toxoid booster or human immune globulin	100%	8
Exception: History of adequate immunization within past 5 years.		
8. Patient discharged and referred to own physician, to physician on call or to outpatient service	100%	
Exception: Presence of extensive or severe tissue damage justifying admission		
9. Patient given written or printed instructions for follow-up care, with patient's signature on hospital's copy of instructions	100%	
Exception: Patient admitted or transferred for care.		
SCHEDULE OF CARE		
10. Documentation of the following information:		
a. Time of arrival at the Emergency Room	100%	
b. Time first seen by a nurse	100%	
c. Time first seen by a physician	100%	
d. Time of departure or transfer from Emergency Room	100%	

SAMPLE

Patients treated in the Emergency Room for suspected or established heat prostration.

REVIEW

Criterion	Standard	Estimated Charge
EVALUATION		
1. Documentation by the Emergency Room nurse of the following:		
a. History, where obtainable, with specific reference to		$ 70
(1) Exposure to hot environment, with estimate of prevailing temperature and duration of exposure	100%	
(2) Onset of weakness, dizziness, vertigo, headache, nausea, blurring of vision, irritability and mild muscular cramps	100%	
(3) Allergies and drug sensitivities	100%	
b. Vital signs	100%	
2. Physical examination with documentation of any of the following:	100%	
a. Patient comatose or unconscious	100%	
b. Skin cold and damp with presence of profuse sweating (diaphoresis)	100%	
c. Presence of hypotension with evidence of peripheral vascular failure	100%	
MANAGEMENT		
3. Acute circulatory failure prevented	100%	
4. Patient placed in reclining position in cool environment with clothing loosened	100%	
5. Cool water taken orally	100%	
6. Isotonic saline solution 1,500 ml administered slowly	0%	20
Exception (Indication): Presence of profound collapse.		
7. Sodium bicarbonate administered	0%	
8. Patient monitored for evidence of complications	100%	
DISPOSITION		
9. Patient discharged and referred to own physician, to physician on call or to outpatient service	100%	
Exception: Presence of condition justifying admission.		
10. Discharged patient given written or printed instructions for follow-up care, with patient's signature on hospital's copy of instructions	100%	
Exception: Patient admitted or transferred for care.		
SCHEDULE OF CARE		
11. Documentation of the following information:		
a. Time of arrival at the Emergency Room	100%	
b. Time first seen by a nurse	100%	
c. Time first seen by a physician	100%	
d. Time of departure or transfer from Emergency Room	100%	

SAMPLE

Patients treated in the Emergency Room for lacerations, bites, puncture wounds, contusions and similar trauma.

REVIEW

Criterion	Standard	Estimated Charge
EVALUATION		
1. Documentation by the Emergency Room nurse of the following:		$ 70
a. History with specific reference to		
(1) Object causing injury and time of injury	100%	
(2) Allergies and drug sensitivities	100%	
(3) Tetanus immunization history	100%	
b. Vital signs	100%	
2. Physical examination with reference to at least the following:		
a. Presence, location and size of laceration, puncture wound, contusion or bite	100%	
b. Before any manipulation or injection of local anesthetic, a search for nerve or tendon injury	100%	
Exception: Site making such investigation irrelevant.		
MANAGEMENT		
3. Cleaning of wound	100%	
4. Wound closure with sutures as indicated	100%	26-74
Exceptions: Punctures, contusions and non-gaping bites.		
5. Dressing with immobilization as indicated	100%	10
6. Transfer to operating suite for surgical repair	0%	
Exceptions (Indications): (a) Presence of extensive or complicated wound; (b) presence of suspected or established nerve or tendon injury.		
7. Administration of tetanus toxoid or human immune globulin	100%	8
Exception: History of adequate immunization within past 12 months.		
8. Administration of prophylactic antibiotic with culture and sensitivity of wound ordered	0%	
Exception (Indication): Presence of contaminated wound.		
DISPOSITION		
9. Patient discharged and referred to own physician, to physician on call or to outpatient service	100%	
Exceptions: (a) Patient admitted for surgical repair; (b) patient's general condition justifies admission.		
10. Discharged patient given written or printed instructions on care of wound and need for follow-up visit to physician, with patient's signature on hospital's copy of instructions	100%	
Exception: Patient admitted.		

SCHEDULE OF CARE

11. Documentation of the following information:

    a. Time of arrival at the Emergency Room   100%
    b. Time first seen by a nurse   100%
    c. Time first seen by a physician   100%
    d. Time of departure or transfer from Emergency Room   100%

EMERGENCY SERVICES
SECOND DEGREE BURNS

SAMPLE

Patients treated in the Emergency Room for burns.

REVIEW

Criterion	Standard	Estimated Charge
EVALUATION		
1. Documentation by the Emergency Room nurse of the following:		$ 70
a. History, where obtainable, with specific reference to		
(1) Circumstances of injury and identification of burning agent	100%	
(2) Allergies and drug sensitivities	100%	
(3) Tetanus immunization history	100%	
b. Vital signs	100%	
2. Physical examination including		
a. Immediate estimation and documentation of degree and extent of burns, using the Rule of 9's	100%	
b. Evaluation of patient's cardiorespiratory status	100%	
Exception: Burn covering less than 5% of body surface area.		
c. Observation of patient for signs of incipient shock as manifested by restlessness, thirst, rise in pulse rate or fall in blood pressure upon being moved from recumbent to sitting position	100%	
Exception: Burn covering less than 5% of body surface area.		
MANAGEMENT		
3. Monitoring of cardiorespiratory status	0%	
Exceptions (Indications): (a) Presence of electrical burn; (b) any burn over more than 15% of the body surface area.		
4. Vein cannulated and blood drawn for hemoglobin, hematocrit, type and cross match for possible transfusion	0%	61
Exception (Indication): Presence of burn covering more than 15% of body surface area.		
5. Intravenous fluids started	0%	20
Exceptions (Indications): (a) Presence of burn involving more than 15% of body surface area; (b) evidence of shock.		
6. Tetanus immunization brought up to date	100%	8
7. Local cleansing and wound care	100%	
DISPOSITION		
8. Patient discharged and referred to own physician, to physician on call or to outpatient service	100%	
Exception: Patient's condition justifies admission or transfer for care.		

9. Patient given written or printed instructions for care, including follow-up visit to physician, with patient's signature on hospital's copy of instructions   100%

    Exception: Patient admitted or transferred for care.

SCHEDULE OF CARE

10. Documentation of the following information:
    a. Time of arrival at Emergency Room   100%
    b. Time first seen by a nurse   100%
    c. Time first seen by a physician   100%
    d. Time of departure or transfer from Emergency Room   100%

SPECIAL MANAGEMENT

Chemical Burns

1. Agent removed from skin immediately and neutralized by appropriate method   100%
2. Swab culture taken   100% $ 41

    Exception: Minor burn involving less than 15% of body surface area.

3. Burned areas cleaned with cold or warm water and a safe and effective antiseptic, then rinsed with sterile isotonic solution   100%
4. Dressing as indicated   100%   7

    Exception: Treatment plan requires open or exposure method.

Respiratory Tract Burns

Tracheostomy   100%   64

    Exception: Absence of laryngeal edema.

Thermal Burns

1. Swab culture taken   100%   41

    Exception: Minor burn covering less than 15% of body surface area.

2. Burned areas cleaned with cold or warm water and a safe and effective antiseptic, then rinsed with sterile isotonic solution   100%
3. Dressing as indicated   100%   7

    Exception: Treatment plan requires open or exposure method.

SAMPLE

Patients who were unconscious upon arrival in the Emergency Room.

REVIEW

Criterion	Standard	Estimated Charge
PRELIMINARY EVALUATION		
1. Documentation by Emergency Room nurse of the following:		$ 70
a. Airway patency ensured	100%	
b. Measures to combat shock if present	100%	
c. History where obtainable with reference to:		
(1) Circumstances of onset of unconsciousness	100%	
(2) Any recent illness	100%	
(3) Any chronic disease	100%	
d. Vital signs including rectal temperature and blood pressure in both arms	100%	
2. Physician's examination with reports on		
a. Search for injection marks	100%	
b. Skin color and search for lesions	100%	
c. Search for evidence of trauma to head or scalp	100%	
d. Eye examination including size of pupils, corneal reflex and funduscopy	100%	
e. Examination of ears, nose and throat with search for escaping blood or cerebrospinal fluid and for scarred or bitten tongue	100%	
f. Type and quality of respiration	100%	
g. Cardiovascular evaluation	100%	
h. Examination for abdominal rigidity or spasm	100%	
i. Neurological evaluation	100%	
DIAGNOSTIC STUDY		
3. Laboratory and other studies including		
a. Blood levels of		135
(1) Hemoglobin	100%	
(2) Sugar	100%	
(3) Blood urea nitrogen (BUN)	100%	
(4) Sodium	100%	
(5) Potassium	100%	
(6) Carbon dioxide	100%	
(7) Chloride	100%	
(8) Bromide	100%	

b. Urine analyzed for $ 35
  (1) Sugar 100%
  (2) Albumin 100%
  (3) Acetone 100%
c. Lumbar puncture 100% 106
 Exception: Diagnosis established by other means.
4. Portable skull x-ray in presence of neurological deficit referable to possible head injury 100% 88

MANAGEMENT

5. Maintenance of airway by means of intubation or tracheostomy 100%
6. Treatment of shock as indicated 100%
7. Administration of oxygen 100%
8. Catheterization 100%
9. Contraindicated
 a. Anything by mouth 0%
 b. Morphine 0%
10. Patient admitted 100%

PROBLEM

Floor culture showing colony count in excess of 20 per Rodac plate.

REVIEW

Criterion	Standard

ROUTINE CLEANING REVIEW OR CONCURRENT SURVEY

Where a second culture performed for the purpose of verification shows a colony count in excess of 20 per Rodac plate,

1. Review of cleaning equipment		
a. Mops washed every day of use		100%
b. Buckets cleaned with steel wool and disinfected each week		100%
c. Vacuum cleaner filters changed upon evidence of clogging, or once a month		100%
Exception: Fixed, non-removable filters.		
d. Cleaning compound for door tops, horizontal surfaces, walls and floors is one of the following:		100%
(1) Quaternary ammonium compound		
(2) Phenolic compound		
e. Silicon-based compounds		0%
2. Review of cleaning procedures		
a. Daily cleaning of floors		
(1) 1 mop used for no more than 4 patient rooms		100%
(2) Each cleaner using 4 mops per day		100%
(3) Dust removed before wet or damp cleaning		100%
(4) Floor wet or damp mopped		100%
Exceptions: Surgery areas, delivery rooms, nursery and carpeted areas.		
(5) Wet vacuum pick-up used in surgery area, delivery rooms and nursery		100%
(6) "Wet Floor" barrier signs placed as needed		100%
b. Daily cleaning of patient rooms		
(1) Door tops dusted and cleaned		100%
(2) Furniture and horizontal surfaces dusted and damp cleaned		100%
(3) Floors dusted and wet mopped		100%
(4) Walls spot cleaned, damp		100%
(5) Washroom or washbowl scrubbed		100%
c. Terminal cleaning		
(1) Following departure of non-isolation patients,		
(a) Linens sent to laundry in closed bags		100%

   (b) Furniture and horizontal surfaces in room, except
     ceiling, washed   100%

   (c) Dust removed from floor   100%

   (d) Floor wet mopped   100%

 (2) Following departure of isolation patients,

   (a) All articles requiring decontamination or sterilization
     sent to Central Services in color-coded closed bags 100%

   (b) Walls, furniture and all surfaces in room except
     ceiling washed to a height of 6 feet   100%

   (c) Washroom or washbowl scrubbed   100%

   (d) Dust removed from floor   100%

   (e) Floor wet mopped   100%

   (f) Housekeeping personnel in room to use the same
     infectious precautions as used by staff during patient's
     occupancy of room   100%

It is recommended that Infection Control personnel carry out periodic concurrent surveys of certain patient care procedures known to be associated with nosocomial infections. The needed data can be gathered by means of direct observation of the manner in which each of these procedures is performed. The purpose of this type of review is to compare actual behavior with the guidelines set forth in the relevant Policy and Procedure Manuals. For use in data collection, a checklist reflecting the criteria to be applied should be prepared and filled in as the observation and data gathering take place. This approach facilitates the documentation of the review findings.

REVIEW

Criterion	Standard

PROBLEMS AND PROCEDURES

Problem: Presence of hospital-acquired urinary tract infection in patients who have been catheterized in the hospital.

CATHETER CARE

Criterion	Standard
1. Perineum exposed and well lighted	100%
2. Closed system Foley catheter used, size 16 where feasible	100%
3. Aseptic technique employed at insertion	100%
a. Operator's hands carefully scrubbed	100%
b. Meatus and surrounding tissues thoroughly scrubbed with 3 successive separate cotton or rayon balls or gauze sponges, soaked in liquid soap or an appropriate disinfectant	100%
c. Tissues rinsed with sterile water	100%
d. Sterile drapes in place	100%
e. Sterile gloves worn after preparation of meatus	100%
f. Catheter lubricated with sterile lubricant from catheter kit	100%
Contraindicated: Use of unsterile lubricant taken from previously opened kit.	
g. Catheter discarded if it touches anything except the sterile gloves, sterile clamp, drapes or meatus	100%
4. Constant downward flow maintained, with collection bag hanging below bladder level at all times	100%
Contraindicated: Collection bag resting on floor below bed.	

Problem: Inflammation or phlebitis at site of intravenous infusion.

INTRAVENOUS THERAPY CARE

Criterion	Standard
1. Vein of forearm or dorsum of hand used	100%
2. Veins of foot or leg	0%
Exception: Absence of another usable site.	
3. Vein cut-down and insertion of cannula	0%
Exception: Usually accessible veins collapsed.	

4. Site of insertion cleaned with an antiseptic   100%
5. Veins distended by means of blood pressure cuff   100%
6. All air removed from tubing before injection   100%
7. Point of needle inserted through skin with bevel pointed upward   100%
8. Needle held parallel and lateral to vein, inserted at oblique angle   100%
9. Rate of flow 120 drops per minute or less   100%
10. Needle strapped in place   100%
11. Filter in place   100%
12. Needle site rotated every 3 days   100%

    Exceptions: (a) Appearance of redness at site earlier, necessitating earlier rotation; (b) catheter in subclavian vein for hyperalimentation.

13. In presence of edema, redness or phlebitis at site, site changed   100%
14. In presence of extravasation of fluid into skin,
    a. Needle removed   100%
    b. Area massaged gently to disperse fluid   100%

Problem: Apparently routine prophylactic administration of antibiotics brought to the attention of the Infection Control Committee.

Review of sample of patients who have received antibiotics prophylactically, with application of criteria reflecting indications for prophylactic use of antibiotics.

INDICATIONS

The presence of any of the following conditions: 100%

1. Scheduled bowel surgery
2. Scheduled pelvic surgery in the presence of pelvic inflammatory disease
3. Scheduled surgery in a patient with a history of rheumatic fever or congenital heart disease
4. Contaminated wound, usually as a result of an accident or an assault

PROBLEM

Culture of clean linens showing a colony count in excess of zero per Rodac plate.

REVIEW

Criterion	Standard

CONCURRENT SURVEY

Where a second culture performed for the purpose of verification shows a colony count in excess of 0 per Rodac plate,

1. Review of laundry environment
   a. Floors washed daily with disinfectant-detergent — 100%
   b. Air colony count not in excess of 30 per Rodac plate — 100%
   c. Air flow moving from "clean" to "dirty" processing areas — 100%
   d. Rooms for storing and sorting soiled linen in laundry separate from other laundry processing rooms — 100%
   e. Rooms for sorting soiled linen under negative pressure, ventilated with 10 room-volumes per hour directly to the outside with no recirculation of air — 100%
   f. All laundry equipment cleaned at end of each work day — 100%
   g. Soiled linen processing areas cleaned and disinfected daily — 100%
   h. Transport carts or "trucks" washed with disinfectant-detergent daily — 100%
   i. Transport carts or "trucks" color coded for clean and soiled — 100%
   j. Bags for linens color coded for clean, soiled and infectious — 100%
   k. Colony count of washing water not in excess of 30 per milliliter of water — 100%
2. Review of laundry procedures
   a. Linens removed from beds with a minimum of agitation — 100%
   b. Used linens bagged in closed color coded bags and removed daily from patient care areas — 100%
      Exception: Removed twice a day in closed color coded bags from nursery.
   c. Bagging of soiled linens performed at location of use — 100%
   d. Soiled linens kept separate from clean linens at all times
      (1) In transport — 100%
      (2) In storage at point of use — 100%
      (3) In laundry — 100%
   e. Washing water temperature above 160 F (71 C) for 25 minutes — 100%
   f. Disinfectant such as quaternary ammonium compound added to wash water — 100%
   g. Clean linens dried and ironed — 100%
   h. Clean linen wrapped for storage — 100%

i. The following items sterilized after washing: 100%
    (1) Linen for severely burned patients
    (2) Linen for the nursery
    (3) Gowns and caps for obstetrical and operating rooms

3. Where applicable, review of infection control maintained by
    contract laundry service
    a. All linen containers or "trucks" are washed and disinfected at
        the end of each working day   100%
    b. All linen containers or "trucks" are equipped with plastic liners   100%
    c. All linen containers or "trucks" are fully enclosed, constructed
        of metal and equipped with snug lids, covers or doors   100%
    d. The hospital's cultures of the laundry service's transport
        equipment reveal colony counts not in excess of 30   100%
        Exception: Cultures not taken.
    e. Air flow and ventilation on the premises of the contract
        laundry service meet the standards that would apply in a
        hospital laundry   100%

ENVIRONMENTAL SERVICES
SECURITY SERVICE

Concurrent survey, either on a regular periodic basis or in response to the emergence of a problem such as an outbreak of pilferage or of vandalism.

SURVEY

Criterion	Standard
1. Access to building(s) and to restricted areas	
a. Entrances that are not under the observation of hospital personnel are kept locked from the outside	100%
b. Doors locked from the outside are equipped with panic bars on the inside	100%
c. Doors locked from the outside and not intended for egress under normal circumstances are equipped with alarm signals as well as signs indicating that the alarm will sound if the door is opened from the inside	100%
d. The following areas are effectively restricted to authorized personnel by means of locks, badge requirements or similar methods of control	
(1) Business offices	100%
(2) Central Services	100%
(3) Kitchens	100%
(4) Laboratories	100%
(5) Medical Record Department	100%
(6) Morgue	100%
(7) Nursery	100%
(8) Nursing stations	100%
(9) Pharmacy	100%
e. After the close of evening visiting hours, anyone not possessing a key to an entrance must be admitted by security personnel	100%
2. Visitors and visiting privileges	
a. No visitors are on patient care floors except during the regular posted visiting hours	100%
Exception: Special provisions applying to the ICU and CCU.	
b. All visitors pass a security observation post on the way to the patient care areas	100%
c. No visitor is permitted to go to a patient care floor or area without a pass issued by security personnel	100%
d. Visitors are limited to two per patient at a time	100%
e. Children under the age of 16 are not permitted in patient care areas as visitors	100%

3. Personnel
   a. No employee is hired before his or her references have been thoroughly investigated, as documented in his or her personnel file — 100%
   b. All hospital personnel wear identification badges displaying their photographs while on hospital premises — 100%
   c. The hospital carries business risk insurance to protect it from loss related to embezzlement or misappropriation of funds — 100%
4. Precautionary activities
   a. Security personnel conduct periodic orientation sessions on security precautions for hospital employees, as documented in security service records — 100%
   b. Nursing personnel advise patients to keep such property as handbags and wallets concealed in a cabinet, preferably locked, near the bed — 100%
   c. Nursing personnel advise patients not to keep jewelry or large amounts of currency in the hospital — 100%
   d. Controlled drugs are stored in locked cabinets that contain nothing else — 100%
5. Parking lots
   a. The hospital's parking lots are well lighted — 100%
   b. Security personnel are available to provide escort service to the parking lots after dusk and before daylight — 100%
6. Incident reports
   a. Records show that incident reports filed during the past 6 months have received prompt responses — 100%
   b. A statistical analysis of incident reports relating to security, identifying the locations and times of day of such incidents, is prepared each month and reviewed by Administration and those responsible for risk control — 100%
   c. No injuries have been sustained on hospital premises or in the hospital parking lot by hospital personnel during the past 12 months — 100%
   d. No injuries have been sustained on hospital premises or in the hospital parking lot by patients during the past 12 months — 100%
   e. No injuries have been sustained on hospital premises or in the hospital parking lot by visitors during the past 12 months — 100%
7. External disaster drills

   Participation of the Security Service in the hospital's last 2 external disaster drills is documented — 100%

SAMPLES

Patients who have received nuclear medicine services.

REVIEW

Criterion	Standard	Estimated Charge
INDICATIONS		
Bone Scan		
Need for at least one of the following:	100%	$ 380
1. Early diagnosis of osteomyelitis		
2. Staging of tumors known to metastasize		
3. Evaluation of (a) an elevated alkaline phosphatase level; (b) pain of skeletal origin; or (c) bone response to therapeutic measures		
4. Differentiation between monostotic and polycystotic primary bone tumors		
Brain Scan, Initial and Delayed		
The presence of at least one of the following elements:	100%	329
1. Need for evaluation of (a) unexplained neurological symptoms and signs; (b) results of cerebral vascular accident; (c) possible subdural hematoma; (d) clinical symptoms and signs of cerebral infectious disease; (e) suspected metastases in the presence of a primary tumor; (f) head trauma or (g) unexplained headache and vertigo		
2. Need for follow-up evaluation after neurosurgery, radiotherapy or chemotherapy for a brain lesion		
Cerebral Blood Flow Scan		
Need for evaluation in the presence of (a) cerebral vascular accident; (b) unexplained neurological symptoms and signs; (c) cardiovascular accident; (d) inflammatory disease or (e) malignancy	100%	293
Circulatory System Studies		
Radionuclide Aortogram		
Need for evaluation of symptoms and signs of abdominal or thoracic aneurysm	100%	
Radionuclide Phlebogram		
The presence of (a) suspected circulatory problems in lower extremities; or (b) symptoms and signs of thrombophlebitis	100%	

Liver, Pancreas and Spleen Studies

Liver Scan (Sulfur Colloid)

Need for at least one of the following: 100%

1. Differential diagnosis in the presence of hepatomegaly and abdominal masses
2. Evaluation of patients with diffuse liver diseases such as cirrhosis and hepatitis
3. Preoperative evaluation for liver metastases in patients with established malignancies
4. Localization of hepatic lesions for needle biopsy or of abscesses for drainage
5. Evaluation of (a) liver position and shape in patients with elevated or abnormally shaped right diaphragm on chest films; (b) ascites of unknown origin; (c) jaundice; (d) suspected hepatic abscess; or (e) suspected liver rupture or hematoma
6. Follow-up evaluation of patients with liver malignancies undergoing chemotherapy, radiotherapy or partial resection, and for follow-up of the course of antibiotic or drainage therapy for hepatic abscess

Rose Bengal Liver Scan

Need for evaluation or differential diagnosis concerning (a) biliary patency; (b) etiology of infantile jaundice; (c) constitutional hyperbilirubinemia; or (d) a space-occupying lesion in the area of the porta hepatis   100% $ 315

Pancreas Scan

Need for evaluation of (a) symptoms and signs suggestive of pancreatic carcinoma; (b) acute and chronic pancreatitis; (c) obstructive jaundice; or (d) evidence of metastatic liver disease without evidence of a primary source   100%   526

Spleen Scan

Need to: 100%   315

a. Depict size, shape and position of spleen
b. Differentiate among left upper quadrant masses
c. Visualize infiltration by such diseases as Hodgkin's Disease, reticulum cell sarcoma or metastatic melanoma or
d. Evaluate the spleen for possible damage resulting from trauma

Lung Studies

Perfusion Lung Scan

Need for evaluation in the presence of (a) possible pulmonary embolization or (b) perfusion changes   100%   268

Ventilation Lung Scan

Need to: 100%   268

a. Evaluate patients with suspected disease of the tracheo-bronchial tree or
b. Differentiate between perfusion defects arising from disease of the bronchial tree and from pulmonary emboli

Myocardial Scan

The presence of at least one of the following: 100% $ 447

1. Need for (a) screening procedure prior to cardiac catheterization or contrast angiography; (b) serial scans as a guide to the effectiveness of therapy; (c) serial scans as a guide to the progression of a disease process; or (d) preoperative and postoperative scans to document the effects of a specific surgical procedure
2. Patient who is (a) sensitive to radiocontrast medium, or (b) too ill to undergo cardiac catheterization or contrast angiography

Renal Scan

The presence of at least one of the following: 100%   409

1. Need for differential diagnosis between (a) renal enlargement and abdominal masses; (b) primary renal tumor and renal cyst; or (c) solitary cysts and multicystic disease
2. Need for evaluation of the renal parenchyma (a) when kidney is visualized by means of intravenous pyelography; (b) in presence of BUN above 30 mg/100 ml; or (c) in a patient allergic to iodine-containing substances
3. Need for evaluation of (a) suspected unilateral renal hypertension; (b) obstructive uropathy; (c) possible renal infarct resulting from thrombosis or embolic phenomena; (d) renal transplant; or (e) suspected renal trauma
4. Need to rule out ureteral involvement in patient with pelvic carcinoma
5. Need for follow-up study in parenchymal renal disease

Hippuran Study
Need to estimate parenchymal function and/or to establish ureteral patency

Tumor Scan (Gallium)

The presence of at least one of the following: 100%   513

1. Need for differential diagnosis of a lesion suspected of malignancy
2. Search for a malignant focus associated with atelectasis and/or pleural effusion in entire hemothorax
3. Need to set up irradiation field in radiotherapy of soft tissue and bone, especially in mediastinal and pelvic areas
4. Need to evaluate response to nonsurgical treatment

DOCUMENTATION OF NUCLEAR MEDICINE SERVICES

Each report is to contain the following items of information: 100%

1. Identity of the patient
2. Consent form where required by hospital policy
3. Identity of the attending physician
4. Identity of the individual administering the radionuclide
5. The date of the study
6. An interpretation of the results signed by a physician
7. The identity of the radionuclide used
8. The amount of the radionuclide used
9. The route of administration

SAMPLES

Departmental records and medical records of patients for whom pathology or clinical laboratory services have been ordered.

REVIEW

Criterion	Standard	Estimated Charge
INDICATIONS FOR PATHOLOGY SERVICES		
1. The need for one or more of the following services, documented in the medical record:	100%	
a. Routine or special laboratory tests		
b. Cytopathologic evaluation		
c. Tissue examination and diagnosis		
d. Transfusion of blood or blood components		
e. Necropsy		
DOCUMENTATION AND TRANSMISSION		
2. All completed laboratory request forms include	100%	
a. Patient's name		
b. Patient's room number		
Exception: Outpatient.		
c. Medical record number		
d. Name of requesting practitioner		
e. Identification of specimen submitted		
f. Test(s) requested		
g. Where tissue specimen is submitted, presumptive diagnosis		
Exception: Absence of tissue specimen.		
h. Date and time specimen was obtained from patient		
Exception: Absence of specimen.		
i. Date and time specimen was received by laboratory		
Exception: Absence of specimen.		
j. Any special handling requirements		
3. Completed laboratory report forms provide the following data:	100%	
a. Patient identification		
b. Test results		
c. Comparative normal values or ranges		
d. As appropriate, sequential and related analyses		
4. Descriptive reports are provided for all tissue specimens submitted	100%	
Exception: Absence of tissue specimen.		
5. All tests are begun on the date desired by the requesting practitioner	100%	
6. Completed laboratory report forms are in the patient's chart at the nursing station within 12 hours of the recording of the test results	100%	

EQUIPMENT AND PROCEDURES

7. Laboratory files contain a complete and current description of each test procedure performed, with such material immediately available to the appropriate laboratory analyst   100%

8. The laboratory has a written quality control system for each laboratory section including routine and/or daily performance and documentation of the following: 100%
    a. Validation of test methodologies
    b. Evaluation of reagents and volumetric equipment
    c. Surveillance of results
    d. Remedial action for all detected deviations from norms
    e. Maintenance, inspection and testing of all equipment and instruments
    f. Monitoring of all temperature control equipment
    g. Evaluation of automated and non-automated analytical equipment and procedures with suitable reference samples
    h. Proper labeling, preparation, dispensing, testing and storage of all solid and liquid reagents and solutions

9. The laboratory maintains records on the calibration of laboratory equipment   100%

10. The laboratory keeps a written preventive maintenance schedule for all laboratory equipment   100%

ANATOMIC PATHOLOGY

11. All specimens received are properly labeled, packaged and identified   100%
12. For all specimens the following information is shown: 100%
    a. Description including identification of tissue and source
    b. Preoperative diagnosis
    c. Postoperative diagnosis

13. A pathologist prepares a report including microscopic analysis and description of findings on all specimens submitted   100%

    Exceptions: (a) Absence of specimen or (b) inclusion of specimen on list of tissues exempt from microscopic analysis requirement.

14. A control mechanism has been established to test stain reactivity with known positive and negative slides   100%

BLOOD TRANSFUSION SERVICE

15. In all refrigerators in which blood is stored, temperature is monitored and maintained at between 1C and 6C   100%
16. Stored blood is inspected daily for contamination or hemolysis   100%
17. The receipt and disposition of all blood products provided to patients is documented   100%
18. Donor blood samples are retained for a time sufficient to assess any transfusion reactions   100%

REVIEWS

Criterion	Standard

MONTHLY SURVEY OF ALL MEDICAL CENTERS AND DRUG STORAGE AREAS IN NURSING STATIONS, EMERGENCY ROOM AND AMBULATORY CARE/OUTPATIENT DEPARTMENT

At least once each month, a survey is conducted by the Pharmacist on the basis of the following criteria:

1. In storage areas, disinfectants, antiseptics and drugs for external use are kept separate from injectible medications and drugs intended for internal use — 100%
2. Vaccines, serums and other biological therapeutic materials are kept refrigerated at 30 F (−1 C) — 100%
3. No outdated, discontinued or recalled drugs are present in drug storage or medication centers — 100%
4. Schedule I, II, III and IV drugs are stored separately from other drugs in locked cabinets that contain nothing else — 100%
5. Any floor stock drugs that are stored at medication centers on floors are listed — 100%

   Exception: Floor stocks not used.
6. Charts of patients receiving antibiotics contain appropriate stop orders and evidence that such stop orders have been followed — 100%
7. All drugs on hand have been approved by the Hospital's Pharmacy and Therapeutics Committee — 100%
8. Each nursing station has a copy of the Hospital Formulary or drug list — 100%

CONCURRENT REVIEW OF PROCEDURES

Concurrent review is conducted on the basis of the following criteria:

1. Before filling an order for a drug, a pharmacist always reviews the original order or a direct copy of it — 100%
2. Drug profiles of both inpatients and outpatients to whom drugs are dispensed are maintained — 100%
3. Before sending a drug cart to a floor, a pharmacist routinely compares each medication with the drug order(s) and the patient's drug profile — 100%
4. Where laminar airflow hoods are used, the equipment is cleaned on each shift — 100%

CONCURRENT REVIEW OF AMBULATORY CARE OR OUTPATIENT PHARMACY SERVICES

Concurrent review is conducted on the basis of the following criteria:

1. Drug profiles are maintained for all patients to whom drugs are dispensed on the order of Medical Staff members — 100%

2. Daily inspection is conducted of drug carts in Emergency Room and Outpatient Department drug storage areas to ensure the adequacy and freshness of supplies — 100%

PERIODIC RETROSPECTIVE REVIEW OF STATUS

1. Absence of adverse medication reactions as found in study of patient's charts — 100%
2. Documented participation of the Pharmacy Service in the Hospital's Quality Assurance program through studies of
   a. Pharmacy operations including timeliness in filling orders — 100%
   b. Utilization and effectiveness of antibiotics with reference to Medical Staff criteria — 100%
   c. Procedures and documentation employed in the dispensing of drugs to outpatients — 100%

PHYSICAL THERAPY SERVICE
INPATIENT AND OUTPATIENT

SAMPLES

Patients who have received physical therapy services.

REVIEW

Criterion	Standard	Estimated Charge
DOCUMENTATION OF SERVICES		
1. Physician's order for physical therapy services specifying:	100%	
a. Diagnosis and reason for treatment order referring to desired outcome		
b. Type of treatment requested		
c. Frequency of treatment		
d. Duration of treatment		
2. Physical therapist's evaluation and treatment plan including reference to desired outcome in record	100%	$ 20
3. Physical therapist's treatment report(s) in record, documenting:	100%	
a. Type of treatment administered		
b. Dates and times of treatments		
c. Specifications of the prescription		
d. Effects of therapy including any adverse reactions		
e. Patient teaching carried out as applicable		
4. Attending physician's documentation in the progress notes of the timely clinical evaluation of the results of therapy	100%	
MODALITIES		
Electrotherapy		
DIATHERMY		
1. Presence of indications including any of the following conditions:	100%	28
a. Arthritis		
b. Chronic muscle spasm		
c. Dysmenorrhea		
d. Myositis		
e. Need for Bennett or reflex heating procedure in Buerger's Disease		
f. Rib injuries		
2. Contraindicated applications including any of the following:	0%	
a. Over skin irritations, rashes or open sores		
b. Over the brain		
c. Over the heart or a pacemaker		

d. Over burned tissues
e. Over metal implants
f. Over tumors
g. During menstruation or pregnancy
h. In the presence of impaired sensation

3. Treatment 30 minutes at 150 milli-amperes   100%
   Exception: Reduced intensity in presence of diabetes.

4. Prevention and management of complications including
   Burning or tissue damage in diabetic patient

   Management

   (1) Diathermy turned off stat   100%
   (2) Patient monitored closely during treatment to prevent
       burning   100%
   (3) Reduced intensity in presence of diabetes   100%
       Exception: Absence of diabetes.

5. Result of treatment: Relaxation of muscle spasm and relief of pain   100%

LUMINOUS INFRA-RED

1. Presence of indications including any of the following conditions: 100% $ 25
   a. Need to promote circulation
   b. For relief of pain and stiffness
   c. To aid in drying open sores and to promote healing of leg
      ulcers, decubiti and skin graft donor sites
   d. Hand injuries
   e. Low back pain syndrome
   f. Cervical whiplash injury
   g. Bursitis
   h. Sprains and strains
   i. Bell's palsy
   j. Tic douloureux
   k. Presence of pain such that the patient cannot tolerate any
      direct contact, e.g., the weight of hot packs upon an inflamed
      bursa

2. Contraindicated applications including either of the following: 0%
   a. Over the eyes
   b. Over desensitized areas such as skin graft receiver sites

3. Treatment parameters
   a. Lamp at a distance of 13 to 14 inches from area being treated   100%
   b. Duration 15 to 20 minutes   100%
   c. Penetration from 1 to 1.5 centimeters   100%
   d. Frequency of 2 or 3 times per day   100%

4. Prevention and management of complications including
   Burning or tissue damage in diabetic patients

   Preventive Management

         Monitoring of patient's reaction   100%

5. Result of treatment: Improvement in local circulation and relief
   of pain   100%

MICRO-WAVE DIATHERMY

1. Presence of indications including any of the following conditions: 100% $ 25
   a. Arthritis, tendonitis or tenosynovitis
   b. Bursitis, fibrositis or myositis
   c. Pelvic inflammatory disease
   d. Sprains and strains
2. Contraindicated applications including any of the following: 0%
   a. Presence of malignancies, edema, effusions, tuberculosis, thrombophlebitis or osteomyelitis
   b. Over the brain
   c. Over the heart
   d. Over pacemakers, metal implants, desensitized areas or dressings
   e. Over the pelvic area during menstruation or pregnancy
3. Precaution to be taken: Eyes protected during teatment   100%
4. Results of treatment
   As applicable,   100%
   a. Improvement in circulation
   b. Relief of pain and stiffness
   c. Drying action on decubiti or leg ulcers

TRANSCUTANEOUS NERVE STIMULATION

1. Presence of severe pain associated with any of the following: 100%   34
   a. Cancer
   b. Causalgia-like pain
   c. Chronic cervical syndrome or torticollis
   d. Chronic low back syndrome
   e. Chronic headache or migraine
   f. Post-herpetic neuralgia
   g. Postoperative pain or complications such as atelectasis or paralytic ileus
   h. Spinal cord injuries
   i. Radiculitis
   j. Bursitis or tennis elbow
   k. Stump and phantom limb pain
2. Contraindicated applications including the presence of any of the following: 0%
   a. Cardiac problem of any kind
   b. Pacemaker
   c. Pain of apparent psychogenic origin
   d. Pregnancy
3. Duration of treatment: 45 to 60 minutes   100%
4. Side effects

   Skin irritation and rash developing beneath or around the electrode in prolonged applications

   Management

   Treatment discontinued until dermatitis clears   100%

5. Result of treatment
   Blocking of perception of pain   100%

ULTRA SOUND THERAPY

1. Presence of indications including any of the following conditions: 100% $ 25
   a. Arthritis
   b. Bursitis, muscle spasm with pain or radiculitis
   c. Epicondylitis
   d. Fibrositis
   e. Frozen shoulder, contractures or joint and muscle stiffness
   f. Plantar warts
   g. Tight scars
2. Contraindicated applications including any of the following: 0%
   a. Over the abdomen or pelvis during pregnancy or menstruation
      or in the presence of an IUD
   b. Directly over the spine
   c. Over metal implants
   d. Over tumors
   e. In patients under 21 years of age, over the joints of the long
      bones
3. Treatment parameters
   a. Average treatment intensity of 1.5 watts per square centimeter   100%
   b. Duration 5 to 8 minutes
4. Prevention and management of complications including pain during
   treatment reflecting excessively high intensity

   Preventive Management
   a. Monitoring of patient's reactions and warning patient to
      verbalize discomfort   100%
   b. Reduction of intensity in presence of discomfort   100%
5. Results of treatment: Relief of pain and stiffness   100%

Heat Therapy and Massage

MASSAGE

1. Presence of indications including any of the following conditions: 100%   25
   a. Acute inflammatory muscle conditions
   b. Acute sciatic and back problems
   c. Fibrositic conditions including bursitis, myositis, tendonitis
      and sprains
   d. Muscle spasm
   e. Need to assist in sedation of extremely tense patient
   f. Torticollis, whiplash injury or stiff neck
2. Contraindicated applications including any of the following: 0%
   a. Acute skin infections, rashes, burns, acne or other skin problems
   b. Over pelvis during menstruation or pregnancy
   c. Over tumors or masses
   d. Presence of thrombophlebitis

e. Presence of varicose veins

f. Presence of an open wound

3. Treatment

   a. Movements to include effleurage, petrissage, kneading, tapotement and/or nerve strokes as indicated   100%

   b. Care of patient to include use of appropriate lubrication, proper positioning, privacy and draping   100%

4. Prevention and management of discomfort due to excessively deep kneading

   Preventive Management

   Monitoring of patient's reactions and facial expression for evidence of pain   100%

5. Results of treatment

   a. Relaxation of tension   100%

   b. Relaxation of muscle spasm and relief of pain   100%

ICE MASSAGE

1. Presence of indications including any of the following conditions: 100% $ 25

   a. Acute rheumatoid arthritis

   b. Post-arthrotomy

   c. Post-menisectomy

   d. Frozen shoulder

   e. Stiff joint with limited range

2. Contraindicated applications including   0%

   History of frostbite or of hypersensitivity to cold

3. Caution to be used in presence of diminished skin sensation   100%

4. Duration of treatment not to exceed 5 minutes   100%

5. Results of treatment

   As applicable,

   a. Reduction of hemorrhage, edema and inflammation   100%

   b. Reduction of pain and muscle spasm   100%

   c. Temporary reduction in spasticity   100%

   d. Neuromuscular facilitation   100%

PARAFFIN GLOVE

1. Presence of indications including any of the following conditions: 100%   25

   a. Need for postoperative care following hand surgery

   b. Presence of Dupuytren's contracture

   c. Arthritis of the hands

   d. Hand injuries

2. Contraindicated applications including any of the following: 0%

   a. Presence of desensitized area

   b. Presence of open sores

   c. Presence of skin infection

   d. Presence of new skin or recently formed scar tissue

3. Treatment parameters
    a. Paraffin temperature between 130 F and 136 F   100%
    b. Immersions: 12 to 16   100%
    c. Glove left on for from 15 to 20 minutes   100%
4. Prevention of burn through touching bottom of paraffin bath

    Preventive Management

    Patient warned of hazard and monitored during treatment   100%
5. Results of treatment
    a. Improvement in local circulation with hyperemia   100%
    b. Relief of pain and joint stiffness   100%
    c. Softening of skin and scar tissue as applicable   100%
    d. Facilitation of passive stretching of the hand   100%

Ultraviolet (Cold Quartz) Therapy

ULTRAVIOLET TREATMENT

1. Presence of indications including any of the following: 100% $ 25
    a. To promote healing and control infection in open sores and
       lesions such as decubiti and leg ulcers
    b. For management of such skin infections as herpes zoster, boils,
       carbuncles, furuncles, folliculitis, fungus infections and
       athlete's foot
    c. For management of psoriasis
2. Contraindicated applications including any of the following: 0%
    a. Over the eyes
    b. Over skin grafts
    c. Over recently formed scar tissue
3. Treatment parameters
    a. Lamp placed from 6 to 12 inches from site to be treated   100%
    b. In facial applications, eyes covered with moistened pads   100%
    c. First exposure 15 seconds, then increased 5 seconds
       O.D. to maximum exposure of 3 minutes   100%
    d. Frequency: one time per day   100%
4. Prevention of complications including burning and ocular damage
   due to exposure to ultraviolet

    Preventive Management

    a. Monitoring of patient   100%
    b. Warning patient to keep eyes closed during treatment, and use
       of moistened eye pads   100%
5. Result of treatment: Drying and healing of lesions   100%

Hydrotherapy

HUBBARD TANK

1. Presence of indications including any of the following conditions: 100%   49
    a. Arthritis
    b. Athletic injuries
    c. Burns
    d. Disc syndrome

281

    e. Hip fracture
    f.   Multiple contusions
    g. Multiple sclerosis
    h. Shoulder injuries

2. Contraindicated applications including the presence of any of the following conditions: 0%
    a. Cardiac disease or cerebral vascular accident
    b. Epilepsy
    c. Head injuries
    d. Hypertension
    e. Infection
    f.   Senility

3. Treatment 15 to 20 minutes at temperature from 98 F to 100 F   100%

4. Management of complications
    a. Falls

      Preventive Management
      Plastic shoes on patient   100%
    b. Chilling of patient

      Preventive Management
      Patient wrapped in blanket after drying   100%
    c. Drowning

      Preventive Management
      Close monitoring of patient   100%
    d. Electrocution

      Preventive Management
      Turbines locked before being turned on   100%
    e. Infections

      Preventive Management
      Preparation with prescribed aseptic technique   100%

5. Results of treatment
As indicated by reason for treatment,
    a. Relaxation of muscle spasm and relief of pain   100%
    b. Debridement   100%

STEAM CABINET

1. Presence of indications including any of the following conditions: 100% $ 49
    a. Acute myositis
    b. Frozen shoulder
    c. Low back injuries
    d. Multiple contusions
    e. Musculo-ligamentous injuries
    f.   Whiplash injury

2. Contraindicated applications including presence of any of the following: 0%
    a. Diabetes
    b. Epilepsy

    c. Head injury

    d. Hypertension or cardiac disease

    e. Infection

    f. Senility

3. Treatment parameters

    a. Steam at ½ pound pressure, temperature to reach 118 F to 120 F   100%

    b. Following steam, shower with water at body temperature for
       2 to 3 minutes   100%

4. Management of complications

    a. Falls

       Preventive Management

       Non-skid shoes on patient   100%

    b. Chills following teatment

       Preventive Management

       Patient supplied with bath blanket   100%

    c. Burns

       Preventive Management

       Patient observed closely and water temperature tested by
       therapist before shower   100%

    d. Overheating

       Preventive Management

       Ice towel applied to patient's face and forehead and changed
       frequently   100%

    e. Infections

       Preventive Management

       Steam boards scrubbed with disinfecting solution and rinsed
       with cold water after each patient   100%

5. Result of treatment relaxation of muscle spasm and relief of pain   100%

WHIRLPOOL TREATMENT

1. Presence of indications including any of the following: 100% $29-49

    a. Contusions

    b. Need for debridement of local burns

    c. Need for cleansing following removal of cast

    d. Strains and sprains

2. Contraindicated applications including presence of any of the
   following: 0%

    a. Hypertension or cardiac disease

    b. Head injuries

    c. Senility

3. Treatment parameters

    a. Treatment 10 to 15 minutes with water temperature from 90 F
       to 110 F   100%

    b. Betadine, pHisoHex or other agents added to water as directed   100%

4. Management of complications
   a. Infections

   Preventive Management
   (1) Tank scrubbed after each patient   100%
   (2) Use of aseptic technique   100%
   b. Falls

   Preventive Management
   Patient assisted and monitored   100%
5. Result of treatment relaxation of muscle spasm with relief of
   stiffness and pain   100%

Rehabilitation Procedures

RANGE OF MOTION EXERCISES

1. Presence of indications including either of the following conditions: 100% $ 15
   a. Need to maintain normal range of motion of joints
   b. Need to prevent contractures
2. Treatment as indicated   100%

Upper Extremity	Joint	Movement of the Joint
	Shoulder	Flexion, extension, hyperextension Internal and external rotation Vertical abduction and adduction Horizontal abduction and adduction
	Elbow joint	Flexion Extension
	Forearm	Supination Pronation
	Wrist	Flexion and extension Ulnar and radial deviation
	Thumb	Flexion and extension Abduction and adduction Opposition
	Fingers	Flexion and extension Abduction and adduction
Lower Extremity	Hip	Flexion, extension, hyperextension Internal and external rotation Abduction and adduction
	Knee joint	Flexion Extension
	Ankle	Dorsi flexion Plantar flexion
	Foot	Inversion Eversion
	Toes	Flexion and extension Abduction and adduction

3. Proper bed positioning maintained so as to permit frequent changes
   in position   100%

4. **Contraindicated:** Forceful or stretching movements of the involved joints — 0%
5. **Treatment schedule:** Short, frequent sessions — 100%
6. **Results of treatment:** Maintenance of normal range of motion of affected joints and prevention of contractures, documented in progress notes and therapist's reports — 100%

TILT TABLE PROCEDURES

1. Presence of indications for treatment, including any of the following conditions preventing or limiting ambulation — 100% $ 15
   a. Cerebral vascular accident
   b. Fractures of lower extremities and hips
   c. Multiple sclerosis
   d. Paraplegia or quadriplegia
   e. Rheumatoid arthritis
2. Treatment
   a. For all patients,
      (1) Vital signs including blood pressure at rest documented — 100%
      (2) Patient secured to tilt table — 100%
      (3) Tilt table brought gradually to vertical position — 100%
      (4) Patient monitored — 100%
         (a) Pulse checked P.R.N. or every 5-15 minutes
         (b) Feet checked for bluish discoloration
             If feet markedly blue, table returned to horizontal position immediately
         (c) Patient checked for evidence of dizziness or diaphoresis
             In presence of such condition, table returned to horizontal position immediately
   b. In presence of non-weight bearing fractures, patient's weight kept off the involved leg by means of one of the following: — 100%
      (1) Placement of sandbags, blocks, towels or small pillows to cause shift of all weight to normal leg
      (2) Placement of pillows beneath affected leg, to elevate it free of footboard so no weight can be placed on it
   c. Fluids pushed during tilt table procedure to aid in kidney and bladder function — 100%
3. Duration of treatment: 20 minutes per session — 100%
   Exception: Patient unable to tolerate vertical or near-vertical position for this long, with treatment period adjusted consistent with patient's tolerance.
4. Results of treatment
   a. Aid in prevention of bone decalcification, decubiti, hypostatic pneumonia and renal calculi — 100%
   b. Patient prepared for ambulation — 100%
   c. Bowel and bladder function stimulated — 100%
   d. Favorable psychological effects with reference to patient's recovery motivation and response to treatment — 100%

GAIT TRAINING

Crutch Gaits

1. Documentation of therapist's plan to train patient in the most appropriate gait(s) for his needs, specified as follows: 100%

Gait	Indications
Three point	Non-weight bearing or partial weight bearing fractures and sprains
Four point	Conditions involving both lower extremities, such as poliomyelitis, multiple sclerosis, arthritis or paraplegia
Two point	Conditions involving both lower extremities
Drag-to gait	Paraplegia
Swing-to gait	Paraplegia
Swing-through gait	Paraplegia

2. Documentation of fact that patient was measured for crutches by means of one of the following methods 100%
   a. Patient standing in parallel bars or reclining supine in bed; measurement taken from axilla down outer border of body to heel with two additional inches added, or
   b. Sixteen inches subtracted from patient's height, or
   c. Measurement taken from axilla to point 6 inches lateral to heel.

3. Documentation of testing for proper fit with patient standing between parallel bars 100%

4. Patient instructed not to place any pressure on the axillary pads of the crutches, but to carry weight on crutch handles only 100%

5. Patient using three point gait instructed to swing involved leg with each step taken with crutches, to prevent hip flexion tightness and contractures 100%
   Exception: Patient not using three point gait.

6. Patient given exercises for strengthening upper extremities 100%

7. Patient instructed in climbing and descending stairs, getting in and out of chairs, crossing curbs and going through doorways 100%

8. Patient given two supervised training sessions per day 100%

9. Safety belt used as indicated 100%

Cane Walking

10. Patient trained to hold cane with hand on side opposite to affected leg 100%

11. Patient trained to step out with affected leg and cane together 100%

Result of Training

12. Patient able to ambulate with assistance 100%

REHABILITATION IN THE PRESENCE OF LOWER EXTREMITY AMPUTATION

1. Performance and documentation of the following steps in the preoperative routine: 100%
   a. Physical therapist's assessment of patient upon notification of impending amputation
   b. Establishment of patient's potential for prosthesis

43

   c. Patient given gait training with crutches or walker $ 25

       Exception: Presence of an impediment such as previous lower extremity amputation or inability to use both hands or arms.

   d. Strengthening exercises begun as indicated for all extremities

   e. Patient given preliminary instruction in details of anticipated postoperative program

   Exception to Criterion No. 1: Emergency surgery not permitting adequate time for preoperative assessment and instruction.

2. Postoperative program

Below the Knee Amputation

a. With Jobst air boot,	100%	25 per day 33 supplies
(1) Ambulation begun one day postoperative		
Exception: Other instructions by physician.		
(2) Rigid splint applied to air boot with pressure increased to 50 mm Hg		
(3) Patient instructed to be 75% weight bearing		
(4) Patient's balance, posture and weight bearing assessed between parallel bars		
(5) Progressive ambulation begun, including stair climbing and transfer techniques		
(6) Strengthening exercises continued for quadriceps of normal leg and triceps		
b. Without Jobst air boot,	100%	25-30 per day
(1) Stump wrapping begun 48 hours postoperative		
(2) Strengthening exercises of stump quads, adductors and normal leg and range of motion exercises to stump performed as tolerated		

Above the Knee Amputation

a. Stump wrapping begun 48 hours postoperative	100%	25-30 per day
b. Strengthening exercises including those for hip extensors and adductors initiated	100%	
c. Ambulation between parallel bars begun 48 hours postoperative	100%	
Exception: Other instruction by physician.		

3. Pain management conducted as indicated for phantom limb pain, upon consultation with attending physician   100%   28
per treatment

4. Physical Therapy Service to obtain prosthetic evaluation no later than 2 weeks postoperative   100%

5. Discussion held by physical therapist with family member or significant other to establish home program, in anticipation of discharge   100%

CARDIAC REHABILITATION FOLLOWING ACUTE MYOCARDIAL INFARCTION

1. Rehabilitation program begun from 3 to 10 days following acute myocardial infarction   100%   420

   Exception: Medically contraindicated within this interval.

2. Patient closely monitored throughout program, as follows:
   a. Pulse rate taken before, approximately 3 minutes into, and after each exercise session 100%
      (1) Pulse rate in excess of 20 beats above resting rate 0%
      (2) Pulse rate in excess of 120 beats per minute 0%
   b. Blood pressure checked before and after each exercise session ... 100%
   c. Patient observed for evidence of orthostatic hypotension upon assuming erect position 100%
3. Where patient is in CCU, monitors frequently observed during treatment 100%
4. Where patient is on telemetry, nursing station informed treatment is to begin prior to start of treatment 100%
5. Patient on telemetry treated on unit, not in Physical Therapy Department 100%
6. Patient encouraged to employ diaphragmatic breathing 100%
7. Exercise program as follows:
   a. Days 1-5 approximately
      Range of motion exercises progressing from passive to active assisted to active with minimal resistance as tolerated
   b. Days 6-10 approximately
      (1) Warm up exercises in sitting position with increasing activity
      (2) Walking progressively increasing distances up to 100 feet on Day 9
      (3) Walking at rate of 88 feet per minute for 1 to 2 minutes to allowed pulse rate on Day 10
   c. Days 11-13 approximately
      (1) Warm up exercises in standing position with increasing demands and activity
      (2) Walking 5 minutes, resting 2 minutes
      (3) Descending flight of stairs Days 11 and 13
   d. Day 14 (discharge day)
      (1) Warm up exercises in standing position as on Day 13
      (2) Walking 5 minutes, resting 2 minutes
      (3) Ascending 1 flight of stairs if required at home
   e. After Day 14, patient permitted to begin progressive conditioning program with bicycle 100%
8. Patient encouraged to return to Physical Therapy Department as an outpatient for continuing rehabilitation 3 times per week .... 100% $ 90 per week

Chest Physical Therapy

POSTURAL DRAINAGE AND PERCUSSION

1. Indications including either of the following conditions: 100%
   a. Chronic obstructive lung disease with secretions
   b. Need for prevention of pneumonia or atelectasis in postoperative or bedridden patient

288

2. Contraindicated applications including the presence of any of the following conditions: 0%
   a. Bleeding
   b. Cardiovascular instability
   c. Empyema
   d. Fractured ribs or flail chest
   e. Increased intracranial pressure such as that associated with head injury
   f. Resectable carcinoma
3. Treatment
   a. Postural drainage for 10 to 15 minutes in each position   100% $ 34
      (1) Upper lobes: Sitting or standing position
      (2) Middle lobe or lingula: Lateral position
      (3) Superior segment of lower lobe: Prone position
      (4) Posterior basilar segment of lower lobe: Jackknife position
      (5) Lateral basilar segment of lower lobe: Sidelying position with affected side uppermost and head slightly down
      (6) Lower lobes: Optional use of tilt table with positioning as indicated above
   b. Percussion to a specific area for 3 to 5 minutes with patient in appropriate postural drainage position   100%
      Exception: Contraindicated in patients with severe osteoporosis, rib fractures or metastases.
   c. Vibration for 6 exhalations following percussion   100%
   d. Chest physical therapy treatments to follow respiratory therapy treatments   100%
4. Instruction in coughing and deep breathing
   a. Patient instructed to take deep breath, hold for 2 seconds and then perform 2-stage or 3-stage cough on same breath   100%
   b. Post-surgical patients instructed to "splint the cough"   100%
      Exception: Patient not post-surgical.
   c. Patient instructed in diaphragmatic breathing   100%
5. Results of treatment
   a. Absence of such complications as pneumonia and atelectasis   100%
   b. Reduction in volume of retained secretions   100%
   c. Increased efficiency in respiration   100%
   d. Patient trained in deep breathing and coughing exercises   100%

REVIEW

Criterion	Standard	Estimated Charge

INDICATIONS FOR RADIOLOGY SERVICE

1. The need for one or more of the following services, documented in the medical record: — **100%**
   a. Routine or special diagnostic study
   b. Therapeutic radiologic services
   c. Visualization during special therapeutic procedures
   d. Determination that a device has been correctly positioned
   e. Follow-up of therapy

DOCUMENTATION AND TRANSMISSION OF REQUESTS AND REPORTS

2. The written request for radiologic service originating from the requesting physician — **100%**
3. Reference to the provisional diagnosis and to the reasons for the service included in the written request — **100%**
4. The radiologic report filed in the medical record within 24 hours following request — **100%**
5. Duplicates of all radiologic reports (a) filed in the radiology department and (b) sent to the attending physician upon request — **100%**

EQUIPMENT AND PROCEDURES

6. All diagnostic radiologic units calibrated at least once a year — **100%**
7. Calibration of each of the following diagnostic units documented: — **100%**
   a. Fixed diagnostic units within the radiology department
   b. Cystoscopic units outside the radiology department
   c. Special procedure units
   d. Fluoroscopic units
   e. Portable units
   f. Dental radiologic units
8. Presence of written evidence that any deficiencies found have been corrected following radiation calibration surveys — **100%**
9. Presence of written policies and procedures covering the following: — **100%**
   a. Scheduling of radiologic services
   b. Preparation of patients for examination
   c. Radiation safety
   d. Safety precautions to be taken against electrical and mechanical hazards
   e. Infection control and the handling of isolation patients
   f. The handling of emergency and critically ill patients

g. Radiologic techniques for each procedure
h. Administration of diagnostic materials

10. Safety measures observed including the following: 100%
    a. Documented periodic evaluation of all gloves, aprons and gonadal shields for defects
    b. Precautions taken to minimize radiation exposure of gonads and fetuses
    c. Assurance that the exposure switches of all fixed diagnostic units cannot be operated outside shielded areas

11. Management of allergic reactions to diagnostic agents
    a. Use of agent discontinued   100%
    b. Reaction treated symptomatically   100%
    c. Alternative investigative method planned   100%

FURTHER EVALUATION

For further evaluation of the utilization of specific radiologic procedure, the reader is referred to the sections on clinical review topics.

RESPIRATORY THERAPY SERVICE

SAMPLES

Patients receiving respiratory therapy services.

REVIEW

Criterion	Standard	Estimated Charge
INDICATIONS FOR RESPIRATORY THERAPY		
1. The presence of any of the following conditions:	100%	
a. Respiratory distress		
b. Bronchitis with dyspnea, persistent cough or tenacious mucous		
c. Emphysema with dyspnea, chronic cough or hypoxia		
d. Pneumonitis with dyspnea, persistent cough, tenacious mucous and/or x-ray evidence of pneumonitis		
e. Atelectasis		
f. Need for preoperative instruction in breathing exercises		
g. Need for postoperative prophylaxis		
INDICATIONS FOR RESPIRATORY STUDIES		
2. For diagnostic purposes to measure pulmonary function or for blood gas analysis	100%	
DOCUMENTATION OF SERVICES		
3. Physician's order for respiratory services specifying the following:	100%	
a. Type of treatment or test		
b. Frequency of treatment		
c. Duration of treatment		
d. Type and dosage of any medication to be used		
4. Respiratory therapist's report in the medical record documenting the following:	100%	
a. Type of test conducted or therapy given		
b. Dates and times of administration		
c. Specifications of the prescription		
d. Effects of therapy including any adverse reactions		
5. Attending physician's documentation in the record of the timely clinical evaluation of the results of therapy	100%	

TREATMENT

Respiratory Distress

Criterion	Standard	Estimated Charge
1. Low-flow oxygen (30%-35%) per nasal cannula Exception: Severe respiratory distress or respiratory failure requiring higher concentration of oxygen.	100%	$ 26 per 8 hours
2. IPPB	100% }	
3. Mist therapy	100% }	44

292

Bronchitis

In the presence of dyspnea, persistent cough and/or tenacious mucous,

1. Mist therapy with ultrasonic nebulizer or heated or cold aerosol and bronchodilator	100%	$ 44
2. Postural drainage and percussion	100%	22

Emphysema

In the presence of dyspnea, chronic cough and/or hypoxia,

1. Tests of pulmonary function such as lung volume and spirometry	100%	20
2. Pending results of blood gas analysis, oxygen at low flow less than 4 liters per minute	100%	26 per 8 hours
3. IPPB	100%	
4. Mist therapy with ultrasonic nebulizer, heated or cold aerosol and bronchodilator as indicated	100%	44
5. Postural drainage	100%	22

Pneumonitis

In the presence of dyspnea, persistent cough, tenacious mucous and/or x-ray evidence of disease,

1. Tests of pulmonary function	100%	20
2. IPPB	100%	
3. Mist therapy with ultrasonic nebulizer or heated or cold aerosol	100%	44
4. Oxygen as indicated	100%	26 per 8 hours
5. Postural drainage and percussion	100%	22

Atelectasis

1. IPPB using air	100%	21
2. Mist therapy with nebulizer or aerosol and bronchodilator	100%	23

Preoperative Services

Instruction in deep breathing, coughing and turning in bed	100%	22

Postoperative Services

1. Instruction in deep breathing, coughing and turning in bed	100%	22
2. IPPB using air	100%	21

Exception: Not indicated because patient ambulatory same day as surgery.

RESULTS OF TREATMENT

The following conditions documented in the medical record: 100%

a. Absence of respiratory distress or dyspnea
b. Reduction in severity of cough
c. Hydration of mucous
d. Absence of hospital-acquired infection associated with use of respiratory therapy equipment

SUGGESTED SAMPLE

Patients discharged during the past six months who had multiple diagnoses and whose hospital stays were longer than fourteen days.

REVIEW

Criterion	Standard	Estimated Charge

SERVICES PROVIDED

1. Presence in the record of the attending physician's request for Social Service consultation, specifying

   a. The patient's primary diagnosis or medical problem — 100%

   b. Any anticipated problem in connection with such matters as transfer of the patient, rehabilitation needs or the need for services of community agencies — 100%

   Exception: Documentation of the attending physician's opinion that the patient is self-sufficient.

2. Social Service evaluation report with reference to the following elements, documented in the medical record:

   a. Patient's intellectual and emotional status — 100%

   b. Patient's financial status with respect to anticipated needs — 100%

   c. Patient's own plans upon his discharge from the hospital — 100%

   Exception: Patient unable to engage in such planning.

   d. Home environment and persons in the household — 100%

   e. Any special needs following discharge from the hospital, such as needs for equipment, prostheses, home nursing care, meal service, housekeeping services, public assistance or the services of community agencies — 100%

   Exception: Documentation in the record of the attending physician's opinion that the patient is self-sufficient

3. Social Service consultation reports or notes in the record reflecting progress in discharge planning including

   a. Contacts with the patient's relatives or significant others in the course of the discharge planning process — 100%

   b. Counseling provided to patient and relatives — 100%

   c. Referral to community agencies as indicated — 100%

   Exception: Patient self-sufficient.

4. Social Service discharge note in the record reflecting

   a. Patient's physical and emotional state — 100%

   b. Complete identification of any community or governmental agencies that are to participate in the patient's care following discharge, with a brief statement of their respective responsibilities — 100%

   c. Identification of the representatives of any agencies that will participate in the patient's care following discharge — 100%

   Exception: Patient self-sufficient.

SUGGESTED SAMPLE

Patients who have experienced cerebrovascular accident, brain damage or surgery or trauma resulting in the loss or compromising of organs used in the reception or production of sound or the articulation of speech.

REVIEW

Criterion	Standard	Estimated Charge
Documentation in the medical record of the following:		
1. Pertinent history	100%	
2. Evaluation		$ 90
a. Language use		
(1) Reception and ability to understand		
Aphasic patient asked to point to pictures to indicate responses		
(2) Expressive ability, with evaluation of		
(a) Patient's ability to frame sentences	100%	
(b) Extent of patient's present vocabulary	100%	
(c) Patient's use of appropriate syntax	100%	
(d) Patient's evident grasp of meanings	100%	
b. Articulation		
Evaluation of the patient's physical ability to produce sounds and to articulate	100%	
c. Description of patient's voice with reference to pitch, loudness and quality	100%	
d. Oral peripheral examination	100%	
e. Evaluation of apparent acuity of hearing	100%	70
3. Plan of care		
a. Assessment of patient's speech rehabilitation potential	100%	
b. Discussion with patient and family for purpose of outlining proposed plan of treatment	100%	
c. Following consultation with attending physician, the schedule of treatment sessions outlined in record	100%	70 per hour
4. Written report with current assessment following each session, included in medical record	100%	

RECORD ANALYST'S GUIDE

Data Element	Location in Medical Record
Patient identification (age, sex, record number, room number)	Outside of file envelope or jacket. Face sheet of record.
Attending physician's ID	Outside of file envelope or jacket. Face sheet of record. Analyst's list of records in audit sample.
Admitting diagnosis	Usually shown on face sheet. Shown at end of history and physical examination report.
Discharge diagnosis	Face sheet, showing code number. Resume as reported by attending physician.
Indications for admission	History. Physical examination report. Physician's admitting note.
Diagnostic or Preoperative Study	Physician's orders showing procedures ordered. Laboratory slips in file showing what tests were carried out and the results.
Laboratory tests	Most hospitals have a fairly standardized set of procedures to be performed on admission. These usually include a panel of blood tests with a complete blood count (CBC) and a urinalysis. The panel report sheet will list each test included, with the results. Urinalysis and other tests will be reported on separate slips.
	Laboratory slips usually show the normal values as well as the patient's reported values for each test.
	Record Analyst: Note whether all procedures ordered were actually performed and recorded.
X-rays	Radiology reports.
EKG	EKG report pages.
Special procedures such as brain and liver scans	Reports in file.
Length of stay (LOS)	File envelope or face sheet showing dates of admission and discharge. Look for Utilization Review Committee's forms. In the cases of patients over 65 and disabled patients, look for Medicare forms in the record.
Mortality	Face sheet Death certificate in file. Death certificate also shows ascribed cause of death.
Management and therapy	Physician's orders. References in progress notes. Nursing care plan. Nurses' notes. Medication, IV and flow charts.
Blood transfusions	Hematology report slips showing blood counts, typing and cross matching of blood. Also should show date, time and

number of units for each transfusion as well as whether whole blood or a component was given.

Record Analyst: Sometimes not all of the blood ordered is used. Be sure to differentiate between the number of units ordered to be ready and the number actually used.

Breathing exercises	Nursing notes and/or respiratory therapy reports.
Medications	Physician's orders. Nursing notes. Medication record page.
Pathology findings	Pathologist's report after surgery or following an investigative procedure that produced a specimen for study.
Physical therapy	Physician's orders. Nursing notes. Physical therapy report pages showing dates, times and duration of treatments.
Respiratory therapy	Physician's orders. Nursing notes. Respiratory therapy record pages showing dates, times and duration of treatments.
Complications	Face sheet and resume. Progress notes. Nursing notes.
Responsive management of complications	Physician's orders. Progress notes. Nursing notes. Consultation reports. Special procedure or treatment reports. Laboratory slips dated after date of onset of complication.
Discharge status	
Health status	Progress notes covering period from 2 to 3 days before discharge. Nursing notes covering period from 2 to 3 days before discharge. Any laboratory report slips covering the period from 2 to 3 days before discharge.

Patient's knowledge and discharge instructions given to patient	This material often is not fully documented.
	Any documentation that may exist will be found in the
	    Progress notes
	    Nursing notes
	    Nursing home transfer form for a patient being transferred to a nursing home.

DIAGNOSTIC DATA

The following clinical and laboratory data and tests are often referred to in the review criteria and in the medical record.

Test or Sign	Normal Value or Range

Vital Signs · *Resting Value*

Pulse

Embryo	150 per minute
At birth	130-140
During 1st year	115-130
During 2nd year	100-115
During 3rd year	90-100
During 7th year	85- 90
About 14th year	80- 85
Middle life	70- 75
Old age	65- 70

Blood Pressure (BP)

Systolic: Usually 100-120
Systolic above 140 usually considered abnormal.

Diastolic: Usually 60-95.
Diastolic above 95 usually considered abnormal.

Pulse pressure: Usually no higher than 50.

In any study in which blood pressure is to be used as a criterion, be sure to ask the Review Committee whether these values will be used as the criterion levels. They may prefer to specify other values.

Respiration

Premature infant	40-90 per minute
Newborn	30-80
1st year	20-40
2nd year	20-30
5th year	20-25
15th year	15-20
Adult	15-20

Temperature

98.6 F or 37 C

Review Committee may consider a level of 99.6 F at discharge as acceptable. Obtain specific level to be used.

Urinalysis-Microscopic

Acetone	0
a-Amino nitrogen	64-199 mg per day (Less than 1.5% total nitrogen)
Amylase	24-76 u./ml
Calcium	150 mg/day or less
Catecholamines	
Epinephrine	Less than 10 μg/day
Norepinephrine	Less than 100 μg/day
Chorionic gonadotropin	0
Copper	0-100 μg/day

Creatine	Less than 100 mg/day or less than 6% creatine
Creatinine	15-25 mg/kg of body weight per day
Creatinine clearance	150-180 L/day/1.73 square meters of body surface area
Cystine or cysteine	0
Hemoglobin and myoglobin	0
Homogentisic acid	0
5-Hydroxindole acetic acid	2-9 mg/24 hours
Lead	.08 µg/ml or 120 µg or less per 24 hours
PSP	At 15 minutes: at least 25% excreted
	At 30 minutes: at least 40% excreted
	At 120 minutes: at least 60% excreted
Phenylpyruvic acid	0
Phosphorus (inorganic)	Average 1 gm/day
Pituitary gonadotropins	Pre-menopause, 6-12 rat units/24 hours
	Post-menopause, over 25 rat units/24 hours
Porphobilinogen	0
Protein	
Quantitative determination	0
Electrophoresis determination	0
Qualitative determination	0

Steroids

	Age	Males	Females
17-Ketosteroids	10	1- 4 mg	1- 4 mg
	20	6-21	4-16
	30	8-26	4-14
	50	5-18	3- 9
	70	2-10	1- 7

17-Hydroxysteroids	3-8 mg/day, with women lower than men
Sugar	
Fructose	0
Pentose	0
Titratable acidity	20-40 mEq/day
Urea clearance	Expressed as % of normal
Urobilinogen	Up to 1.0 Ehrlich u.
Uroporphyrin	0
VMA	Up to 9 mg/24 hours

Urinalysis—Specific Gravity

Specific gravity	Usually, 1.015-1.025 specific gravity

Often shown as only the last 2 digits on laboratory slips. Thus, for example, the normal range may appear as 15-25.

CBC and Differential Count

pH	7.35-7.45
Hematocrit (Hct)	Male: 42%-50% Female: 40%-48%

Hemoglobin (Hgb)	Male: 13-16 gm/100 ml
	Female: 12-15 gm/100 ml
White blood cells (WBC)	4,800-10,800/cu. mm
Red blood cells (RBC)	4.2-5.9 million/cu. mm
Red blood cell indices	
Mean corpuscular volume (MCV)	80-94 cu. microns
Mean corpuscular hemoglobin (MCH)	27-32 micro micrograms
Mean corpuscular hemoglobin concentration (MCHC)	33%-38%
Platelet count	200,000-350,000/cu. mm
Reticulocytes	0.5%-1.5% of red cells

Coagulation Profile

PTT (partial thromboplastin time, activated)	22-37 seconds
Prothrombin time (Quick)	Less than 2 seconds' deviation from control

Cardiac Enzymes

CPK (creatine phosphokinase)	Male: 5-35 u./ml
	Female: 5-25 u./ml
LDH (lactic dehydrogenase)	60-100 u./ml
SGOT (serum glutamic oxalacetic transaminase)	10-40 u./ml

Electrolytes

Chlorides	100-106 mEq/L
Potassium	3.5-5.0 mEq/L
Sodium	136-145 mEq/L

Lipids

Cholesterol	150-280 micrograms/100 ml serum
Cholesterol esters	60%-75% of cholesterol
Phospholipids	9-16 mg/100 ml as lipid phosphorus
Triglycerides	40-150 mg/100 ml serum
Total fatty acids	190-420 mg/100 ml serum
Total lipids	450-1,000 mg/100 ml serum

Rh Factor

Rh factor	Positive (+)

Serology

VDRL or PTA-ABS test	Result shown as negative

Blood Gas Analysis

CO_2	20-25 mEq/L or 45-55 ml/100 ml blood
Arterial O_2 saturation	96%-98%
Arterial PCO_2 or pCO_2	37-41 mm Hg
pH (Arterial plasma)	7.39-7.41
PO_2	75-100 mm Hg

Iron

Iron	50-150 μg/100 ml serum
Iron binding capacity (IBC)	250-410 mg/100 ml serum
Blood urea nitrogen (BUN)	8-25 mg/100 ml whole blood
	Urea = BUN × 2.14

SMA 6, 12, 18 and 20   Battery or panel of computerized blood tests that give results for 6, 12, 18 or 20 components on a printed form showing normal and abnormal values

Newborn Tests and Signs

Dextrostick test	45 mg
PKU	Result shown as negative
Serology (VDRL)	Result shown as negative

MEDICINE AND SURGERY

Term	Meaning and Example of Use
Afebrile	Without fever. Temperature no higher than 98.6 F, usually for a period of at least 36 hours. *Where the Review Committee uses "Afebrile" as a criterion, ask them to specify the temperature level that is to be considered acceptable for purposes of the study.*
Ambulatory	Able to walk. Where this is used as a criterion, as in connection with discharge status, an exception would occur in the case of a patient who, due to some unrelated pre-existing condition, had been unable to walk at the time of admission to the hospital.
Angina pectoris	Pain and oppression about the heart, usually paroxysmal in occurrence. May radiate from the heart to the left shoulder and down the left arm.
Anorexia	Loss of appetite.
Apnea	Breathlessness. May follow exercise, or may be related to depressive effect of certain drugs, especially during sleep.
Ascites	Excessive accumulation of serous fluid in peritoneal cavity (abdomen). Manifested by swelling of abdomen.
Asthenia	Severe generalized weakness.
Atelectasis	Collapsed or airless condition of the lung. May be caused by obstruction due to a foreign body, mucous plugs, excessive thick secretions or by compression due to a tumor in the chest.
Atrophy	A wasting and reduction in the size of an organ or muscle.
Azotemia	Condition characterized by the presence of nitrogenous bodies, especially increased amounts of urea, in the blood.
Babinski reflex	Characteristic involuntary spreading of the toes when sole of the relaxed foot is stroked. Normally present in infants less than 6 months old. Presence in an individual beyond this age usually indicates some disorder of the cortico-spinal tract.
Bradycardia	Slow heart beat.
Bradypnea	Slow breathing.
Bruit	Abnormal sounds or murmurs arising from blood vessels.
Cachexia	General debility or ill health with malnutrition.
Calculus Pl.: calculi	A stone formed within an organ. Ex.: Renal calculi, kidney stones.
Cephalalgia	Headache.
Cicatrix	Scar.
Colic	Spasm in any hollow or tubular soft organ accompanied by severe pain. Ex.: Biliary colic in gallbladder disease.
Coma	A state of unconsciousness from which the patient cannot be aroused, even by powerful stimulation.

Conservative management	A course of therapy involving principally the observation and support of the patient with measures to alleviate his symptoms and discomfort. It involves refraining from the use of surgical or other aggressive procedures in an effort to permit the body's natural recuperative processes to take effect.
Culture	An artificial growth of bacteria in a sample of blood, urine, sputum, nose or throat secretions or stool, or of material from an abscess. The purpose of the culture is to identify the bacteria causing an infection.
Cyanosis	A dark bluish, dusky or purplish coloration of the skin and mucous membranes due to inadequate oxygenation of the blood.
Dehiscence (of a wound)	The bursting open of a wound following surgical closure.
Diaphoresis	Profuse, abnormal sweating.
Dyspnea	Marked shortness of breath, rapid and/or labored breathing. Respiration above 20/minute in an adult.
Edema	Condition in which body tissues contain an excessive amount of fluid. Sometimes called dropsy or anasarca.
Embolism	Obstruction of a blood vessel by foreign substances or, more usually, by a blood clot.
Embolus	A clot or other plug brought by the blood from another vessel and forced into a smaller one, thus obstructing the circulation.
Epistaxis	Nose bleed.
Evisceration	A weakening or opening of a surgically repaired abdominal wall such that the viscera (abdominal contents) tend to protrude.
Fistula	An abnormal tube-like passage from a normal cavity to a free surface or to another tube. May occur as a congenital anomaly, as a result of trauma, or as a postoperative complication.
Frequency (of urination)	A condition characterized by the need or desire to urinate more often than the patient considers normal or comfortable.
Hallucination	A false perception having no relation to reality and not accounted for by any existing external stimuli.
Hematemesis	Vomiting of blood.
Hematochezia	Bloody stool. Also refer to "Melena."
Hematuria	Bloody urine.
Hemoptysis	Expectoration of blood arising from hemorrhage of the larynx, trachea, bronchi or lungs.
Hepatomegaly	Enlargement of the liver. The physical examination report may include a reference to the physician's assessment of the size of the liver in terms of a specified number of finger breadths below the costal margin (lower edge of the ribs).
Icterus	Yellowish coloring of tissues, membranes and secretions, due to bile pigments. Syn.: Jaundice.
Infarct, infarction	Death of tissue resulting from absence of blood supply to any organ or part. Ex.: Myocardial infarction.
Jaundice	Yellowish coloring of tissues, membranes and secretions due to bile pigments. Syn.: Icterus.
Malaise	Generalized discomfort, uneasiness, indisposition, often indicative of an infection.

305

Melena	Passage of dark stools, stained with blood pigments or with altered blood.
Metastasis	Movement of bacteria or body cells, especially cancer cells, from one part of the body to another. Usually used to refer to the spread of cancer cells via the blood or lymphatic stream.
Nausea	Discomfort preceding vomiting, inclination to vomit.
Neurological deficit	Condition characterized by a derangement of neuromusculatory function. May occur as a complication following neurological or orthopedic surgery. Progress notes may refer to muscular weakness or paralysis.
Nocturia	Excessively frequent urination at night, significantly interfering with sleep.
Obese	Extremely fat, from 20% to 30% over the average weight for the individual's age, sex and height.
Obesity	Presence of an abnormal amount of fat on the body.
Palliative	Having the effect of relieving or alleviating a symptom without necessarily curing the disorder. The term may be applied to medications or to surgery.
Petechiae	Minute areas of hemorrhage under the skin or in an organ.
Rales	Abnormal respiratory sound heard in auscultation, classified as either dry or moist and also as to site of origin.
Sensorium	The sensory apparatus of the body taken as a whole. The term is sometimes used to represent a patient's senses of sight, hearing, smell, taste and touch or feeling. Thus, a patient's chart may contain a statement to the effect that his sensorium was "clear" or that it was "clouded."
Syncope	Transient loss of consciousness due to inadequate blood flow to the brain; fainting.
Tachypnea	Rapid breathing. Not identical with difficult or labored breathing or dyspnea.

OBSTETRICS AND GYNECOLOGY

Female Reproductive System

Stem or Term	Meaning and Example of Use
Cervix uteri	Neck of the uterus. Ex.: Cervicitis, an inflammation of the cervix.
Clitoris	Female homologue of the penis. Ex.: Clitoridectomy, excision of the clitoris.
Colpos	Vagina, the canal leading to the uterus. Ex.: Colpocele, hernia into the vagina.
Cystis	Relating to the bladder. Ex.: Cystitis, inflammation of the bladder.
Galact	Milk. Ex.: Galactedema, swelling of the breast due to an accumulation of milk within it.
Hymen	Fold of mucous membrane partially occluding the vagina. Ex.: Hymenorrhaphy, suturing of the hymen.
Hystera	Womb or uterus. Ex.: Hysterectomy, excision of the uterus.
Labia majora	Labia majora are the hairy skin folds on either side of the vulva.
Labia minora	Labia minora are mucous membrane folds within the labia majora.
Lochios	Lochia, discharge following childbirth. Ex.: Lochiorrhagia, excessive flow of lochia.
Mamma	Relating to the breast. Ex.: Mammary gland.

306

Mastos	Breast. Ex.: Mastopexy, surgical fixation of a pendulous breast.
Metra	Womb or uterus. Ex.: Metritis, inflammation of the uterus.
Nymphe	Nymphae, the labia minora of the vulva. Ex.: Nymphoncus, swelling or tumor of the nymphae.
Ovarian	Relating to the ovary, the egg-producing organ of the female. Ex.: Oophorectomy, excision of the ovary.
Oviduct	The tube passing from the uterus to the ovary, commonly called the Fallopian tube, named for the Italian anatomist Gabriele Fallopio.
Papilla	Nipple. Ex.: Papillate, shaped like a nipple.
Para-, endo- and myometrium	Parametrium: Outside covering of the uterus. Endometrium: Inside lining of the uterus. Myometrium: Muscular structure of the uterus.
Perineum	The region between the anus and the structures beginning at the pelvic outlet in the female.
Salpinx	Fallopian tube. Ex.: Salpingitis, inflammation of the Fallopian tube.
Thel	Relating to the nipple. Ex.: Thelalgia, pain in the nipple.
Trachel	Neck of the uterus or cervix. Ex.: Trachelotomy, cutting of the uterine neck.
Uterus	Womb. Ex.: Uterine gestation, the carrying of a child in the womb.
Vagina	Canal extending from the opening of the vulva to the mouth of the uterus. Ex.: Vaginitis, inflammation of the vagina.
Vulva	The labia and the skin covering the opening of the vagina.

Fetal Structures

Stem or Term	Meaning and Example of Use
Amnion	The membrane enclosing the fetus. Ex.: Amniocentesis, the removal of amniotic fluid for chemical study.
Chorion	The outer membrane covering the fetal structure.
Fetus, foetus	The unborn child.
Placenta	A round, flat organ within the uterus during pregnancy, connecting mother and child by means of the umbilical cord. The placenta provides nourishment for the fetus. Ex.: Placenta praevia, detachment of the placenta from the uterine wall prior to the birth of the child, usually causing severe hemorrhage.

Normal and Abnormal Conditions

Term	Meaning and Example of Use
Ablatio placentae	Premature separation of the placenta.
Abortion	Spontaneous or induced delivery of the fetus before it is viable.
Amenorrhea	Absence or cessation of menstruation.
Dysmenorrhea	Painful menstruation. Ex.: "Cramps."
Eclampsia	A toxemia of pregnancy characterized by severe hypertension, headaches, albuminuria and edema of the lower extremities.
Ectopic pregnancy	A condition in which the fertilized ovum is implanted and develops outside the uterine cavity. Ex.: Tubal pregnancy.
Kraurosis	A degenerative disease of the vulva associated with atrophy of the tissues. The skin layer becomes thin and parchment-like.

Leukoplakia	A pre-cancerous degenerative disease of the vulva associated early with hyperplasia and later with atrophy of the tissues. The labial folds flatten and assume an opaque white aspect. The introitus (entrance to the vagina) shrinks.
Menarche	Onset of menstruation.
Menopause	Natural or medically induced (e.g., following hysterectomy) cessation of menstruation.
Menorrhagia	Excessive flow during the menstrual period.
Metrorrhagia	Abnormal uterine bleeding during the intermenstrual period.
Multigravida	A woman who has been pregnant more than once. For example, the term "gravida 2, para 1" signifies a woman who has had one child and is in her second pregnancy.
Multipara	A woman who has had two or more babies. In the suffix "para" the letter "p" symbolizes the number of *pregnancies* experienced, the letter "a" the number of *abortions* and the letters "ra" the number of children *remaining* (born) *alive*.
	Thus, "multipara 2-0-3" describes a woman who has had 2 pregnancies, zero abortions and 3 children born alive including a set of twins.
Nullipara	A woman who has never given birth to a child.
Placenta praevia	A condition in which the placenta develops in the region of the surgical os and complicates delivery by becoming separated from the uterine wall prior to the birth of the child. The condition is associated with heavy bleeding or hemorrhage.

Positions of the fetus in various presentations

Cephalic Presentation

1. Vertex: Occiput the point of direction

Left occipito-anterior	L.O.A.
Left occipito-transverse	L.O.T.
Right occipito-posterior	R.O.P.
Right occipito-transverse	R.O.T.
Right occipito-anterior	R.O.A.
Left occipito-posterior	L.O.P.

2. Face: Chin the point of direction

Right mento-posterior	R.M.P.
Left mento-anterior	L.M.A.
Right mento-transverse	R.M.T.
Right mento-anterior	R.M.A.
Left mento-transverse	L.M.T.
Left mento-posterior	L.M.P.

3. Brow the point of direction

Right fronto-posterior	R.F.P.
Left fronto-anterior	L.F.A.
Right fronto-transverse	R.F.T.
Right fronto-anterior	R.F.A.
Left fronto-transverse	L.F.T.
Left fronto-posterior	L.F.P.

Breech or Pelvic Presentation

1. Complete breech: Sacrum the point of direction with feet crossed and thighs flexed on abdomen

Left sacro-anterior	L.S.A.
Left sacro-transverse	L.S.T.
Right sacro-posterior	R.S.P.
Right sacro-anterior	R.S.A.
Right sacro-transverse	R.S.T.
Left sacro-posterior	L.S.P.

2. Incomplete breech: Sacrum the point of direction. Same designations as above, adding the qualifiers "footling," "knee," etc.

Transverse Lie or Shoulder Presentation

Shoulder: Scapula the point of direction

Back Anterior Positions

Left scapulo-anterior	L.Sc.A.
Right scapulo-anterior	R.Sc.A.

Back Posterior Positions

Right scapulo-posterior	R.Sc.P.
Left scapulo-posterior	L.Sc.P.

Post partum hemorrhage	Hemorrhage following the delivery of a child.
Pre-eclampsia	A toxemia of pregnancy characterized by increasing hypertension, headaches, albuminuria and edema of the lower extremities. If pre-eclampsia is not properly treated it may develop into true eclampsia.
Precipitate labor and delivery	A condition in which the separation and expulsion of the child and placenta occur before the usual retraction of the uterus can take place.
Primigravida	Woman in her first pregnancy.
Primipara	Woman who is having her first baby.
Pruritus of the vulva	Excessive itching of the vulva.
Puerperium	The period from delivery to the return of the uterus to its normal pre-gravid size and function, usually about 6 weeks.
Trimester	One-third of the period of gestation, or 3 months.

Pelvic Diameters

Term and Meaning	Normal Value or Range
I. External	
Interspinous Distance between the outer edges of the anterior superior iliac spines.	26 cm (10¼ in.)
Intercristal Distance between the outer edges of the most prominent portion of the iliac crests.	28 cm (11 in.)
Intertrochanteric Distance between the most prominent points of the femoral trochanters.	32 cm (12½ in.)

309

Oblique, right and left
    Distance from one posterior superior iliac spine to the opposite
    anterior superior iliac spine.
                                        22 cm (8½ in.)

External conjugate
    Distance from undersurface of the spinous process of the last lumbar
    vertebra to the upper margin of the anterior suface of the symphesis
    publis.
                                        20 cm (7⅞ in.)

II. *Internal*

True conjugate
    The Most Important Diamter of All.
    Anterior-posterior diameter of pelvic inlet.
                                        11 cm (4¼ in.)

Diagonal conjugate
    A measurement that is 2 cm (¾ in.) less than the height and
    inclination of the symphesis.
                                        13 cm (5⅛ in.)

Transverse
    Distance between the ischial tuberosities.
                                        11 cm (4¼ in.)

Anterior-posterior of outlet
    Distance between lower border of symphesis and tip of sacrum.
                                        11 cm (4¼ in.)

Anterior sagittal
    Distance from undersurface of symphesis to center of line between
    ischial tuberosities.
                                        7 cm (2¾ in.)

Posterior sagittal
    Distance from the center of the line between ischial tuberosities to
    the tip of the sacrum.
                                        10 cm (4 in.)

ABBREVIATIONS

The following list contains some commonly used abbreviations. For further information refer to your hospital's list of approved abbreviations. This list is kept in the Medical Record Department. Any abbreviation used in a medical record should appear on the hospital's list of approved abbreviations.

AC	Before meals.
ABP	Arterial blood pressure.
AD	Right ear.
ADL	Activities of daily living.
AFB	Acid fast bacteria.
AGNO$_3$	Silver nitrate.
AK	Above the knee.
AMA	Against medical advice. Often used when a patient signs himself out of the hospital before his physician considers him ready to be discharged.
A&P	Anterior and posterior.
AS	Left ear.
ASHD	Arteriosclerotic heart disease.
AV	Atrioventricular.
A-V	Arteriovenous.
b.i.d.	Twice daily.
BK	Below the knee.
BMR	Basal metabolic rate.
BP	Blood pressure.
BRP	Bathroom privileges.
BUN	Blood urea nitrogen.
c̄	With.
Ca	Carcinoma.
CBC	Complete blood count.
CHF	Congestive heart failure.
CNS	Central nervous system.
CO$_2$	Carbon dioxide.
CPK	Creatinine phosphatase.
CSF	Cerebrospinal fluid.
CVA	Cerebral vascular accident, or stroke.
D&C	Dilatation and curettage.
Dx	Diagnosis.
D/W	Dextrose in water.
ECG or EKG	Electrocardiogram.

ECT	Electroconvulsive therapy, or electroshock therapy.
EEG	Electroencephalogram.
EMG	Electromyogram.
ESR	Erythrocyte sedimentation rate.
ETOH	Alcohol.
FBS	Fasting blood sugar.
FH	Family history.
FUO	Fever of unknown origin.
Fx	Fracture.
GI	Gastrointestinal.
gtt.	Drop(s).
GU	Genitourinary.
Hct	Hematocrit.
HCVD	Hypertensive cardiovascular disease.
Hgb	Hemoglobin.
Hpn	Hypertension.
HS	Bedtime care.
Hx	History.
ICU	Intensive care unit.
I&D	Incision and drainage (of an abscess).
IM	Intramuscular.
I&O	Intake and output.
IPPB	Intermittent positive pressure breathing.
IV	Intravenous.
IVP	Intravenous pyelogram.
KUB	Kidney, ureter and bladder.
LBBB	Left bundle branch block.
LDH	Lactic dehydrogenase.
LLQ	Left lower quadrant.
LMP	Last menstrual period.
LUQ	Left upper quadrant.
MCV	Mean corpuscular volume.
mEq	Milliequivalent(s).

mg	Milligram(s).	S	Without.
μg	Microgram(s).	SBE	Subacute bacterial endocarditis.
NG	Nasogastric.		
Noct.	Night.	SGOT	Serum glutamic oxalacetic transaminase.
NPO	Nothing by mouth.		
O₂	Oxygen.	SH	Social history.
OD	Right eye.	SO	Significant other. Usually refers to a family member or someone else who will help to take care of the patient at home.
OR	Operating room.		
OS	Left eye.		
PBI	Protein bound iodine.		
PC	After meals.		
PERLA	Pupils equal, reactive to light and accommodation.		
		SOB	Short of breath.
		Soln.	Solution.
PH	Past history.	SSE	Soap suds enema.
PID	Pelvic inflammatory disease.	Subcut.	Subcutaneously.
PKU	Phenylketonuria.	T&A	Tonsillectomy and adenoidectomy.
PO	Postoperative.		
PRN	As needed. Usually refers to medication or treatment.	TID	Three times a day.
		TLC	Tender loving care.
PT	Physical Therapy.	TPR	Temperature, pulse and respiration.
PTA	Prior to admission.		
PTD	Prior to discharge.	TWE	Tap water enema.
q. 4 hours	Every 4 hours.	URI	Upper respiratory infection.
q.i.d.	Four times a day.	UTI	Urinary tract infection.
RBBB	Right bundle branch block.	VD	Venereal disease.
RBC	Red blood cell.	VS	Vital signs (temperature, pulse, respiration and blood pressure).
RLQ	Right lower quadrant.		
ROM	Range of motion, as in range of motion exercises.		
		WBC	White blood cell.
RR	Recovery Room.	WNL	Within normal limits.
RUQ	Right upper quadrant.		

APPENDIX

HEMODIALYSIS CENTER PROTOCOL*
Northwestern Memorial Hospital

I. PURPOSE AND DESCRIPTION

The Dialysis Center consists of an in-Hospital Dialysis Unit and a Satellite Unit. The in-hospital facility is staffed and equipped to provide dialysis care for hospitalized patients with acute and chronic renal failure, cases of drug overdosage, renal transplant patients requiring dialysis and unstable chronic outpatients. The Satellite Dialysis Unit is utilized entirely for outpatient dialysis and home dialysis training. Both hemo and peritoneal dialysis, as well as diafiltration (sequential ultrafiltration) are performed at both units. Hemoperfusion is performed at the hospital unit.

II. ORGANIZATION

A. **Medical Staff:** The Physician Director has responsibility for general direction of the Center. In discharging his responsibilities, the Physician Director is assisted by the Assistant Director, the Nursing Supervisor and the Administrator—Renal Services. These latter two individuals have reporting relationships to the Nursing Service and Hospital Administration respectively. The Medical Staff of the Center consists of physicians who are members of the Hospital staff and of the Section of Nephrology/Hypertension. These physicians report directly to the Director.

B. **House Staff:** Medical Students, interns, resident and fellows assigned to the Nephrology Service follow the patients in the in-Hospital Dialysis Center. A house staff call schedule is issued monthly. House staff are permitted to take call at home. No house staff coverage is provided for the Satellite Unit except for scheduled visits by the Nephrology fellow, and for acute emergencies as outlined below.

C. **Nursing Staff:** The Department of Nursing is responsible for all nursing personnel and technicians assigned to the Dialysis Center and for the development of Nursing Policies and Procedures. The nurses and technicians of the Dialysis Center are responsible to their respective Head Nurses who report to the Nursing Supervisor. The Nursing Supervisor is jointly responsible for patient care, to the Medical Director and Assistant Medical Director of the Center and to the respective Nursing Department Director.

III. CRITERIA FOR ADMISSION

A. Patients with acute renal failure unresponsive to conservative management;

B. Patients with acute drug intoxication unresponsive to conservative management;

C. Patients with chronic end-stage renal failure, including possible candidates for renal transplantation, home dialysis training or both;

D. Renal transplant recipients with acute or chronic allograft rejection causing severe renal insufficiency;

E. Patients with other conditions which are potentially benefited by hemodialysis, as for example intractable edema;

F. Patients needing dialysis immediately prior to undergoing a renal transplant operation.

IV. CRITERIA FOR DISCHARGE

A. Stable chronic outpatients are discharged by the Charge Nurse providing vital signs are stable;

---

*This protocol is used with the permission of Northwestern Memorial Hospital, Chicago, Illinois.

B. Unstable chronic outpatients are discharged by the Charge Nurse only after consultation with the physician on call or the patient's personal physician;

C. Stable chronic inpatients are discharged to the floor by the Charge Nurse after report is given to the Charge Nurse of the floor to which patient is being transferred;

D. ICU patients will be transferred from Dialysis to ICU, after optimal stabilization for transfer has been achieved, accompanied by a member of the managing service house staff; a dialysis nurse if available will also accompany the patient. A Dialysis Staff Nurse will give report to the ICU Charge Nurse at or before time of transfer;

E. Acute inpatients not from ICU will be discharged from Dialysis to the floor by an R.N. providing vital signs are stable and nursing report has been given. If the patient is unstable in the opinion of dialysis Medical Staff or Charge Nurse, a member of the managing house staff shall accompany the patient from Dialysis to the floor, or to ICU if this is felt to be indicated by Medical Staff.

V. OPERATIONAL PROCEDURES—PHYSICIANS

A. **Patients with Acute Renal Failure, Acute Drug Intoxication, or with Conditions Potentially Treatable by Hemodialysis:** Prior to transfer to the Dialysis Center from another area of NMH, each patient must be evaluated by one of the staff nephrologist-physicians of the Center. As soon as need for hemodialysis has been established, the physician consults the Director or the Assistant Director and asks to schedule the procedure. The nephrologist-physician retains full responsibility for the dialysis care with the consent and concurrence of the patient's attending physician. He also determines whether or not future hemodialyses are indicated after initial treatment on the artificial kidney. Performance and supervision of acute dialysis is under the close supervision of nephrologists. Transfers or acceptance of outpatients or referrals of patients from outside hospitals or physicians are not accepted by any member of the dialysis or nephrology staff until confirmation of availability of dialysis space has been obtained from the Director or the Assistant Director.

B. **Patients with Chronic End-Stage Renal Failure:** Prior to admission to the program each patient must be evaluated by one of the nephrologists of the Center staff. The nephrologist assembles all clinical and laboratory data which are pertinent and consults with the Director and the Assistant Director regarding clinical circumstances of the patient and availability of dialysis space. No patient, acute or chronic, may be scheduled or accepted into the Northwestern Memorial Hospital Dialysis Program without prior consultation with, and approval by, the Director or in his absence by the Assistant Director. The nephrologist will attempt to determine whether or not the patient is a suitable candidate for in-center dialysis, outpatient dialysis, renal transplantation or home dialysis training. The transplant surgeon will evaluate all new patients who fulfill primary criteria of suitability for transplantation prior to presentation to the Medical Review Board. All cases, whether suitable for maintenance dialysis or for transplantation are presented to and reviewed by the Dialysis-Transplant Medical Review Board. After acceptance of the patient into the chronic dialysis program, the patient's nephrologist maintains continuing responsibility for care. In the event he/she should wish to decline further responsibility, the patient will be assigned in a rotating order to a member of the Center's Medical staff willing to accept such new patients for continuing care. After stabilization in the in-Hospital facility, patients are transferred to the outpatient facility for continuing dialysis care. Decisions regarding transfer of patients between Hospital and Satellite units are made by the Director or Assistant Director, after consultation with the patient's attending nephrologist. Assignment of patients to particular dialysis shifts will be based on availability of space and staff, and will be made by the Director or Assistant Director, with the assistance of the Head Nurse of each unit.

C. **Patients with Chronic, End-Stage Renal Failure Suitable for Home Dialysis:** These patients are transferred to the facility in the Satellite Unit by the Director or Assistant Director, after initial equilibration in the hospital, if necessary.

1. *Nursing Responsibilities:* Home training nurse-clinician provides 24 hour coverage for patients dialyzed at home. If the nurse-clinician is not available, or if physician consultation is needed, the attending physician on-call for the Dialysis Center will be contacted. A plan of care is established in conjunction with the patient and his/her family and continuity of care and follow-up care is arranged by the Home Training Clinician.

D. **Renal Transplant Patients in Need of Hemodialysis:** Two dialysis beds will be designated as dialysis-transplant beds. These beds will be available to transplant patients 2 shifts per day, 6 days per week. Sunday dialysis will be performed only on an emergency basis.

1. The use of these stations for transplant patients will be at the discretion of the Chief, Division of Transplantation or his designee. However, the stations may be used by the Section of Nephrology for non-transplant patients if the need arises and if circumstances allow, e.g., stations not utilized in full for transplant patients. The Chief, Division of Transplantation, and Chief, Section of Nephrology, who is also Director of the Dialysis Center, will work out appropriate procedures to maintain availability of these stations to transplant patients at all times, avoiding at the same time, that such stations are under-utilized.

2. The Chief of the Section of Nephrology will select and assign a nephrologist to provide medical consultation to the Division of Transplantation. It is understood that this Nephrologist, as a member of the Department of Medicine and of the Section of Nephrology, will be responsible to the Chief, Section of Nephrology and to the Chairman, Department of Medicine.

E. **Initiation of Dialysis:** Undertaking hemodialysis requires access to the circulation by percutaneous cannulation of blood vessels (Seldinger technique), by insertion of special needles into A-V fistula branches, or by connection of external shunt. The Seldinger technique is performed by one of the staff nephrologists of the Center or by the Nephrology Fellow under close supervision of the staff nephrologist.

F. **Patient Assignments:** All chronic dialysis patients are assigned a member of the attending Medical Staff of the Center as their primary care physician.

G. **Call Schedule:** A call schedule for physicians is distributed by the Director at least ten (10) days in advance of each monthly call period. A Staff Nurse and Technician from the Main Unit staff are scheduled to be on non-restrictive call by the Head Nurse each week of the monthly schedule. Physicians, nurses and technicians are provided with a long-range radio-pager for use when on call. The assigned physician, nurse and technician are responsible, and remain available by telephone or pager for the duration of the shift he/she is scheduled to cover.

H. **Emergencies:** In case of an emergency notify telecommunications on the emergency telephones located in each unit.

1. *In-Hospital Unit:* In the event of cardiac arrest, the cardiac arrest team for the Wesley Pavilion is notified immediately. The house staff members on first or second call for the Nephrology-Hypertension service are also notified by the Charge Nurse. In addition, the attending nephrologist on call for the Dialysis Center will respond as well.

2. *Outpatient Unit:* In the event of cardiac arrest, the Olson Pavilion cardiac arrest team will be notified and will respond. The Nephrology-Hypertension physician on first or second call will, during daytime hours, be carrying an Olson Pavilion cardiac arrest pager, and will also respond; during evening or night time hours, the Nephrology-Hypertension house staff physician on first or second call will keep Northwestern Memorial Hospital telecommunications advised of his location, will be notified immediately in event of cardiac arrest, and will also immediately respond. The Chicago

Fire Department paramedics will be notified by telecommunications upon receipt of the cardiac arrest call, and will also respond, assisted by management by the Olson Pavilion Emergency Room for further monitoring. An attending nephrologist is always on call for each shift at the Satellite unit, and he will also be notified. The arrest will be managed by the Olson Pavilion cardiac arrest team until the Nephrologist-Hypertension house staff member or attending nephrologist on call reach the scene to relieve them. After the patient is stabilized, he will be transferred by the Fire Department paramedics to the hospital Emergency Room. Staff personnel assigned to the out-patient unit are trained in the technique of cardiopulmonary resuscitation, and the necessary equipment is available in the unit. For medical problems not requiring the full cardiac arrest team, the attending nephrologist on call for the particular shift at the Satellite unit, or the attending nephrologist on call for the Nephrology-Hypertension service at Northwestern Memorial Hospital, will be contacted.

VI. INFECTION CONTROL

The Northwestern Memorial Hospital Policy entitled "Communicable Disease and Infectious Conditions-Infection Control Program," Policy 5.15, will be followed.

A. Quality of care, including nursing care and use of monitoring and other special equipment, will not be compromised for any patient whose condition requires isolation.

B. Hepatitis
1. *Laboratory Tests:*
   a. All new employees will have an SMA 20 and HBs Ag checked before starting to work in the unit and quarterly thereafter. Laboratory studies will be done monthly, or more frequently if indicated, if there has been question of increased risk of exposure.
   b. Each new acute or chronic dialysis patient will have SMA 20 HBs Ag checked before starting on the program and monthly thereafter.
2. *Equipment:*
   a. Needles and syringes will be placed in a plastic bottle which will be incinerated at the end of each day. If necessary to remove a needle from syringes or bloodlines, hemostats will be used.
   b. Chux will be used under the cannulated arm to protect linen or chairs from blood spillage.
   c. Detailed procedures for sterilization of machines and equipment are contained in Dialysis Center Policies and Procedures.
3. *Staff:*
   a. Staff will wear gloves on the initiation of dialysis, termination of dialysis, and when wiping up blood spills.
   b. Staff are not permitted to smoke, eat, or drink in the dialysis area.
   c. Staff members will wash hands or change gloves between procedures with different patients.
   d. Staff members with breaks in the skin of the hands may not assist with the care of known HBs Ag positive patients.
   e. Staff members who are known to be pregnant will not be allowed to assist with the care of HBs Ag positive patients.
   f. Hospital scrub clothing will be provided for the staff, and will be worn while participating in patient care activities.
   g. Incident reports and prompt evaluation by NMH Employee Health Service Physician will be made for any needle sticks or contact with blood in eyes, mouth, or cuts.

4. *Care of HBs Ag Positive Patients:*

   a. HBs Ag positive patients will be dialyzed only in the Hospital isolation unit. No HBs Ag positive patients will be dialyzed in the outpatient Satellite unit.

   b. A separate isolation room will be provided in the Hospital unit, and will be used exclusively for HBs Ag positive patients.

   c. Detailed Policies and Procedures for care of HBs Ag positive patients are contained in Dialysis Center Policies and Procedures.

5. *Personnel Policies for HBs Ag Positive Staff:*

   a. Any HBs Ag positive staff member will not be permitted to have direct patient contact for a period of 2 months following reversal of the HBs Ag. Other suitable tasks will be found for such personnel if they are able to work or if not, they will be paid in accordance with the Illinois Workman's Compensation law. Permission to return to work and the type of work is at the discretion of the employee's attending physician, the NMH Health Service physician, the Medical Director, the Assistant Director, and the Nursing Supervisor, of the Dialysis Center.

   b. Any staff member receiving injury from potentially contaminated supplies or equipment which results in loss of skin integrity will have HBs Ag and SMA 20 determinations every 2 weeks for a period of 6 months.

VII. VISITING

Permission for visiting is given by the nurse in charge, and depends on the condition of the patient and of the Unit in general. Visiting in the Hospital unit will be limited to a maximum of one visitor per patient for no more than 5 to 10 minutes per hour. Visiting in the Satellite outpatient unit will be limited to no more than one visitor per patient for a maximum of 15 to 20 minutes per hour. Visitors will not be permitted in the unit while patients are being placed on dialysis or being taken off dialysis. Visitors may be asked to leave the Dialysis Unit by the Physician or nurse in charge at any time if in their opinion any patient is too unstable to permit visitors, or if the condition of the unit has become too congested to permit safe dialysis. Non-relatives are not allowed to visit unless specifically requested by the patient with permission of one of the Dialysis Center staff physicians.

VIII. MISCELLANEOUS

Personal phone calls are not allowed in the Hospital Unit. However, such calls are permitted in the Outpatient Unit to the extent that they are not disturbing or disruptive to other patients and are permitted by the Assistant Director. Patients are not permitted entry into food preparation or food storage areas. Food or beverages will not be served to patients in the Outpatient Dialysis Unit. However, patients may bring food into the Outpatient Unit for their own personal consumption during dialysis. No food may be stored in the Dialysis Center and none may be shared between patients in the Dialysis Center. Flowers are not allowed. Radios are allowed only if provided with individual headsets. Only television sets available in the facility may be used. Smoking is not permitted. Private duty nurses are not permitted to give care in the facility except by permission of a Center staff physician.

I. OBJECTIVE

The objective of the Quality Assurance Plan is to preserve and enhance the high quality of patient care at the _____ Hospital in part by ensuring that:

- Patient care personnel are qualified and effectively supervised;
- Patient care services are appropriately organized with clear channels of supervision, responsibility and accountability;
- Patient care appropriate to the needs of patients is delivered in a timely manner, is optimal within the range of available resources, is consistent with achievable goals and is properly documented;
- Patient care is delivered in as cost-effective a manner as possible;
- Documentation facilitates the continuity of care and the evaluation of services;
- All elements entering into the care of patients are subjected to periodic review, either retrospective or concurrent, with the use of pre-established objective criteria and documentation of findings; and
- The findings of patient care review are utilized by the hospital in concrete ways to fulfill the objectives of the hospital's Quality Assurance Program.

It is the responsibility of the Board of Directors to establish, maintain and support, through the Executive Director and the President of the Medical Staff, an ongoing Quality Assurance Program that includes effective mechanisms for reviewing and evaluating patient care and that provides for effective responses to the findings of such evaluation. Toward this end the hospital will establish a Quality Assurance Committee. The following activities will be incorporated in the Quality Assurance Program:

- Identification of potential problems or concerns in the delivery of health care services;
- Objective assessment of the cause and scope of each problem;
- Implementation of decisions and plans designed to resolve observed problems;
- Monitoring activities designed to ensure that the desired results have been achieved;
- Documentation substantiating the effectiveness of the program in improving patient care and ensuring sound clinical performance;
- Reporting of findings to the Medical Staff, the Executive Director and the Board of Directors; and
- Annual appraisal of the effectiveness of the Quality Assurance Program.

II. SCOPE AND COVERAGE OF THE QUALITY ASSURANCE PROGRAM

A. Services Covered

All services that have a bearing upon the care of patients will be included in the Quality Assurance Program. Such services and groups include but are not limited to the following:

1. Administration
2. Medical Staff
3. Nursing Service
4. Emergency and Outpatient Services *(Divide these if appropriate.)*
5. Central Services
6. Environmental Services
7. Food Services
8. Maintenance and Engineering Services
9. Medical Record Service
10. Pharmacy Service

11. Physical Therapy Service *(Or Rehabilitation Services if appropriate.)*
12. Respiratory Therapy Service
13. Safety and Risk Management Services
14. Security Service *(Combine with Safety function if appropriate.)*
15. Social Services

B. Types of Review to Be Performed

The Quality Assurance Program will be implemented through the performing of a variety of analytical studies of the nature and quality of patient care services and the manner of their delivery. Patient care evaluation studies may be either retrospective or concurrent. Where possible, such studies will be focused upon potential or established problems in the delivery of services.

The principal sources of data used in this process will include but need not be limited to medical records, departmental records, treatment records, hospital billing records and the records of the preventive maintenance and safety inspections of plant and equipment.

A study may be addressed to problems arising in connection with a diagnosis, a procedure, a treatment modality or the operation of a department or service. Identification of suitable topics may be based upon evidence of problems revealed through previous studies as well as upon the observations and insights of members of the various professional staffs and services.

III. ORGANIZATION, DUTIES AND MEETINGS OF THE QUALITY ASSURANCE COMMITTEE

A. Membership of the Quality Assurance Committee

The Quality Assurance Committee will consist of the hospital's Executive Director, the President of the Medical Staff and two other Medical Staff members appointed by the President, the Director of Nursing Services and one other member of the Nursing Service appointed by the Director, the Director of the Medical Record Service and the Quality Assurance Coordinator.

The Chairman of the Committee will be appointed by *[the President of the Medical Staff or the hospital's Executive Director]. Note: This varies.*

Representatives of other departments and services will participate in the Committee's deliberations, by invitation, on those occasions when the Committee is planning or reviewing studies involving their services.

B. Lines of Authority

The Quality Assurance Committee will report on a quarterly basis to the Board of Directors through the Executive Director and the President of the Medical Staff.

C. Duties

Among the duties of the Quality Assurance Committee will be the following:

- Establishing a schedule of quality review studies for the hospital on an annual basis;
- Reviewing and approving the choice of study topics and criteria submitted to it by the various services responsible for performing quality review studies;
- Reviewing and accepting the reports of all quality review studies performed in the hospital;
- Reporting on the findings of quality review studies to the Medical Staff and the Board of Directors;
- Referring all matters requiring educational or corrective action to the appropriate service heads with recommendations and target dates for follow-up;
- Conducting an annual evaluation of the effectiveness of the Quality Assurance Program; and
- Providing general direction and coordination to all quality assurance activities of the hospital.

D. Assistance to the Quality Assurance Committee

The Committee will be assisted in its activities by the Quality Assurance Coordinator, who will have ongoing responsibility for the administrative aspects of the program.

Outside aid such as consultants may be called upon from time to time for the performance of quality assessment activities and to identify and assess the extent of observed problems, as agents of the Quality Assurance Committee. However, reaching and implementing solutions to problems in the delivery of patient care services is a responsibility of the Board of Directors, the Medical Staff and the Executive Director.

E. Meetings of the Quality Assurance Committee

Monthly meetings of the Committee will be held on a regularly scheduled day at a regular time which is to be determined at the first meeting of the year, commencing in the month of _____ each year. Minutes of all meetings will be kept. A log book will be maintained by the Quality Assurance Coordinator, listing all evaluation studies, actions taken, monitoring activities and dates of Committee reports to the Medical Staff, Executive Director and Board of Directors.

IV. IMPLEMENTATION

The following schedule of department/service and Medical Staff review will be observed:[1]

Frequency	Review
Annually	Dietetic Service
Semi-annually	Ambulatory Care Service
	Social Service
Quarterly	Anesthesia Service
	Blood Utilization
	Medical Record Service
	Nursing Service
	Pharmacy and Therapeutics
	Physical Therapy Service
	Respiratory Care Service
	Special Care Units
Bi-monthly	Infection Control Summary Report
Monthly	Antibiotic Utilization
	Emergency Services
	Tissue/Surgical Case Review
As needed	Other patient care studies
Quarterly	Summaries of studies reported to Medical Staff Executive Committee, Medical Staff and Board of Directors

A. Medical Staff Review Activities

The following traditional review activities of the Medical Staff will be continued.

1. Infection Control

The activities of the Infection Control Coordinator will be carried on under the general direction of the Administration and the Infection Control Committee. Reports of infection monitoring activities will be submitted on at least a bi-monthly basis to the Infection Control Committee and by that committee to the Quality Assurance Committee.

2. Antibiotic Utilization Review

Review of the utilization of antibiotics, as well as of other drugs, is the responsibility of the Pharmacy and Therapeutics Committee. Reports summarizing the findings of ongoing monitoring of

---

[1] This list reflects the review requirements specified in the standards of the Joint Commission on Accreditation of Hospitals. A hospital planning to include such departments as Environmental Services, Food Services, Maintenance and Engineering and Safety and Security in its comprehensive quality assurance and risk control program might establish semi-annual reviews of departmental performance for these departments or services.

antibiotic utilization will be submitted by the Pharmacy and Therapeutics Committee to the Quality Assurance Committee on a monthly basis, for later reporting to the Board of Directors.

Review criteria will apply to the use of antibiotics for both inpatients and outpatients. Criteria to be adopted will be consistent with any guidelines established in the Rules and Regulations of the Medical Staff.

3. *Blood Utilization Review*

Review of the use of blood and blood components will be performed on an ongoing basis. Reports of the findings of such review will be submitted to the Quality Assurance Committee on at least a quarterly basis. Topics to be included in such review include the use of whole blood, the use of blood components, the amounts of blood ordered, the amounts of blood used and the amounts of blood wasted. Criteria employed will apply to the indications for transfusion as well as to the prevention and management of transfusion reactions and complications.

4. *Tissue Review*

Surgical case review will be performed on a monthly basis and documented in written reports. Review samples will include all records showing major discrepancies between the pre- and post-operative diagnoses. Cases involving the absence of specimens for tissue study are to be included in the study samples, as well as those in which a pathologist's report is present. Criteria to be applied will include indications for surgery, to be established prior to the review.

5. *Pharmacy and Therapeutics Review*

The surveillance of adherence to the hospital's pharmacy and therapeutics policies, especially with respect to the selection, intra-hospital distribution and safe administration of drugs, is a responsibility of the Pharmacy and Therapeutics Committee, working in collaboration with the Pharmacy, the Nursing Service and Administration. Review is to be performed at least quarterly and documented in written reports.

6. *Medical Record Review*

The quality of the medical record is primarily a responsibility of the Medical Staff. Maintenance of high quality involves the collaboration of the Nursing Service and other professional personnel involved in the care of the patient. The Medical Record Committee is responsible for working with the Director of Medical Records to develop guidelines for evaluating medical records. This review and evaluation will be performed on at least a quarterly basis and documented in written reports submitted to the Quality Assurance Committee.

B. Schedule

The number and frequency of quality review studies performed by the Medical Staff, the Nursing Service and the other departments and services within the hospital will be consistent with the policies and accreditation requirements of the Joint Commission on Accreditation of Hospitals as well as with any applicable requirements that may be formulated by the Professional Standards Review Organization.

V. EVALUATION OF THE EFFECTIVENESS OF THE QUALITY ASSURANCE PROGRAM

At least once each year the Quality Assurance Committee will conduct a review of the degree to which any deficiencies found in the course of patient care studies, concurrent monitoring and other evaluative procedures have been corrected. This program evaluation will involve the use of measurable criteria of change during the relevant time period. The evaluation of the program's effectiveness will be documented in a comprehensive report to be submitted to the Board of Directors, the Executive Director and the Medical Staff. As a result of its findings, the Committee will make recommendations for further improvement to the various groups concerned.

QUALITY ASSURANCE PROGRAM
ACCOUNTABILITY MODEL

Patient Care Review or Study	Frequency	Responsible Committee	Documented by	Reported to	Documented by
Dietetic Service	Annually	Dietetic Service	Report	QA Committee	Minutes
Social Service	Semi-annually	Social Service	Report	QA Committee	Minutes
Anesthesia Service	Quarterly	Anesthesia Service	Report	QA Committee	Minutes
Blood Utilization	Quarterly	Medical Review or Tissue	Report	QA Committee	Minutes
Medical Records	Quarterly	Medical Record	Report	QA Committee	Minutes
Nursing Service	Quarterly	Nursing Review	Report	QA Committee	Minutes
Pharmacy and Therapeutics	Quarterly	Pharmacy and Therapeutics	Report	QA Committee	Minutes
Rehabilitation Service	Quarterly	Rehabilitation Service	Report	QA Committee	Minutes
Respiratory Care	Quarterly	Respiratory Care Service	Report	QA Committee	Minutes
Infection Control	Bi-monthly	Infection Control	Report	QA Committee	Minutes
Antibiotic Usage	Monthly	P&T or Medical Review	Report	QA Committee	Minutes
Emergency Service	Monthly	Emergency Service	Report	QA Committee	Minutes
Surgical Case (Tissue)	Monthly	Tissue Committee	Report	QA Committee	Minutes
Other Clinical Studies	As needed	Medical Review	Reports	QA Committee	Minutes
Summaries of studies	Monthly or quarterly	QA Committee	Summary reports	Medical Staff, Executive Committee & Administration	Minutes
Summaries of studies	Quarterly	Medical Staff and Administration	Summary reports	Governing Body	Minutes

This table is intended only as an illustrative model showing the way the quality assurance reporting requirements could be met. In any given hospital, the names of the review groups responsible for the various studies might vary from those shown here.

INDEX